SCOTLAND AND NATIONALISM

Reviews of previous editions:

'This is a brilliant book, packed with learning and imagination.'
Neal Ascherson, *The Scotsman*

'. . . witty, penetrating and frequently provocative overview of Scots culture and politics during the last three centuries'
History Today

'. . . a brilliant book full of provocative insights'
Vernon Bogdanor, *Political Studies*

'*Scotland and Nationalism* provides a bold and imaginative lead into difficult territory and has more ideas within a page or two than many a definitive work in its entirety.'
Paul Addison, *The Times Literary Supplement*

With the first elections for the Scottish Parliament scheduled for early May 1999, and the Scottish National Party ahead of Labour in the opinion polls, this new edition brings *Scotland and Nationalism* entirely up-to-date. In particular the lead up to and implications of the 1997 referendum are analysed, together with the development of nationalist feeling in a wider context.

Christopher Harvie is Professor of British and Irish Studies at the University of Tübingen. His other books include *The Rise of Regional Europe*, also published by Routledge.

SCOTLAND AND NATIONALISM

Scottish Society and Politics
1707 to the Present

Third Edition

Christopher Harvie

ROUTLEDGE

London and New York

First published 1977 by George Allen & Unwin

Second edition published 1994
by Routledge
11 New Fetter Lane, London EC4P 4EE

Simultaneously published in the USA and Canada
by Routledge
29 West 35th Street, New York, NY 10001

Reprinted 1995

Third edition 1998

Typeset in 10/12 pt Palatino by The Florence Group, Stoodleigh, Devon

Printed and bound in Great Britain by
T.J. International Ltd, Padstow, Cornwall

British Library Cataloguing in Publication data
A catalogue record for this book is available from the
British Library

Library of Congress Cataloguing in Publication data
Harvie, Christopher T.
Scotland and nationalism : Scottish society and politics
1707–present / Christopher Harvie. – 3rd ed.
p. cm.
Includes bibliographical references and index
1. Scotland – Politics and government.   2. Nationalism –
Scotland – History.   3. Scotland – Social conditions.
I. Title.
DA765.H37   1998

320.9411–dc21   98–23255

ISBN 0–415–19524–1 (hbk)   0–415–19525–X (pbk)

To Kenneth Morgan
and in memory of
Jane Morgan and Kenneth MacKenzie

CONTENTS

ix

PREFACE AND ACKNOWLEDGEMENTS

Revising a book after fifteen years is a vertiginous business: a partnership with an immature, cocky younger self who occasionally manages feats of generalisation and insight which middle age is no longer up to. Revising *Scotland and Nationalism* had all these problems, and more: the fact that in this interval one's contemporaries and juniors made good so many of the historical and interpretative *lacunae* of which the book complained.

The book was prolix, young Harvie apparently having Lloyd George's idea that an argument could only be got across to politicians by endless repetition. In an ideological sense, it was also strongly anti-nationalist, or at least hostile to what it saw as the simplicities of the nationalist picture of a martyred nation. This led some reviewers to regard it as opposing the devolution policy which eventually foundered on 1 March 1979. Where it succeeded, the book did so for reasons which were collective rather than individualistic: the 'common sense' which possessed a generation in Scotland that its own past had been forgotten, as much by nationalists as by unionists; that the culture of the country was the result of a peculiar dialogue between community and enterprise, Calvinism and rationalism, Scotland and 'Britain', between the peoples and regions of a complicated, argumentative nation.

This may explain why the study of Scotland seems to be regarded as significant throughout Europe, despite the country's legendary lethargy in actually netting the ball of autonomy. Like Columbus, the Scots may have located something more important *en route* to their Indies. Not for the first time, Scotland seems both to symbolise and make accessible more widespread European problems; it is 'Englishness' which seems to tail off into the discussion of stereotypes and the commercial mystifications of 'heritage'. David McCrone noted in his critique of *Scotland and Nationalism* that the author always seemed to be casting a sidelong glance at an English opinion he somehow expected to be more sophisticated. I get his point. There was a feeling that if Scotland was in contact with anywhere else, it had to happen *through* England – something the 'renaissance' itself fed by being so dependent on London publishers and publicity. The 'British' experience was the necessary catalyst, but matters didn't stop there. Two things have happened to this view. One: Britain was never only England, but a construction which, by opening out to the Empire and to America, rather dissolved the constrictions of conventional nationalism. Two: the European connection remained much more important than I judged in 1977, both through Scots' experiences of Europe and through the world of the immigrant communities.

The crucial area was the nineteenth century, which in 1977 seemed such a dismal swamp of redundant religious arguments and sentimental persiflage. The work in the interval of Robert Anderson, Jay Brown, William Donaldson, Hamish Fraser, Helen Meller and many others has opened this up as a period of continuing originality and energy of speculation and creative effort. Thus the Enlightenment and the renaissance can be linked up in a continuity. Getting Victorian Scotland right meant reworking much of the book. In the more recent period, my concentration on the Scottish National Party in the 1977 edition had to be modified by the fact that nationalist ideas became disseminated far more widely over the political scene.

As *Scotland and Nationalism* succeeded in appealing to the elusive 'general reader' I have replaced footnotes with a bibliographical essay directing him or her to more detailed reading, particularly the remarkable output of the 1980s.

ACKNOWLEDGEMENTS

In preparing the 1977 edition I was grateful for the advice, encouragement, criticism and hospitality of Clive Emsley, the late Julie Brotherstone, Jack Brand, Neal Ascherson, Graham Martin, John Bright-Holmes, Irene Hatt, Jackie Baldick, Jean Jordan, Gavin Kennedy, Christopher Smout, Tom Nairn,

Nicholas Phillipson, Keith Webb, John Simpson, Gordon Brown (now MP), Owen Dudley Edwards, Henry Cowper, Joan Christodoulou, Chris MacWhirter, Stephen Maxwell, Bob Bell, Robin Cook MP, Angus Calder, Ian Jordan, Gwyn A Williams, Geoffrey Best, Ian MacDougall, Arthur Marwick, Robert Tait, Iain McLean, the late Alex Aitken, the late Dr Archie Lamont and the late William Marwick. I was also greatly in the debt of the staff of the Open University Library, the National Library of Scotland, and Edinburgh University Library.

In reworking the second edition, I would like to thank my editors at Routledge, Claire L'Enfant and Emma Cotter, and Jane Mayer, who converted the first edition into a disc for rewriting. This edition has benefitted a great deal from journalistic and broadcasting assignments, and academic contacts made in the 1980s. So, thanks to: John Milne and Ken Cargill of the BBC, Tom Gallagher, John Osmond, Peter Jones and the late Bobby Campbell of the *Scotsman*, Hans-Gustav Klaus, Ursula Kimpel, Thomas Kleinknecht, Allan MacCartney MEP, Bernard Crick, Lindsay Paterson, George Rosie, Jim Ross, Jim Sillars, Lord Steel, James Douglas-Hamilton MP, Alex Salmond MP, John McGrath, Hamish Henderson, Cairns Craig, Paddy Bort and Carola Ehrlich. My sister Jane George compiled the index. My especial thanks to her, to my family in Scotland, and to my wife Virginia and my daughter Alison.

For the third edition I have divided the last chapter and extended the material to take account of the 1997 general election, the devolution referendum and the Scotland Act. This implies greater attention being paid, in the new Chapter 7, to the social forces which were, in the 1980s and 1990s, pulling the country in contrary directions: towards a servitor role for the new international affluence, and towards solidarity with the far more numerous victims of MacDiarmid's 'Wunds wi' warlds to swing'. In this I have been greatly helped by Richard Finlay, Ken Ferguson, Mike Russell, Mark Lazarowicz, Anja Sandersfeld, Colin Matthew and Mathias Kothe.

As the 'acknowledgements' in the 1977 edition records, Kenneth Morgan started me off as a Scottish historian. To my original dedication I add his name, and that of his wife Jane. Jane died tragically young, like Kenneth MacKenzie. The contribution of both was such that 'What would they have thought?' remains a touchstone.

INTRODUCTION
A sad nuisance

'We were all assembled to hear Winston make his funeral oration on Roosevelt, but before he started an absurd incident occurred,' Sir Harold Nicolson wrote to his son Nigel in April 1945:

> A young man of the name of McIntyre had been elected as Scottish Nationalist for Motherwell. He refused to be introduced by any sponsors, since he does not recognise the Mother of Parliaments and wishes to advertise himself. He advanced to the Bar without sponsors and the Speaker told him that he could not take his oath, as that was contrary to Standing Orders. At which many Members rose offering to sponsor the cub and put an end to the shaming incident, but he refused. He was therefore told to go away and think it over, which he did, shrugging vain shoulders. Next day he thought better of it and accepted sponsors; but even then, as he reached the box, he said, 'I do this under protest', which was not liked at all. He is going to be a sad nuisance and pose as a martyr.

Sir Harold did not approve of Dr Robert McIntyre. Descended from the gentry of Lowland Scotland, his father a former head of the Foreign Office, Nicolson had mirrored the evolution of establishment politics between the wars – from Toryism, through National Labour, to membership of the Labour Party after 1945. Dr McIntyre, a rather dour young medical officer for the county in which the Nicolsons held their title, Stirlingshire, was a son of the manse, pacifist in outlook, who denied that the Mother of Parliaments had any right to order Scotsmen into the

1

war. The encounter was apposite. It was not only between two men, or two parties, but between two Scotlands.

This book is about both Scotlands – the achieving society, the defensive community – and the relationships between them. It is concerned with political nationalism, why it remained apparently in abeyance for two and a half centuries, and why it became relevant in the second half of the twentieth century. The Scottish component of the Union, despite its surface resemblance to the rest of Britain, is distinctive: a house whose familiar façade conceals a quite different construction. Nicolson did not question the Union at all, McIntyre saw it purely as an instrument of oppression. But it had both encompassed and separated two quite different societies. McIntyre's election, however, was a prelude to its most fundamental challenge yet, and one which it may not survive.

Dr McIntyre's career as MP lasted only six weeks. Both he and Nicolson were thrown out at the general election. The episode was eccentric, as McIntyre had been supported by Conservatives, who could not, because of the wartime electoral truce, run their own candidate. Westminster did not hear about him for nearly twenty years but when he did emerge again it was as president of a movement which threatened the supremacy of the House whose patience he had tried, sorely if briefly, in 1945. The fortunes of the SNP rose and fell decade by decade; but the decline in support for the Union was consistent. In 1945, in an early Gallup poll, 9 per cent supported independence; even in the 1970s this had only risen to 20 per cent. By 1992 between 35 and 40 per cent, almost double the Scottish National Party's poll, wanted out.

Even at the nadir of devolution in 1979 William Miller, Professor of Politics at Glasgow University, could write of 'the end of British politics', reflecting the fact that nationalism had skewed the Scottish political scene. Issues at elections, once similar to those agitated south of the border, had given way to a new politics, in which divisions between unionists and home rulers supplemented those between right and left, and were made even more complex by the manoeuvring of the ambitious with their eye on power in the eventual political settlement. Even the Major government's *Scotland in the Union* exercise in March 1993, intended to check demands for a legislature, had to emphasise the Union as a partnership, not an incorporation.

Much attention was paid to the ominous question of cultural identity and, intriguingly, the word Britain appeared only once in a 56-page document.

The Scottish National Party was the initial beneficiary. Its leaders, once dismissed as eccentrics, were able three times to talk confidently about imminent independence; with their rivals internally divided or weak. Three times this prospect unhelpfully dissolved. Yet a new consensus has been created; other parties, and non-political groups, have moved towards substantial devolution; many Scots, particularly the young, simply no longer think of themselves as British. The probability increases that the cumulative failures of London government will lead to an overwhelming movement for secession.

Has the home rule movement been merely a protest? Or a self-interested attempt to grab oil revenues from the North Sea? The SNP has survived and matured in a way that no protest party would be capable of, but paradoxically home rule remains low down on voters' priorities, despite its permeation of the language of politics. Does this language, then, reflect reality? If it is a distortion of some fundamental economic or class reality by 'false consciousness', why does it persist at election after election?

This reflects a complex social situation. Economic base and political superstructure in Scotland depend on historical factors. So, to determine the prospects – if any – for the Union, we have to distinguish between direct responses to Anglo-Scottish crises and the underlying relationships that maintained the Union as a balance of assimilation and autonomy, allowing Scottish nationality to survive through a distinct pattern of government and society. Pervaded by parallel dualisms between the cosmopolitan and the native, the individual and the social, the nature of the settlement was familiar from the thinking of one European socialist 'discovered' by a Scot – Hamish Henderson – and influential in Scotland in the 1970s, Antonio Gramsci, leader of the Italian Communists until his imprisonment by Mussolini. Gramsci was a Sardinian – from the Italian equivalent of the Highlands. Influenced by Croce, he challenged Marx's crude generalisations about nationalism, and the way in which the masses were persuaded to integrate themselves in the 'civil society' (a phrase originating in eighteenth-century Scotland) which sustained the dominant political and economic groups.

He attributed this critical function to the intellectuals, whose history thus becomes the key to understanding why nationalist movements emerge.

Or do not emerge. For the uniqueness of Scotland lies in the power of a civil society divorced from political nationalism, and in an intelligentsia which, lacking a political centre, was divided between two loyalties. Borrowing from Gwyn A. Williams – another Gramsci man, this time Welsh – on Goya and Spain in the time of Napoleon, I christened them the red and the black. The red Scots were cosmopolitan, self-avowedly enlightened and, given a chance, authoritarian, expanding into and exploiting bigger and more bountiful fields than their own country could provide. Back home lurked their black brothers, demotic, parochial, sensitive about community to the point of reaction, but keeping the ladder of social promotion open, resisting the encroachments of the English governing class. In uneasy alliance, they controlled the rate of their own assimilation to the greater world, the balance which underlay their integration in 'Britain'; they also guaranteed a moral purposiveness which went beyond nationalism, something recognised by one of its most uncomfortable products, Thomas Carlyle:

> A country where the entire people is, or even once has been, laid hold of, filled to the heart with an infinite religious idea, has 'made a step from which it cannot retrograde'. Thought, conscience, the sense that man is denizen of a Universe, creature of an Eternity, has penetrated to the remotest cottage, to the simplest heart.

After World War II, the balance changed. The attractions of 'Britain' declined with the effectiveness of the economy and the political elite; insensitive attempts at social engineering, right and left, brought the Union to a state in which its stability fluctuated from year to year, and sometimes from by-election to by-election. But one cannot understand the intricate moves of the current political transactions without casting a backward glance at the politics of nearly three centuries of unionism – and a Scottish history which, although it profoundly affected the idea of nationalism, rarely conformed to its orthodoxies. The Scots have, man for man, probably done more to create the modern world than any other nation. They owe it an explanation.

4

Part I

1

THE BALLADS OF A NATION
Political nationalism, 1707–1945

Oldbuck: I'll supply you with a subject – The battle between the Caledonians and the Romans – the Caledoniad;
or, Invasion Repelled. Let that be the title – it will suit the
present taste, and you may throw in a touch of the times.
Lovel: But the invasion of Agricola was *not* repelled.
Oldbuck: No; but you are a poet – free of the corporation, and as little bound to truth or probability as Virgil
himself – You may defeat the Romans in spite of Tacitus.
Sir Walter Scott, *The Antiquary* (1816)

THE USES OF LIBERTY

In 1704, on the eve of the Union, Andrew Fletcher of Saltoun,
the most energetic champion of the doomed Scottish
Parliament, published anonymously his *Account of a Conversation
concerning a Right Regulation of Governments for the Common Good
of Mankind*. One sentence of this tract was to be prophetic in
describing the course of Scottish nationalism over the next 250
years:

> I knew a very wise man so much of Sir Christopher
> [Neville]'s sentiment that he believed that if a man were
> permitted to make all the ballads, he need not care who
> should make the laws of a nation.

Nationalist tradition has, to the present day, regarded Fletcher
as the parent of Scottish democracy. The cultural nationalist
Saltire Society runs an annual Andrew Fletcher lecture; wreaths
are laid at the family tomb in Saltoun kirkyard. Fletcher was a
man of his unruly time, a patriot in the mould of Machiavellian

'civic humanism', a talented, choleric soldier, whose scheme for the economic revival of Scotland involved reinforcing serfdom. His anti-English interventions in the Scottish Parliament probably accelerated the Union which he loathed. Yet he accurately predicted the way Scottish nationalism, on the margin of British and European politics, would survive.

Poetic tradition had given a logic of its own to Scottish development during the Middle Ages. Two national epics treated the War of Independence, 1296–1328, not as a chivalric episode but as a popular struggle which was also libertarian. The myth was underlain by reality. On the edge of Europe, composed of a variety of races and affected by the cultural traditions of Roman and Christian Europe, Welsh, Irish and Norsemen, Scotland had evolved by the thirteenth century, in advance of England and France, the institutions of a national community. These were in the main aristocratic, derived from Anglo-Norman feudal practice, but their local identity was so secure that when the male royal line of Scotland expired in 1286, the Scots nobility thought that joining England under a dual monarchy implied no major risk to it. Instead, the collapse of this scheme, and English invasion, made patriots of the mass of the population.

In 1320, six years after the defeat of Edward II at Bannockburn, the Scots nobility, along with 'the other barons and freeholders and the whole community of the realm of Scotland', petitioned the Pope to recognise Scotland as independent and Robert the Bruce as king. The Declaration of Arbroath, 'the most impressive manifesto of nationalism that medieval Europe produced', culminated with the words:

> We are bound to him [King Robert] for the maintaining of our freedom both by his right and his merits, as to him by whom salvation has been wrought unto our people, and by him, come what may, we mean to stand. Yet if he should give up what he has begun, seeking to make us or our kingdom subject to the king of England or the English, we would strive at once to drive him out as our enemy and a subverter of his own right and ours, and we would make some other man who was able to defend us our king; for, as long as a hundred of us remain alive, we will never on any conditions be subjected to the lordship of the English. For we fight not for glory, nor riches, nor honour, but for

freedom alone, which no good man gives up except with his life.

This absolute 'freedom from unfreedom' – not the 'liberties' of a privileged class – reflected the experience of a war intense enough to have given most groups in society a stake in its outcome: a type of popular nationalism rare in Europe before the French Revolution.

It was not to last. There was little popular involvement in the politics of the two grim centuries which followed, disfigured by royal minorities and the nobility dismembering the state. After the Reformation of 1559–60, religion altered the matrices both of nationalism and of liberty. But the poets preserved and transmitted the memory of the war and its ideals: the praise of freedom in Archdeacon Barbour's *The Bruce* in 1375:

> A! fredome is a noble thing
> Fredome mays man to haiff liking;
> Fredome all solace to man giffis
> He levys at es that frely levys.

was, a century later, joined by Blind Harry's glorification of Bruce's more obscure predecessor, William Wallace. Both epics were printed and reprinted from the sixteenth century onwards; their echoes carried through to the mobs which rioted against the Union in 1707 and against the malt tax in 1713, and which lynched Captain Porteous in 1736. They were picked up by the Jacobin Burns and condensed in 1793 – *after* the execution of Louis XVI – into the powerful stanzas of 'Bruce to his Troops on the eve of the Battle of Bannock-burn':

> Scots, wha hae wi' Wallace bled,
> Scots, wham Bruce has aften led;
> Welcome to your gory bed,
> Or to victorie.
>
> Now's the day, and now's the hour,
> See the front o' battle lour;
> See approach proud Edward's power –
> Chains and slaverie!
>
> Wha for Scotland's king and law

Freedom's sword will strongly draw,
Free-man stand, or Free-man fa',
Let him follow me!

Bannockburn, Arbroath and Wallace's reputed birthplace at Elderslie remain places of nationalist pilgrimage – though rivalled since 1979 by the empty Parliament building on Edinburgh's Calton Hill.

Burns's attitude to Scottish nationalism was ambiguous. In 1894 the Glasgow professor John Nichol, the friend of Kossuth and Mazzini, described him as writing the requiem of Lowland Scotland 'as a distinct nationality', while being the prophet of a new and universal democratic order. Burns's poetry became part of the liberal radicalism – the German Freiligarth's 'Trotz Alledem', sung by the crowds of 1848, is 'A Man's a Man for a' that'. But, allied with industrialisation, mass society overthrew much of Scottish political distinctiveness, and with it the basis for a nationalist movement. The internationalist, elitist Goethe, writing to Carlyle in 1828, was strongly conscious of Scottish identity; the Marxist Georg Lukács, a century later, assimilated the country to 'England'.

OUT OF SYNC

Elie Kedourie characterised nationalism as amalgamating the politics of the French Revolution, vesting sovereignty in the people, and the philosophy of German idealism, 'realising' the individual will in the service of the state. Yet nationalism also drew on earlier tendencies. In the seventeenth and eighteenth centuries absolute rulers tried to crush aristocratic localism and provincial loyalties, dangerous centrifugal forces during the late middle ages and the wars of religion. Monarchs shaped future nations, when they suppressed the estates of the clergy, nobles and burgesses; conversely, where they failed, or compromised, a smaller-scale nationality could develop around what survived. Such institutional cultures marked what mid-nineteenth-century radicals, notably Marx and Engels, called the 'historic' nationalities. Through them, and in defiance of the conservative multinational empires, the Poles and the Hungarians evolved towards capitalism and democracy.

For the groups which failed to sustain such institutions, or had none to sustain, Marx and Engels had little time: 'peoples without history' were a threat to social progress:

> There is no country in Europe that does not possess, in some remote corner, at least one remnant-people, left over from an earlier population, forced back and subjugated by the nation which later became the repository of historical development. These remnants of a nation, mercilessly crushed, as Hegel said, by the course of history, this 'national refuse', is always the fanatical representative of the counter-revolution and remains so until it is completely exterminated or de-nationalised, as its whole existence is in itself a protest against a great historical revolution.

Amongst Slavs, Basques and Bretons they numbered the Gaels, 'supporters of the Stuarts from 1640 to 1745'. Scots as Scots appeared in their discussions only to show how they had eluded the great generalisations. The Lowlanders lacked the constitutional focus – or determination to secure it – of 'historic nationality'; but despite the shared Parliament and language, they were indelibly separate from the English. 'The preponderance of enjoyment lies on the more credulous side,' the polymath Hugh Miller, a man of the Highland line, wrote of the latter. 'I never yet encountered a better-pleased people . . . Unthinking, unsuspicious, blue-eyed, fair-complexioned, honest Saxons.' For the Scots had made the *conscious* decision to supersede nationalism by ideology.

From the standpoint of 'British' history, the Union of 1707 resembled contemporary continental developments: the suppression of a schismatic nobility in the interests of dynastic security. After it, in the words of Lord Dacre, 'intelligent Scotchmen rejoiced in the removal of their national politics to London' and got on with the real business of improving their country. Accurate enough about English attitudes, this is as misleading about Scotland as the nationalist myth of a representative assembly cut down in its prime. Although dominated by nobles and their factions, the Scottish Parliament had since 1688 claimed a hitherto unprecedented national role. Its problem was twofold. First, it had to cope with economic disaster in the 1690s: two years of crop failure and famine, and the catastrophic colonial enterprise at Darien. Second, it was not indispensable. For a century and a half, it had had a rival – the Kirk.

CALVINISM IN ONE COUNTRY

In *The Scot in History*, the American historian Wallace Notestein contended that 'in explaining Scottish character nothing is more important than religion'. The country's uniquely influential reformation created a new politics and a new concept of freedom. The corruption of the Catholic Church, coupled with a European diplomatic revolution which allied the great Catholic powers of Spain and France against Elizabeth's England, made the Scots opt for drastic religious innovation, guaranteed by agreement with England. This brought to an end the French alliance which had endured since the War of Independence, and effectively foreshadowed the Union. The social gospel of Calvinism gradually overlaid the ideals of national independence and individual freedom which the ballads had celebrated.

A European crisis coincided with the weakening of central authority in a peripheral state; an *émigré* intelligentsia returned to impose its own ideology. Like the Russian Communists after 1917, the Scots Calvinists proclaimed a 'positive' liberty, achieved within society. This was not capricious – George Buchanan and Samuel Rutherford had a strong sense of popular sovereignty – but neither was it conspicuously tolerant:

> No man may be permitted to live as best pleaseth him within the Church of God; but every man must be constrained by fraternal admonition and correction to bestow his labours when of the Church they are required, to the edification of others [otherwise] discipline must proceed against them, provided that the civil magistrate concur with the judgement and election of the Church.

The claims of the Kirk were confirmed by the Revolution of 1688, not before the Calvinists had tried to impose their will on all the Stuart dominions. 1688 meant compromise – 'Calvinism in one country' – with religion allowed to prevail over a precocious political nationality, a victory confirmed in 1707. The writers and singers of the ballads didn't just provide parallels with European nationalism: 'Ossian' MacPherson, Burns and Scott gave it much of its ideological pabulum. But at home, for the next two centuries, they were on their own. During the great age of European nationalism, Scottish religion took centre stage.

NORTH BRITISH RADICALISM

The ideology which triumphed in 1707 was not anti-Scottish. 'Principled' unionists like William Carstares, leader of the Kirk, and William Paterson, founder of the Bank of England *and* the Bank of Scotland, regarded Parliament as only *one* national 'estate', offered up for the safety and effectiveness of the Kirk, the law and the educational system. As Sir Robert Rait and Professor A. V. Dicey wrote in their apologia *Thoughts on the Union* in 1920, one could be both a sincere nationalist and an advocate of the Union. Would any English government have tolerated a parliament open to Jacobite and French intrigue? Its suppression – say in 1745 – would probably have doomed all the independent semi-Scots 'estates'.

Still, the Union was unpopular even among politicians favourable to the principle. They wanted a looser federation; instead they got only nominal representation at Westminster, through forty-five MPs, mainly government placemen. A more drastic integration might have brought a competent bureaucracy, but taking over English political traditions – party patronage and local initiative paradoxically meant that Scottish local and church government could go its own way. In time of economic depression, 'semi-independence' seemed a poor substitute for a sovereign Parliament, but it satisfied enough of the estates to inhibit any hostile alliances.

These would have been difficult anyway. The discontents of the two Scotlands were too distinctive: trade and religion in the Lowlands; clan conflict and subsistence for the third of the population which lived beyond the Highland line. The latter erupted periodically in Jacobite revolts, a doomed aristocratic localism. After the failure of the last of these in 1745–6, Lowland Scotland accelerated the 'improvement' which by 1800 brought it abreast of its southern neighbour in economic performance and ahead in 'Enlightenment', accelerating the denationalisation that Cumberland's guns began on Culloden Moor.

Aristocratic Scottish nationalism then vanished. The rather intellectualised efforts of the (thoroughly Hanoverian) literati in the 1760s – Adam Ferguson and his cronies of the 'Poker Club' – to reanimate a Scottish militia on 'Machiavellian' lines foundered. 1745 was still too close. Protests against interference with

Scots law in the 1780s appealed to nationalism, but implicitly demanded political convergence with the south. By 1789 Jacobitism could be celebrated by a radical like Burns, because it was harmless. Thomas Paine mattered; Cardinal Henry Stuart, the last Pretender, didn't. The revolutionary French toyed with promoting Scots separatism, and some Scots radicals concurred, such as the laird of Huntershill, Thomas Muir, whom persecution drove to accept French aid, but on the whole reformers wanted to strengthen rather than to subvert the Union. The campaign of the Scottish 'Friends of the People', whose 'British Convention' was held in Edinburgh in November 1793, demonstrated close collaboration between Scottish and English radicals, something which persisted when the Scots-Irish, Enlightenment-inspired, radicalism of the United Irishmen broke down. In the reform agitation which succeeded the peace in 1815, there was certainly a nationalist element in the skirmish of the 'Radical War' of 1820, but English agitators like Cobbett and Cartwright were enthusiastically welcomed in Scotland, and the traditions of seventeenth-century English parliamentarianism were celebrated by the founding of Hampden Clubs. By the mid-nineteenth century Lowland Scotland had qualified democratic presbyterianism with a markedly anti-Irish streak.

Whatever Scots radicals thought about the principle of the Union, they preferred alliance with Englishmen to persecution by their native judiciary. The bourgeoisie, which in Europe acted as the main sponsor of nationalism, was either cowed by the government or forced to look for allies in the south, as in the case of its leading cadre, the young Whigs who founded the *Edinburgh Review* in 1811. Their road to freedom lay through assimilation to the English franchise. To Gladstone, speaking in the 1880s, the Reform Act of 1832 was the 'political birth' of Scotland, 'the beginning of a duty and power, neither of which had attached to the Scottish nation in the preceding period'. But this had little to do with nationality: the end of 'management', effectively the subordination of the remaining Scottish political institutions to British representative government, was regretted by few. Where the Whigs led, a multitude of Scots Chartists followed, their eyes fixed on Westminster. A decade later, no region organised more energetically in the anti-French Volunteer Movement of 1859 – the amateur soldiers in their kilts and trews fulfilling a century later the demands of the Poker Club. For the fifty years the Liberals dominated Scotland, the Union was only once a political issue.

EIGHTEEN EIGHTY-SIX

It is wrong to discount altogether the existence of a Scottish political ideology. Elements of the 'civic virtue' of the Buchanan–Fletcher epoch surface during the nineteenth century, in the 'theoretical histories' of Galt, in Thomas Chalmers's attempt to revive the active parish, in the conservative *étatisme* of Thomas Erskine of Linlathen and his friend Carlyle. The key example, however, is the legal philosopher James Lorimer, whose commitment to educational reform, female suffrage and European Union (he drew up the first scheme for a federal Europe in 1884) and cultural nationalism were both original and exemplary. The title, however, of a pamphlet of Lorimer's, *Political Progress not necessarily Democratic* (1858) gives the game away. The civic tradition was didactic: it accorded ill with the egalitarian hopes of the age of Mazzini, Jackson and Marx.

Scottish Liberalism was democratic and unionist. Happily for Britain, because its dominance also coincided with a change in European nationalism. The 'peoples without history' began to acquire national identity, written literature, political programmes. Older radicals looked balefully on the organisation of the likes of the Slavs of the Habsburg Empire, seeing a gambit of the conservative powers, out to create a Jacquerie of reaction. Marx and Engels muttered about waging wars of genocide against 'national refuse'. Yet, by destroying the last feudal servitudes, the revolutions of 1848 created the basis for an influential non-socialist populism. This alliance between a 'free' peasantry coping with agricultural depression, emigration and urbanisation and a nationalist intelligentsia was also potent in Ireland and Wales, especially after the 1870s. But not in Scotland. Here, the agricultural population was smaller (only 6 per cent in 1901, compared with 20 per cent in Ireland), the depression less severe and mitigated by industrial growth.

But this international upheaval echoed around the birth of the movement for legislative devolution. In the early 1880s Gaelic Scotland took on the landlords it had endured for over a century. Goaded by the example of the Land League in Ireland,

15

crofters in the Highlands stood and fought against eviction. The Scottish administration lurched from coercion to conciliation, ordering gunboats and police north, then sending the Napier Commission, which promised security of tenure, the settlement of rent arrears, and a Land Court. The Highlanders used their new voting power, expelled their Whig MPs and returned five independent 'Crofter' MPs, one of whom, Gavin Clark, had ironically been a founder with Marx of the International. This radicalism would later help establish the Scottish socialist movement, with home rule firmly on its programme, but the main pressure for devolution came from more influential and less nationalist sources.

If land agitation paralleled, albeit feebly, European peasant nationalism, the concurrent campaign for a Scottish Secretary (a post which had been suppressed in 1746) seemed a reversion to aristocratic localism. It was headed by the Earl of Rosebery and supported by the Duke of Argyll, the arch-enemy of land reform, and the Earl of Fife – and by both main parties. A verbose plutocrat, who had stage-managed Gladstone's Midlothian campaign in 1878–80, Rosebery wanted to establish himself, like Joseph Chamberlain and Charles Stewart Parnell, as the leader of a territorial interest. He chose the right time. The Commons was congested with legislation, made worse by Irish and Tory obstruction. Local government reforms, which might have helped by transferring powers to county councils, were themselves trapped, and delays in Scottish legislation and the Land War gave weight to his propaganda.

Gladstone found concession to the propertied safer than the Irish alternative: nationalism plus land agitation. In 1884, he carried the Secretaryship against Scottish administrators worried at a political (and Westminster) headship; the implications of this were sufficiently unradical for the Tories to take the work over when the Liberals fell. Lord Salisbury offered the new post to the Duke of Richmond and Gordon. The Duke thought it 'quite unnecessary' but Salisbury's nephew, Arthur Balfour, urged him to persist: 'The effulgence of two Dukedoms and the best salmon river in Scotland will go a long way.' The Duke accepted.

The agitation for the Secretaryship was as ambiguous as the 'defence' of Scots law a century earlier. The Secretary actually increased the subordination of Scottish affairs to English party politics: most obviously when the Conservatives (a minority in Scotland) stayed in power after 1886. By then the Liberals had split over Irish home rule, and some were canvassing home rule for Scotland. Gladstone uttered a gnomic endorsement of their efforts in 1886:

> Scotland, which for a century and a quarter after her Union was refused all taste of a real representative system, may begin to ask herself whether, if at the first she felt something of an unreasoning antipathy, she may not latterly have drifted into a superstitious worship, or at least an irreflective acquiescence.

He followed it with an equally gnomic disclaimer in 1889, to the relief of most of his front bench. But the Scottish Liberal Association adopted home rule in 1888. After swallowing an Irish policy they had campaigned fiercely against before 1886, anything was possible.

An 'all-party' Scottish Home Rule Association was formed in 1886. For twenty-eight years it displayed most of the (ineffective) characteristics of later groups – and, indeed, trained many of their activists, starting rather ominously with the young Ramsay MacDonald. But it courted consensus out of weakness; barely keeping together romantic conservatives like the Marquess of Bute and Professor John Stuart Blackie, unionists who used Scottish home rule sentiment against the Irish, radicals who equated it with land nationalisation and the eight-hour day and, most significant and most demoralising of all, Gladstonians who believed that – pending the re-election of the GOM – 'Ireland blocked the way'.

Scottish home rule bobbed about in the slipstream of the Irish: it did not have their motive power. The Irish, as Conor Cruise O'Brien has observed, regarded home rule as a barely tolerable compromise, sanctified by the opposition of men whom they loathed. Discontents of all sorts – political, religious, linguistic and agrarian – pulled in more extreme directions. Parnell's parliamentary leadership focused these, and concentrated them behind a movement, a programme and a man. But Scottish grievances, such as the land issue, were less acute; there could be no language politics when barely 5 per cent spoke Gaelic; some radical causes – notably the Liberal campaign after 1887 to disestablish the Kirk – would actually damage the traditional estates. And there was no Scottish Parnell.

There could scarcely be when the Scottish Liberals, in their selection of candidates, massively endorsed the Union. Gladstone sat for Midlothian, Morley for Montrose, Asquith for East Fife and Trevelyan for Glasgow Bridgeton. James Bryce, Professor of Civil Law at Oxford, a lucid and original constitutionalist, was MP for South Aberdeen from 1885 to 1906; he surfaced about twice a year 'delivering addresses on political, literary or educational topics and always setting apart one day for callers who might wish to see him on business of any kind'. By 1906 over half of Scots MPs were English; most lived in the south. Such a tolerant electorate might favour constitutional innovation. But it wouldn't be bigoted about it.

Scottish Liberalism was conservative and deferential. After 1886 it was to suffer for this. In that year the Welsh and Irish confirmed their radicalism, and the Scots started to backslide. This began with the secession of the Liberal Unionists, and by 1900 they and the Conservatives had a majority in Scotland. Unlike Wales, there was no large-scale radical nationalist movement: no Tom Ellis, no Lloyd George. New Liberal thinking came from the right, from collectivist-inclined imperialists like R. B. Haldane, who had little time for home rule. Along with antivivisectionism, women's suffrage and disarmament, it became part of the repertory of party 'faddists' and socialists such as Keir Hardie and Don Roberto Cunninghame-Graham, who founded the Scottish Labour Party in 1888, on ground otherwise stony for radical politics. The SLP was soon in sectarian dissarray, and Hardie headed south to the more promising politics of radical London.

In fact 1886 drove the Liberals even further from a logical policy of devolution. If Professor John Vincent has identified the central concern of mid-Victorian Liberalism as restructuring politics to incorporate new classes and interests – and the Radical Programme of 1885 followed this by proposing regional governments large enough to sustain the activity and pulling-power of parliamentary politics – Gladstone favoured instead the 'great moral issue' of Irish home rule (and his own leadership). Ireland could not generate support indefinitely, and into the vacuum came socialist and imperialist initiatives, strongly centralising in tendency.

The Liberals recovered spectacularly in 1906, but although there were subsequent paper majorities for Scottish home rule, the task was too complex. Only Winston Churchill, characteristically, was prepared to attempt it, with a scheme (borrowed, perhaps, from H. G. Wells) for parliaments for Scotland, Ireland and Wales, and seven English regions, all with equal legislative powers, but he moved from the Home Office to the Admiralty in 1911. The Liberal leadership was wedded to centralisation, party cohesion and elite control – even at the price of collectivism and class politics. No amount of motions in favour of Scottish home rule would make it throw these advantages away, though Scots never tired of passing them.

Scottish nationalism was probably much more profoundly affected by the consequences of an incident at Hampden Park on 30 October 1886 than by anything that happened at Westminster that year. During a third-round Football Association Cup match between Preston North End and Queen's Park, Jimmy Ross, a Scots player with Preston, fouled Harrower, the Queen's Park centre-forward, before a crowd of 15,000. The pitch was invaded by Queen's Park supporters (a rather genteel bunch, if truth be told) and Ross had to be smuggled out of the ground. The incident brought to a head differences between the Football Association and the Scottish Football Association; the SFA announced on 10 May 1887 'that clubs belonging to this Association shall not be members of any other National Association', and Scottish teams withdrew from the FA Cup.

This declaration of independence came at a crucial moment. The rather aristocratic amateurism which had dominated the game since the late 1860s was, in England, rapidly giving way to professionalism. Although most of the early professionals were Scots like Ross, the SFA, which had strong links with the Volunteer Movement and its junior branch the Boys' Brigade, stood out for amateurism, and this issue underlay the schism of 1887. The SFA gave in on professionalism by 1893, but the organisation of the Scottish and English Leagues had crystallised. The new proletarian, professional game was organised on national, not on British, lines. When Professor James Kellas writes that: 'working class nationalism is generally related to culture and football, not politics', he highlights something that stemmed from the 1880s. Had a British League then come into operation, things might have been different. Independence in football meant the fostering of the distinctively Scottish political–religious conflicts of the big city teams, an anti-national element, as it detracted from notions of unified community. But, in a nation which always read its newspapers from the back, it gave the press a good financial reason to emphasise its Scottishness. To this day, sales of English dailies are low in the north, save where, like Rupert Murdoch's *Sun*, they bow to the customs of the country.

'Nationalism' in sport paralleled the dualism of the Union. In 1884 Irish nationalists had created the Gaelic Athletic Association to organise games – hurling and Gaelic football – which the English did not play. The GAA banned its members from playing 'garrison games' – football or rugby – and its members were later to become some of the most militant supporters of Sinn Fein. Such was the power of sport. In Wales rugby provided the 'reborn nation' with its greatest triumph, in the (unique) defeat of the New Zealand All Blacks at Cardiff Arms Park in 1905. In Scotland, however, subjective separateness combined with economic and political links with England to produce the ritual conflict of two nations playing the same game.

'THE STRATEGY OF NOISY INACTION'

A paradox remains. If, after 1832, Scottish party politics, in and out of Parliament, fitted snugly into the Union mould, why did recurrent agitations harping on national injustices get so much popular support? In the 1820s, while the Whigs were driving towards integration, Sir Walter Scott, as 'Malachi Malagrowther', stirred up national sentiment to protect the note-issuing powers of Scottish banks, threatened by a government proposal to grant a monopoly to the Bank of England. In the 1850s grievances over English heraldic aggressions (always a sensitive area with the more romantic) combined with social and educational discontents to create a National Association for the Vindication of Scottish Rights. This proved ephemeral, but by 1860 national identity was incarnated in the prickly Wallace Monument on the Abbey Craig at Stirling, from which the decisive battlefields of the War of Independence could be viewed. Similar emotions were ventilated at intervals until they merged with the home rule movement after 1886.

Were such outbreaks part of an implicit strategy of 'noisy inaction' directed, or at least sanctioned, by those committed to assimilation *on their own terms*? Dr Nicholas Phillipson has argued that nationalist emotion, directed at symbolic targets like banknotes or flags, surfaced when assimilation seemed to acquire a momentum of its own: the banknote crisis when 'management' was in its death throes; Scottish Rights when the new settlement was skewed by the Disruption of 1843 and increasing centralisation (which caused similar localist reactions in England). In both cases the lowest common denominator of nationalism, resentment of the English, was served by such historic nationalist ideology as came to hand. This was frequently more unpredictable than its canny sponsors had bargained for.

Patriotic agitation gave continuing legitimacy to fringe groups – Jacobites, Gaelic enthusiasts, Catholics, even Tories – who could tap emotions which the ruling consensus neglected. In due course, and helped by external sources like Queen Victoria and the tourist industry, patriotism evolved into Tom Nairn's great Tartan monster, the populist subculture which eventually issued forth in the music halls and the sentimentality of the Kailyard school. The political returns to 'real' nationalism were, like the Secretaryship, limited; but by the 1880s the Scottish landscape sprouted hotels, railway stations and public buildings in that baronial style immortalised by Osbert Lancaster:

Spiral staircases of a steepness and gloom that rendered oubliettes unnecessary; small windows which made up for the amount of light they kept out by the amount of wind they let in; drains which conformed to medieval standards with an accuracy which in the rest of the structure remained an eagerly desired but as yet unattained ideal.

The middle classes wore kilts on Sundays. They smothered the use of 'Scotch' or 'North British', or England instead of Britain. Under the patronage of the egregious Rosebery, Burns Clubs multiplied after 1885, as did Caledonian associations among emigrants, anxious to evade the unpopularity of the British at their imperial zenith – as well as salivating at the chance to consume quantities of legally distilled whisky and export ale. Black Scotland had in fact become an essential complement of red Scotland, a fruitful schizophrenia which enabled the Scots to run with the ethnic hare and hunt with the imperial hounds.

The entente between emotive nationalism and effective unionism gelded any political movement. It lacked the economic grievances on which Irish and Welsh nationalism fed; the religious and educational estates, which steered economic change and political response, were committed to Union and Empire. Left-wing home rulers in the Young Scots' Society – founded as a pro-Boer pressure group in 1900 – propagandised against 'English' MPs and in favour of a 'new Liberal' programme before 1914, but the momentum of social and economic development continually frustrated them.

Home rule stood a chance of success only when the confidence of Westminster faltered. This came closest in the Irish home rule crisis between 1910 and 1914, less through radical pressure in Scotland, than through unionist fears of total constitutional breakdown. These were voiced by an energetic Scots imperialist, F. S. Oliver (grandson of the Victorian radical leader Duncan MacLaren) in a series of *Times* letters in 1910, and formed the basis of the settlement that Lloyd George and Churchill hoped might gain Tory support. Had war not broken out, the Scots might have been presented with a Parliament. But did they know what they wanted to do with it?

If war adjourned the Irish crisis – which resumed with enhanced ferocity in 1918 – it postponed indefinitely the regionalisation of British politics. Another 'great moral issue' moved in, but this time Liberal Britain died and Ireland escaped. Scottish devolution had to find its place in an altogether new political order.

DEVOLUTION IN A COLD CLIMATE

Total war – sustaining its impact and adjusting to its consequences – dominated British politics for fifty years, distorting old loyalties and institutions. Formal war aims promised recompense for sacrifice; unforeseen social changes were engendered by the intensity of the conflict. Yet war, even taken at the strength of 1914–18 and 1939–45, was complex and catalytic, not absolute and uniform.

Nowhere more so than in Anglo-Scottish relations. For example, devolution *could* have come in 1914; war aims in 1918 sanctioned the principle of national autonomy. Yet Scotland was by then firmly under southern control. In World War II, by contrast, centralised planning and control was legitimised as part of a continuing welfare capitalism, yet Scotland acquired an unprecedented degree of administrative devolution. Between the changes that total war unleashed and Scottish politics was a layer in which political manoeuvre was critical. It was here that the activities of nationalists at last gained relevance.

World War I ended the devolution option. Although a Speaker's Conference examined it in 1919, the secession of southern Ireland and the collapse of the Liberals fatally weakened it. War boosted British agencies, and the takeover of Scottish institutions. As William Ferguson wrote, 'in 1914 the Scottish economy was a reality, but by the 1920s the phrase, while still in use, could be taken to mean only a depressed sector of a none-too-robust British economy'. Between 1918 and 1923 the five railway companies, most of the banks and shipping companies were taken over by English concerns, while a depressed international market afflicted manufacturing industry. The nationalists had to combine an interventionist economic and social programme with the traditional arguments for devolution. This they failed to do.

The home rule movement had no power in itself, nor was politics predictable. Although a form of autonomous socialism was ventilated during and just after the war by the Marxist pedagogue John Maclean and the Jacobite Catholic aristocrat Ruaraidh Erskine of Mar, they were articulate rather than influential. There was little or no organisation. The Scottish Home Rule Association had lapsed by 1914, along with the various Liberal pressure groups, and its revival in September 1918 came only two months before the general election, too late for sustained propaganda. It was also difficult to second-guess an agile electorate which voted overwhelmingly for the Conservative coalition in 1918, swung left in 1922, further left in 1923, then back to the right in 1924. Most candidates said they favoured home rule in some shape or form, but they were never in the same place long enough to do anything about it.

The Labour Party, which had supplanted the Liberals, exemplified this. Its Scottish Council, and the Scottish Trades Union Congress, favoured home rule, but they were marginalised by the growth of non-Scottish trade unions and growing industrial confrontation. The case of railway amalgamation in 1921–3 was critical. The government proposed a Scottish railway company, but was forced to alter its plans by Scottish railway shareholders and trade unionists, the first fearing (with reason) that they would take over a hopelessly uneconomic system, the second remembering vindictive old Scots managements. For both, security appeared to lie in unity with the south. As other amalgamations in the textile, chemical and engineering industries showed, this logic was by no means unique.

The home rulers were not totally to blame for the failure to get devolution on to the party manifestos. For if devolution were to mean collective control, over railways for instance, an executive framework was necessary. It scarcely existed. Government departments and boards, still divided between Edinburgh and London, were restricted to supervising local government and the traditional estates, themselves badly in need of reform. Devolution before 1914 was an answer to constitutional crisis, but now the crisis had shifted to society and the economy. This was vividly underlined by the General Strike in May 1926. Although unsuccessful, it powerfully reinforced class-consciousness and Labour organisation, demonstrating the political archaism of the Liberal agenda, home rule included.

THE NATIONALISM OF THE LITERATI

These misfortunes were aggravated by changes within the national movement. The first home rule bill moved by a Labour MP, in 1924, was semi-federal, similar to pre-war Liberal proposals. But the next, in 1927, came from the enthusiasts of the Scottish Home Rule Association, and demanded a status like that of the Irish Free State. It was briskly dismissed by the Commons, but Ireland, the emergent nations in Europe and the revolutionary discontinuities in Russia and Italy deeply affected younger, leftish nationalists. James Connolly, the martyr of the Dublin Easter Rising of 1916, had been born in Edinburgh, played an active part on the Scottish left and was *Forward*'s Irish correspondent. John Maclean had been appointed Soviet consul in Scotland by Lenin himself. The memory of both – for Maclean died, worn out, shortly after he broke with the British Communists to found his own revolutionary party – was used by publicists like Erskine of Mar to fuse nationalism to revolution.

24

The leader of the 'Scottish Renaissance', the poet and critic C. M. Grieve (Hugh MacDiarmid) in his manifesto of 1927, *Albyn, or Scotland and the Future*, even claimed that the death of devolution – 'the last step in the assimilation of Scotland to England' – was essential for nationalism to triumph. The creation of an independent national party wasn't a response to Westminster's failure to pass home rule; it was an alternative to home rule itself.

Between 1925 and 1927, Grieve produced, besides *Albyn, A Drunk Man Looks at the Thistle* and *Contemporary Scottish Studies*, subjecting the state of Scottish culture to a sustained and devastating analysis. He was no traditionalist, out after traducers of national myths, but a European of the artistic and political revolutions, who regarded England as irredeemably provincial. Grieve had been reared in the exotic left which centred on A. R. Orage's *New Age*, and he extolled, with little regard for consistency, every force that made for action – Communism, Fascism, nationalism or Social Credit. He idealised contradiction – his 'Caledonian Antisyzygy' – borrowing this monstrous phrase from Gregory Smith's study of Scots literature. And inconsistency summed up the qualities of the national movement he helped create.

On 23 June 1928 the National Party of Scotland was formally inaugurated at Stirling: an independent movement, distinct from any British political party. In this it paralleled the founding in Wales, three years earlier, of Plaid Cymru. Both mobilised students and intellectuals; both stressed linguistic distinctiveness and a native tradition of decentralised democracy, currently under threat. But the *Blaid* followed a nationalist renaissance in Wales which had lasted for some sixty years. Its career was to be bedevilled by its association with forces – the Welsh language, nonconformist radicalism and temperance – now waning but still able to frustrate any consensus in favour of home rule. In Scotland the *absence* of an effective nationalist tradition was, paradoxically, a source of strength. In the eyes of its younger and more radical supporters, the new movement was a catalyst; its consequences unprecedented and unpredictable. As MacDiarmid wrote:

O Scotland is
The barren fig

Up, carles, up,
And round it jig!
A miracle's
Oor only chance.
Up, carles, up
And let us dance!

The National Party (NPS) fused traditional nationalists to Catholic intellectuals, students, journalists and discontented members of the Independent Labour Party (ILP). Its first Chairman and its Secretary, Roland Muirhead and John MacCormick, were refugees like Grieve from the ILP, in the 1920s a nursery of unorthodox radicalism and a training school for Labour organisers. This legacy – Muirhead's loyalty and cash and MacCormick's organisational ability – kept a potentially fissile party together, but it could not resolve the contradictions between political nationalism and the Scottish context.

Nationalist weakness echoed its own complaint that talent drained away from Scotland. The NPS was at best a reserve team. The politically competent – Robert Horne and Walter Elliot on the right, Sir Archibald Sinclair in the Liberal Party, James Maxton and Tom Johnston on the left – still immersed themselves in Westminster, although John Buchan was rumoured sympathetic. There was no structure of Scottish politics to which they could relate, so the organisational ability of individual nationalists could easily slip into opportunism or eccentricity – something evident in the NPS's leading personalities, John MacCormick and Roland Muirhead. Both were isolated from the main arena. MacCormick, a gifted student politician at Glasgow University, would have gone into Labour politics, had they not shifted south. He sensed the vacuum and through a series of shrewd publicity coups established nationalism as an alternative focus. Without a parliamentary presence, however, he could not sustain these initiatives. Instead, he tried to ally with traditional representatives of Scottish Liberalism, and was branded as an opportunist. Muirhead, a wealthy tanner of left-wing sympathies, could remember Keir Hardie founding the Scottish Labour Party. A dour supporter of socialism of a rather anarchistic type, pacifism and colonial liberation, he bankrolled anyone with such aims, whatever their effectiveness. The coexistence of the two kept the NPS and its successor together in the 1930s, but it also ensured that its achievements were, to say the least, limited.

Ideologically, the NPS had its own antisyzygy. During World War I nationalism had taken on a new meaning: liberation from imperialism. Muirhead approved, equating Scotland with the exploited colonies, but the notion of home rule *qua* imperial federation was still important to those who longed for the pre-war balance. Such an alliance was plausible, but the enthusiasm of the young, and the profits of Muirhead's Gryfe Tannery, had to be tapped. The same problem affected the NPS's domestic policy. Should it provide collectivist remedies, or should it appeal to the Scottish establishment, worried about the drain of authority to the south? When in the 1930s its leaders opted for the latter, even sympathetic observers like the poet and critic Edwin Muir found it difficult to forgive them. In the face of the misery of the depression, their politics seemed irrelevant compared with the drastic remedies of the socialists:

> Even if the country were governed by Scotsmen, the economic conflicts within it could still generate the same intestine hatreds as they do now, and would still deserve to do so.

Yet the options before the NPS were limited. The Scottish electorate was temperamentally conservative, and a move to the left would alienate many potential supporters, particularly former Liberals. If it took on the trade-union-backed Labour Party, which could still play the home rule card, it would end up simply as the weakest section of the Scottish left. This was shown by the 1929 general election, when it polled less than 5 per cent in two seats. Even in Glasgow St Rollox, where locomotive building had been severely hit by contraction and the transfer of work south, it only got 15 per cent.

After the débâcle of its second government proclaimed its ideological bankruptcy, Labour fell from from 37 to 7 MPs, four of whom shortly seceded with the ILP. The only possibility of success seemed to lie in an appeal to traditionalists. The latter were certainly perturbed enough. Besides business amalgamations, much of the Scottish civil service was now directly under government control and centralised in London. Church politics had been quieted by the re-union of the Kirk and the Free Church in 1929, and in the same year there had also been a particularly ruthless local government reform, abolishing parish councils. The overwhelming victory of the National government in 1931 seemed to show that integration was out of control.

Then strange things happened. Ramsay MacDonald reverted to his home rule infancy, prompted perhaps by the incalculable Buchan, perhaps by Lord Beaverbrook, who had just started the *Scottish Daily Express*. The business community reacted with hostility and unease, writing *en masse* to *The Times*. This, in turn, started a revolt in the heartland of the Scots bourgeoisie, the Unionist Association in Glasgow Cathcart, in favour of imperial devolution, 'the Milner programme of the pre-war years with a dash of Lord Beaverbrook added'. The rebels were joined by Sir Henry Keith, the Tory doyen of local government, Sir Alexander MacEwen, a prominent Highland Liberal and by Andrew Dewar Gibb, Regius Professor of Scots Law at Glasgow University and former Unionist candidate for Hamilton, who drew up an appeal to the Duke of Montrose, a convert to Liberalism who was known to look sympathetically on home rule. The result was the formation in 1932 of the Scottish Self-Government Party.

MacCormick had advised the organisers of the new party on policy and, through the agency of the novelist Neil Gunn and Beaverbrook's aide George Malcolm Thomson, quickly came to an agreement with them, even at the cost of a split within the NPS and the expulsion of MacDiarmid. In 1934 the two parties merged, with a programme which accentuated home rule and underplayed independence – although it never discarded it completely. The Scottish National Party performed creditably at the 1935 general election, contesting eight seats and polling an average of 16 per cent, and in 1938 MacCormick negotiated a pact with the Scottish Liberals which would give the party a straight run in twelve constituencies of its own choice. Against this, however, the move to a consensus position lost it many activists. From a membership peak of over 10,000 in 1934 it declined to below 2,000 by 1939. Respectable and centrist, MacCormick's policy helped to make nationalism an alternative polarity to socialism in planning Scotland's future. Few of the numerous economic, amenity and social service organisations which were set up in the 1930s by 'middle opinion' in Scotland – the National Trust for Scotland (1931), the Saltire Society (1936), and the Scottish Council for Social Service (1939) – lacked con-

28

tact with the nationalist consensus. But it left the activists and the ideologues isolated.

TOM JOHNSTON AT ST ANDREW'S HOUSE

In 1937 the Gilmour Committee recommended the transfer of the Scottish government departments to an Edinburgh head-quarters. Although the obsession that 'the bomber will always get through' was probably more influential than nationalism in securing this, nationalism of a rather conservative sort had certainly played its part. The Scottish National Development Council had been set up in 1930 by the same group which later founded the Scottish Party. Rather surprisingly, it was bank-rolled by the industrialist, and strong unionist, Sir James Lithgow, and then got enough government assistance, through the Commissioner for the Scottish Special Area, to take on some economic advisory functions. Through its offshoot, the Scottish Economic Committee of 1935, it began to give the Secretary of State a role, albeit indirectly, in economic policy.

In 1939, St Andrew's House – a formidable building resem-bling a Central European railway station – was opened as the Scottish Whitehall. James Kellas has seen this as the critical transition which 'accelerated the movement towards political separatism', but in fact it gave Edinburgh only what Dublin had been left with in 1801. St Andrew's House rapidly assumed the persona of Dublin Castle, the impersonal medium of alien gov-ernment. But the Scottish administration was beginning to move beyond its traditional fields: agriculture and fisheries, law and order, health and education. Administrative devolution came at the end of a period of economic and political stagnation, and even conservatives were envisaging a great expansion in the sphere of government. Would such responsibilities as social and physical planning also be conceded, or would they be centralised in the south?

The invasion of Poland in September 1939 killed the SNP's plan for an all-party Scottish Convention to discuss home rule. The war itself ought logically to have killed nationalism *tout court*. The centralisation of British decision-making was drastic; in Europe small nations fell like ninepins. Nationalists reacted gloomily. Yet by 1945 they had played a prominent part in wartime politics, and executive devolution managed to keep pace with the expansion of government activity. No single group played a critical role. The context of wartime politics was more important than the actors, and its disappearance exposed their relative immaturity. But the line had been held: a combination of political agitation, non-political nationalism and executive determination at last brought nationalism to terms with the reality of collectivism.

Nationalism's resilience was remarkable, considering the eccentric behaviour of the SNP. With its dwindling membership, it was scarcely strong in 1939. MacCormick then gambled on achieving an entente with the moderate left, a policy which the appointment of Tom Johnston, Labour MP for West Stirlingshire, as Secretary of State in February 1941 seemed to endorse. But, within sight of success, he was challenged by the party's remaining fundamentalists. In 1937 they had pledged the party to oppose conscription, save when carried out by a Scottish government. When the war came this commitment was put to the test by the Chairman of the Aberdeen branch, Douglas Young. Educated at public school (Merchiston Castle) and Oxford, poet, socialist and lecturer in Greek at the university, Young was a picturesque and charming eccentric in the tradition of John Stuart Blackie. He wrote to Muirhead in 1940 saying that the Allies would lose the war and that the Scots should think of a separate peace:

> The Germans will look around for aborigines to run Scotland, and it is to be wished that the eventual administration consist of people who have in the past shown themselves to care for the interests of Scotland.

Young was actually charged with refusing to register either for military service or as a conscientious objector, on the terms of the 1937 resolution. In 1940 and 1941, through a protracted legal battle, he began to attain the status of a martyr, attracting the support of those penalised by the arbitrary acts of wartime government. Memories of a disproportionately high Scottish death rate in World War I were revived; the conscription of Scottish women to work in Midlands munitions factories added insult to the injury of the depression. Both sides surfaced at the SNP annual conference in June 1942, when MacCormick proposed that the party cease contesting elections and concentrate instead on cultivating an all-party commitment to home rule at the end of the war. He was defeated and angrily withdrew from the conference to found his own movement, Scottish Union, later Scottish Convention. Its time was to come, but not yet.

The splitting of one small movement into two could not be expected to enhance the nationalist cause, yet it did. In February 1944 Young nearly won Kirkcaldy Burghs; the following April the party's secretary, Dr Robert McIntyre, won Motherwell. With the exception of the North Midlothian election in early 1943, the main English third force, Common Wealth, made little impact north of the border. Criticism of the way the war was being run was seen as nationalist criticism, which the Scottish Secretary, Thomas Johnston, shrewdly orchestrated to gain increased freedom of action. The Home Secretary, Herbert Morrison, marvelled at the way Johnston used a 'Sinn Fein' threat in Cabinet committee to extort an advanced social programme from the government. Yet the nationalists were not simply useful bogeymen. Johnston had for long been associated with home rule, and his programme differed little from MacCormick's. By fusing this to administrative acumen and political opportunity, Johnston created for the first time the institutions on which bourgeois nationalists could build.

The factors which made up Johnston's political background were those which led Scottish radicals of earlier generations – and many of his own contemporaries – to quit the country. He was born into a lower middle-class family at Kirkintilloch, just outside Glasgow, in 1881. While at Glasgow University he became a member of the ILP and the Fabian Society then, in 1905, inherited a small printing firm. In a series of pioneering, if partisan, histories, *Our Scots Noble Families* (1909) and *A History of the Working Classes in Scotland* (1922), he began to reinterpret the myth-laden Scottish past. Aided by various veterans of the old Scottish Labour Party and west of Scotland radicals, he founded *Forward* in 1906 and made it the leading periodical of the ILP. Much more influential than the Marxism of John MacLean, *Forward* preached the pacifistic, humanitarian radicalism which the Clydeside MPs took south in 1922. Yet Johnston did not follow them in their disillusion with the parliamentary process, nor did he break his links with Scottish home rule and local government politics. As a junior member of the minority Labour government of 1929–31 and a director of the Empire Marketing Board, he shifted towards the political centre. While the ILP walked into the political wilderness he made close contact with 'middle opinion' groups which sought social reconstruction through bipartisan policies of physical planning and economic growth. As a sponsor of the Saltire Society and a leader of self-government pressure groups within the Labour Party, he gave such developments a specifically Scottish slant.

Churchill gave Johnston his chance in February 1941. Johnston was able to name his terms and got what amounted to a promise of *de facto* home rule for the duration of the war. He was to have a Scottish Council of State, consisting of all the ex-Secretaries of State, who would vet legislation proposed for Scotland. If it received their approval, it was to go through Parliament without delay. The Scottish Grand Committee of MPs was to meet, experimentally, in Edinburgh. A Scottish Council on Industry was to be set up to involve businessmen, bankers, trade unionists and local government leaders in planning industrial development – virtually taking over the role of the Board of Trade in Scotland. The prospect suited the convenience of Westminster as well as the Scottish administration. Parliament did not have to absorb itself with Scottish legislation; the need for frequent communication with the south was obviated. Not all of Johnston's proposals worked. The Scottish MPs – most of them still Tories – showed little interest in meeting in Edinburgh and after a couple of attempts the meetings lapsed, being replaced by the Scottish Council. But the commitment to conform to Scottish opinion, where that opinion was manifest, was adhered to by Whitehall. Johnston got sanction for the North of Scotland Hydro-Electric Board, for the transfer of planning powers to the Scottish Office, for the extension of agricultural intervention and forestry development and for the imaginative management of health and welfare schemes. 'We had got Scotland's wishes and opinions respected and listened to,' he wrote later, 'as they had not been respected or listened to since the Union.'

Johnston left office and Parliament in 1945. His achievement stopped short of home rule, and he probably contributed to its deferment. Always a 'doer' rather than a 'talker', his absorption in boards, committees and *ad hoc* authorities seemed to make him prefer such consensus to the divisiveness of elected assemblies. The assailant of 'Our Noble Families' became something of a territorial magnate himself, as Chairman of the Hydro

Board and the Scottish Forestry Commission. Rather than fight for further devolution in Attlee's Cabinet he preferred to consolidate the institutions he had set up.

Johnston's success in devising *ad hoc* authorities made these into alternatives to legislative devolution. If the quarter-century after 1940 was the age of enlightened, centrist 'Butskellism', he ensured that executive authority was not concentrated in Whitehall, but was at least shadowed in Scotland. In 1940–41, according to Paul Addison, 'middle opinion' took power in England; Johnston ensured that a specifically Scottish 'middle opinion' – his colleagues on the Saltire Society, the Scottish Council for Social Service, and the various Labour self-government groups – gained influence during the war years.

In the long run the shift was more drastic. The growth of the Scottish Office meant that the preoccupations of Scottish politicians were increasingly contained within the country. The age of the carpet-bagger was nearly at an end. This might be reflected only by the mediocrity – if *native* mediocrity – of Scottish MPs, but after almost 250 years, during which the central concerns of economic life had eluded nationalist politics, the components of 'developmental' nationalism were at last perceptible in Scotland. As the country, its industrial base as lopsided as ever, lurched into the post-war world, its future was, as never before, linked to the performance of its devolved executive government.

2

AN ACHIEVING SOCIETY
Unionist Scotland, 1707–1945

Scotland is unique among European nations in its failure to
develop a nationalist sentiment strong enough to be a vital
factor in its affairs – a failure inconsistent alike with our
traditional love of country and reputation for practicality.
The reason probably lies in the fact that no comprehensive-
enough agency has emerged; and the common-sense of
our people has rejected one-sided expedients incapable of
addressing the organic complexity of our national life. For
it must be recognised that the absence of Scottish nationalism is, paradoxically enough, a form of Scottish self-
determination.

C. M. Grieve, *Albyn, or Scotland and
the Future* (1927)

NON-NATIONAL NATIONALISM

Out of step with nationalism elsewhere in the world, the Scots
were until the later twentieth century judged and dismissed by
its criteria. Yet something remained which was, perhaps, more
important. Scotland after 1707 wasn't the self-referential,
Manichaean world of 'autistic' nationalism whose community is
continually threatened by external enemies and internal traitors.
Even 'absolute' nationalists were unobtrusive, wary of complex
and morally ambiguous politics, of 'common' experiences –
industrialisation and imperialism – generically similar but still
markedly different from England's. Myths were important,
even positive, such as the conviction, in Professor H. J. Paton's
words, that 'the passion for liberty runs right through Scottish
literature and political thinking'. But they could also be danger-

ous, as Yeats regretted when a nationalism which exalted feeling over fact plunged his country into civil war in 1922–3:

> We had fed the heart on fantasies,
> The heart's frown brutal with the fare;
> More substance in our enmities
> Than in our love; O honey-bees,
> Come build in the empty house of the stare.

The Irish myth was centred round a country forced into union in 1801 and denied home rule after 1886: Cathleen ni Houlihan, the old woman who would be rejuvenated by liberty. There was no such Scottish persona, largely because, for most of the post-1707 epoch, the Union functioned with the co-operation and enthusiasm of the Scottish people. Discovering the terms of this consent is complicated by the competing myth – fashionable until very recently – of 'unionist history'. Marching in step with Whitehall, and its projection of Britain abroad, this has lazily assumed that within a United Kingdom dominated by a sovereign Parliament, Scottish affairs are merely minor variations on British themes.

The two myths are complementary. The 'political homogeneity' which underlay post-war British politics – and the resulting insensitivity – reinforced the simpler forms of nationalism. To find concepts which fit the facts of Anglo-Scottish politics since the Union, we have to retreat to a period when confidence in central government was less whole-hearted: to the assault on the sovereign state – Harold Laski's 'modern Baal to which the citizen must bow a heedless knee' – in the 1900 to 1920 period. 'Pluralist' political thinkers, who wished to substitute a range of near-autonomous authorities for the state, drew attention to the 'semi-independence' that Scottish institutions – 'the estates' – had enjoyed since the Union, just when their status was being threatened by the centralising impulse of World War I.

Given his involvement with the semi-syndicalist Guild Socialists, who thought along such lines, it is not surprising that Grieve, in *Albyn*, considered that the Scots – or at least their ruling groups – had secured their own national settlement *within* the Union. In this he echoed Laski who argued in *Studies in the Problems of Sovereignty* (1917) that the presbyterians who had in 1843 withdrawn from the Kirk to found the Free Church recognised the Union as purely a contractual agreement:

They were fighting a State which had taken over bodily the principles and ideals of the medieval theocracy. They urged the essential federalism of society, the impossibility of confining sovereignty to any one of its constituent parts.

Arch-unionists and ideologues of parliamentary sovereignty that they were, even Dicey and Rait, in their *Thoughts on the Union*, stressed how the Act of 1707 had, through constitutional conventions, been interpreted as preserving Scottish nationalism. The estates – legal, educational and religious – remained remarkably free from southern interference; in turn they nurtured those who exploited the opportunities provided by the Union. That such studies were by English scholars, or scholars trained in England, betrayed a deficiency in Scottish consciousness: Laski found that the country of Burnet, Hume and Robertson had not produced by 1916 an adequate history of the Disruption of 1843. The weakness came when historians were supposedly the pedagogues of the new nations, something which both attenuated political nationalism and stemmed directly from the 'Scottishness' which the Union guaranteed.

Post-Union Scotland was gripped in a complex cultural dialectic. On one side were the estates and civil society, both recognisably Scottish. On the other were industry and Empire. The outcome was, however, not 'British' but protean; after about a century of Union it ceased to be geographically centred in Scotland, and went beyond any national historiography. Before about 1830 the Scottish literary-historical tradition could deal with a society which was both lived-in and 'improving'. After 1920, economic reverses and literary revivals animated 'orthodox' nationalism. The problem is the near-century during which industrialisation and liberalism almost blindly created the social structure and the functional politics of modern Scotland.

ENGLISH GOLD

K. W. Deutsch, the American sociologist, defined nation-states as 'diffuse, particularistic and ascriptive'. *Diffuse* because their key institutions are not specialised but generally competent; *particularistic* because only their citizens are entitled to use these; and *ascriptive* 'because you are who you are, you will be presumed to have certain qualities'. Such a national society:

offers few choices to the individual, but it also imposes few burdens. The member does not have to worry about how to choose his course; most things and relationships are more or less given.

Its opposite is a society in which institutions are functional, with open access and universal validity, and status is determined by achievement.

It is difficult to recognise post-Union Scotland in either scenario. The compromises of unionism complicate matters for a start, but even the 'Scottish' context is opaque. The lack of a Parliament meant that the nation was not omnicompetent, yet the estates claimed an authority beyond their specific functions. There was, theoretically, a common citizenship, yet the Scots had privileges in Scotland denied to the English. The Union enhanced aristocratic control of politics, yet accelerated the social mobility of the ambitious and talented from the lower classes. It created a society in which national and universal elements were uniquely combined.

Later apologists would credit the men of 1707 with a prescience which that 'parcel of rogues in a nation' would never have claimed. Burns's jibe is fair enough: their motives were short-term and selfish. Even Daniel Defoe, who had worked hard to promote the Union, was appalled at the outcome:

> The great men are posting to London for places and honours, every man full of his own merit and afraid of everyone near him: I never saw so much trick, sham, pride, jealousy and cutting of friends' throats as there is among the noblemen.

If principle played little part in forging the Union, it would have played even less in its repeal, which was nearly carried at Westminster six years later. The year 1707 involved the manoeuvres of the great territorial magnates, the Dukes of Argyll, Hamilton, Atholl and Queensberry, and the leaders of the English parties, anxious to secure their northern flank and the Protestant succession against the French and the Stuart Pretender. Political parties in Scotland, if they could be dignified with the name, were tools of aristocratic intrigue, or responses to it. The estates were treated at best as clients, or simply ignored.

Despite this, most responsible Scots believed that lasting Union was inevitable. Even Lord Belhaven, whose 'Vision' speech – 'I think I see our ancient mother Caledonia, like Caesar, sitting in the midst of our senate . . . attending the final blow' – was the only great oratory of the whole affair, mourned the state of the country. Against the opulence of England, he admitted:

> We are an obscure, poor, people, though formerly of better account, removed to a remote corner of the world, without name and without alliances, our ports mean and precarious so that I profess I do not think any one port of the kingdom worth the bringing after.

Economic backwardness, as Professor Tom Devine has shown, can be exaggerated, but the setbacks of the 1690s had halted the country's modernisation. In Europe the terms of trade shifted against traditional Scots exports. Austere independence had few takers; nobleman and merchant alike looked south, respectively eyeing power and patronage, an expanding English market and the liquidation of Darien losses. 'The motives will be, Trade with most, Hanover with some, ease and security with others,' wrote the Earl of Roxburghe in 1705. He and his party, the Squadrone Volante, had opposed earlier Union negotiations; then, foreseeing English determination and Scots acquiescence, he switched sides, expedited the business, and became a Duke.

This mixture of opportunism and fatalism was predictable. Before 1688 the King controlled the Scots Parliament through the 'Lords of the Articles', which minimised conflict with Westminster, and aggravated it in Scotland. Once freed from this constraint, the two legislatures turned on each other. Their leaders had to find a substitute for royal authority as arbiter in a conflict which the weaker legislature could not win. For power groups in Scotland, there were worse options than Union. Presbyterians and Whigs distrusted the independence offered by the Stuarts; noblemen remembered that instability could, given rebellion or civil war, lead to an English takeover.

Some still recalled nine years during which they had been ruled – on the whole efficiently and equitably – by eight commissioners 'of the Parliament of England for ordering and managing the affairs of Scotland'. Cromwell's officers had felt no inhibitions about interfering with Scots religion and Scots law, enforcing toleration and breaking the authority of ministers and lairds. Mixing social revolution and assimilation, one of them, the Welsh regicide Colonel John Jones, wrote:

> It is the interest of the Commonwealth of England to break the interest of the great men in Scotland, and to settle the interest of the common people upon a different foot from that of their lords and masters . . . The great men will never be faithful to you so long as you propound freedom to the people and relief against their tyranny.

Given a few more years of such direct rule, the power of the Scottish estates might have been eradicated, and assimilation become irresistible. Instead the struggle against James II promised a further accession of demotic nationalism. Federalism was popular among the people and forcefully advocated in Parliament House by Andrew Fletcher. But the people did not dispose of power; if the Union settlement recognised the rights of Church, law and nobility, the estates had no wish to share them with a legislature.

'SEMI-INDEPENDENCE'

The Union won few friends. The Scots regarded the Treaty as a fundamental law, a constitution for the United Kingdom, but it was subject to the autonomy of a sovereign Westminster, which abolished the Scottish Privy Council in 1708, assimilated the law on treason to that of England in 1709 and restored ecclesiastical patronage in 1712. English perfidy and arrogance? In fact the first and third were the result of intrigues by Scots politicians: the Squadrone wanted the Privy Council suppressed before it could become a platform for Jacobites; the Jacobites, headed by Lockhart of Carnwath, a fierce opponent of the Union, used a Tory victory to re-establish patronage as a stepping-stone to the return of episcopacy. The change in the treason law was an understandable over-reaction to the Jacobite menace. Party contests breached the Union settlement – and could have overthrown it completely. What endured was aristocratic involvement in United Kingdom politics and presbyterian hostility to the Stuarts. What if the Pretenders had been diplomatic enough to conciliate Scots religious sentiments? Had they been diplomats they would not have been Pretenders. Until 1715 the margin was narrow but decisive: Hanover and the Kirk were better than Stuart and the Parliament. After 1715 the Union was strengthened by the evolving capacities of a new system of government. Political management and the estates became the cornerstones of Scottish 'semi-independence', the structure that nurtured the economic and social forces which ultimately overwhelmed it.

'Semi-independence' was pivoted on a political system which differed from that of England not in degree but in principle. English constituencies were far from symmetrical, but the ideal of representation was cherished, and in some places was even real. Up to 1832, one Englishman in 30 could vote. The equivalent figure for Scotland was one in 600. Scarcely 3,000 'county freeholders' voted for the 30 county MPs; the 15 burgh MPs were elected by groups of town councils, a self-selecting oligarchy. With a total electorate smaller than many *individual* English boroughs or counties, the Scottish MPs represented no one but their paymaster, usually the confidant of the government who managed Scottish affairs. Bluntly, they were there to be bought, the quid pro quo being that the 'Scotch manager' would square government demands with Scottish interests and patronage. Which he did: before the Union was a score or so years old, Scots legislation was being discussed in Edinburgh between the manager, the Scots law officers, the Faculty of Advocates, the Convention of Royal Burghs, the county freeholders and the Church. Once agreed, it could be carried at Westminster and enforced in Scotland.

This institutional federalism was essentially pluralistic. Westminster abrogated its theoretical sovereignty and acquiesced in Scottish autonomy in enforcing law, even if this meant that the Scots to a great extent legislated for themselves. This spirit even survived the decline of 'semi-independence' after 1830: the Scots interpreted public health and poor law legislation imaginatively, applying their own variations to United Kingdom enactments. This flexibility helps to explain the paradox of Scotland in the 'age of improvement': the coexistence of intellectual and social vitality and apparent political servility. By Deutsch's definition the 'diffuse' nation-state was moribund, and local government little better. But these deferred to estates which were both 'Scottish' and functional; creating an effective, unobtrusive politics and encouraging a scale of values, in social and intellectual life, which went beyond the nation: the vertebrae of an achieving society.

The practical politics of post-Union Scotland revolved round the law and the Kirk, which mediated between authority and the potential anarchy of popular feeling in a way the formal electoral system was incapable of doing. Between 1688 and 1707 law consolidated its doctrines and autonomy. Its theory, rooted in Roman law, was made explicit by Viscount Stair in his *Institutions of the Law of Scotland*, published in 1681, just when the autonomy of the Faculty of Advocates was recognised after energetic internal struggles. The Faculty became a forum for the discussion of legislation; and, later on, as the 'territorial jurisdictions' of the north and west were abolished, transmitted the skills of 'management' to the legal families – the Forbeses, Dundases and Erskines – which took over from the noblemen. This hegemony lasted; until the creation of the Secretaryship in 1885 the Lord Advocate, head of the Scottish legal profession, was the chief government agent in the north.

Stair warily followed Buchanan and Rutherford in advocating a limited monarchy. He wrote in 1660:

I have been persuaded that it was both against the interest and duty of kings to use arbitrary government; that both kings and subjects had their title and rights by law, and that an equal balance of prerogative and liberty was necessary for the happiness of a commonwealth.

This was reflected in a partnership which the manager had to maintain by continual adjustments. Sir Walter Scott dramatised the process in *The Heart of Midlothian* (1818), that brilliant documentary of the early years of the Union, which centres on the Porteous Riot of 1736. Porteous, the captain of Edinburgh's town guard, was sentenced to death for ordering his men to fire on a crowd at a smuggler's execution. His reprieve by royal prerogative was regarded as an infringement of Scottish liberties, and in a well-organised uprising he was taken from the Tolbooth and hanged. Parliament enacted severe penalties for Edinburgh, but these were mitigated after intervention by the Duke of Argyll, whose brother, the Earl of Islay, was the Scottish manager. Argyll's policy was less consistent than Scott's depiction, although his power was such that his defection cost Walpole his Prime-Ministership in 1742. But Scott realised that Scottish identity depended on a sort of contract, in which the informal pressures of mob violence and patronage played as active a role as that of the great institutions of state.

The politics of 'semi-independence' were patrician – popular only when the mob intervened. But suppose such interventions gained independent momentum? In religion, authority confronted a popular claim, articulate and persistent. The Kirk, under the rule of the Moderates – ministers who were liberal in theology and philosophy, but prudently conservative in politics – controlled education and poor relief; its ministers and laymen debated politics as well as religion at the annual General Assembly in Edinburgh. But its link to landed power was secured by a breach of presbyterian principle: the restoration of patronage in 1712. In *The Wealth of Nations* in 1776 Adam Smith, a Moderate and deist, commended the non-hierarchical organisation of presbyterianism as giving its clergy 'more influence over the minds of the common people than perhaps the clergy of any other established church'; he also upheld patronage as a security against fundamentalist zealots. Whig rationalism applauded the offspring of a Jacobite intrigue. Yet this betrayal of the Covenant was to agitate the religious estate for over a century until, in 1843, it split it down the middle.

Religious politics and divisions were quite different from the south. English dissent dated from the time of the Commonwealth, and meant a clean break with state-sponsored religion. After the Restoration, and the exclusion of nonconformists from government, the ideal of the self-governing congregation holding to its own variety of belief became linked with the encouragement of manufacture and entrepreneurship, notably among Quakers, Unitarians and Congregationalists. In Wales 'new dissent' – mainly Methodism – overtook the establishment, and pervaded the democratic nationalism of the nineteenth century. In all these cases, the road from religion to politics was indirect. Sects decided for themselves to ignore the establishment, try to get concessions from it, or attack its very existence; their political affiliations resulted from these decisions. But in Scotland religious disputes centred on the political issue of who controlled the establishment. The various secessionist groups did not retreat into their own private theologies. Each was convinced that it was the true legatee of the Covenanters of 1638.

English dissent provided motives for self-realisation in commerce, and useful family networks. In Scotland this was inverted: the tranquillity that Adam Smith commended existed because dissenters did *not* withdraw from politics. They abused the establishment but they never challenged the principle. The world of the Calvinist zealot Davie Deans, in *The Heart of Midlothian*, peopled with martyrs for the Covenant, was valid to him: a surrogate politics which consoled the defeated. Brawling over patronage was a source of disorder, but the discontent was only symbolic and left the modernisation of society, encouraged by the Kirk, unchecked. The Reverend Micah Balwhidder, the worldly Moderate minister of Dalmailing in John Galt's *Annals of the Parish*, is 'intruded' in 1760, to the accompaniment of a riot. When he quits it fifty years later, having helped it evolve into an industrial town, the dissenters turn up to his final service, out of respect.

CATCHING UP AND HOLDING DOWN

Both managed politics and Moderate religion had latent weaknesses, but they provided security for the economic growth of Lowland Scotland. After 1746 they were unchallenged. Although Webster's census in 1750 found that about 30 per cent of the population still lived beyond the Highland line, the relationships which held its society together rapidly disintegrated. The judicial powers of the chiefs were abolished, the missionary activities of the Kirk were increased. Where Highland society maintained itself – by burning kelp for fertiliser, cattle raising and herring fishing, the population grew for another century – it did so through Lowland finance and a Lowland market. More often its surplus population, accumulating on subdivided crofts and feeding itself on potatoes (which increased the nutritive yield of the land by 300 per cent, compared with oats), simply supplied the new industrial areas with the manpower they required.

In the course of his analysis of 'the Celtic fringe in British national development', the American sociologist Michael Hechter discovered a process of 'internal colonisation' in which:

The movement of peripheral labour is determined largely by forces exogeneous to the periphery . . . Economic dependence is reinforced through juridical, political and military measures. There is a relative lack of services, lower standard of living, and higher level of frustration . . . [and] national discrimination on the basis of language, religion, or other cultural forms.

Something like this certainly happened in the Highlands after 1746 but the internal colonisers were Scots. More Scots had fought for Cumberland than for Charles Edward; more Scots than English soldiers thereafter wasted the glens; it was Scots landlords and factors, not Englishmen, who forced the Highlanders on to the emigrant ships. Not until later could the Highlanders look south for pity, while their bards commemorated them, with dignity and rare beauty, in the last flowering of a dying tongue. The Canadian Boat Song of 1829 had both:

> When the bold kindred, in time long vanished,
> Conquered the soil and fortified the keep,
> No seer foretold the children might be banished
> That a degenerate lord might boast his sheep.

Though the bitterness and eloquence were – probably – those of an Irishman, Tom Moore.

The lairds and bailies of the Lowlands who had done their best to ignore Charles Edward, were even then preoccupied with the economy, and once it really started to expand, in the 1780s, political union rapidly became economic integration. Industrialisation, until 1914 *the* great discontinuity, seemed to create a common history for England and Scotland, separating them from their continental neighbours (and from Ireland, whose melancholy statistics were never allowed to pollute those of the United Kingdom). But how much was this due to the Union? Many economic historians described the Scottish experience by extrapolating from British statistics to produce a marginal variant. Since accurate figures for production and employment came *after* integration, this is understandable, but a profession increasingly preoccupied with quantification may have neglected other routes that the Scots could follow to attain this end. The success of economic integration also meant that nationalists steered clear of it, apart from condemning its social shortcomings. But the assumption that Scotland was pulled along by innovations and market forces generated in England may be rather too facile.

Before 1830 the manufacturing sections of both Scottish and English economies were dominated by textiles; thereafter Scottish distinctiveness was treated as an aspect of regional product specialisation. Yet there were significant differences, even in the ultimate integration. Scotland sustained, throughout her industrialisation, higher rates of urbanisation than England – but also far higher rates of emigration. Had natural increase taken its course, as in the south, the population in 1900 would have been 6 million instead of 4.5 million. Partly as a result, Scotland did not build up a market for consumer-goods-oriented industry. Although average wages became comparable, per capita income fell as the wealthy moved south; and the physical state, accommodation and health of the working class were significantly poorer than in England. Further, economic development lacked continuity, lurching from crisis to crisis, from one industry to another. Linen and the banks were in trouble in the late 1760s, the American trade collapsed in 1776, the cotton industry stagnated after 1815. To the instabilities of the international economy the Scots added variations of their own.

Was this as an aspect of internal colonialism – English entrepreneurs building up marginal capacity which could be discarded in times of recession? There were incomer entrepreneurs, but at each crisis it was the Scots who seized on new options: cotton in the 1780s, iron in the 1820s, ships in the 1860s, steel in the 1880s. This adaptability was only possible within a society which commended it as a social and educational goal, and provided the sort of infrastructure that made it possible. One hypothesis about the ingredients of industrial progress may be relevant. The French economic historian François Crouzet has attributed the structural innovations which accelerated British industrialisation to production 'bottlenecks' present in Britain but not in France. These difficulties stimulated innovations, neglected by the entrepreneurs who lived off the bounty of France, which had previously enjoyed an equivalent growth rate. If this works for Britain, it is even more relevant to Scotland, where per capita income as late as 1867 was much lower than south of the border – £23 10s. compared with £32 – an indication that supplies of capital and the home market would be limited. Growth was therefore likely to depend more on the conscious creation of 'social overhead capital' than on the arbitrary operation of market forces.

Because it culminated in *The Wealth of Nations* (1776) the economic philosophy of the Scottish Enlightenment is often assumed to be individualism, free competition and a distrust of the state. Yet the development of the Scottish economy in Adam Smith's time emphasised the governing principle of his moral philosophy, 'sympathy': the capacity for altruistic conduct and for promoting the general good. The institutions of Scottish economic life represented less the triumph of individualism than the determination of public bodies to secure its stable development. Smith himself admitted that Scotland was backward compared with England, yet attributed her advance to such factors as the absence of party politics and a court, which checked strife and luxury; the flexibility of poor relief, which meant that labour was mobile; and the system of public education, which supplied a docile and adaptable work-force. The sort of road-mending and school-building government he envisaged was a 'local or provincial administration' very like the one he lived under.

In England industrial development proceeded despite government, or through its abstention. The merchant and banking society of London was only marginally interested in it. In Scotland, by contrast, influential organisations were corporate rather than competitive, and depended on close links with the manager and the estates. Despite its failure, Darien and the Company of Scotland had provided a precedent for economic advance as a concern of the governing elite, later expressed in such statutory bodies as the Board of Trustees for Manufactures and Fisheries, set up in 1727. This played an important role in expanding the linen industry, in government funding of roads, harbours and waterways, in the administration of forfeited Jacobite estates in the Highlands and in encouraging the fishing industry through bounties. Not all these measures were successful – and the real take-off still came with southern textile technology in the 1780s – but they concentrated attention on acquiring appropriate equipment and trained manpower.

Government efforts were supplemented by voluntary bodies, some ephemeral, some long-lived, of which the Society for Propagating Christian Knowledge in Scotland (1708), the spearhead of the attack on Gaelic culture, was as important in its way as the Society for Improving the Knowledge of Agriculture

(1723–45); and by joint-stock concerns providing infrastructure – banks, insurance companies and canal companies. The frontiers between these and government were fluid, and their efforts also overlapped with those of individual lawyers, academics, merchants and landowners, always eager to offer instruction to their contemporaries through pamphlets and patronage. Even the entail, the hereditary mortgage on an estate, which south of the border was usually seen as a fund for aristocratic high living, became in Scotland the means towards investment whose benefits might only be realised by future generations. 'Be ay sticking in a tree; it will be growing, Jock, when ye're sleeping.' Scott's Laird of Dumbiedykes may have been uncouth, but he typified the men who, over a century, transformed the Scottish landscape.

Industrialisation, in fact, had its roots in the land. Between 1745 and 1845 Scottish lairds pursued a conscious strategy of creating new villages – some 150 in all – which would provide hand- or even factory-work for a rising population while also allowing agricultural modernisation. In other words, the early stages of economic growth were a 'controlled' process of what has been called 'proto-industrialisation' in which productivity was increased while traditional relationships remained. Hence the popularity of Robert Owen's super-paternalist New Lanark. So absolute was the control of the lairds that even the serfs of Russia – who could at least elect their head-man – seem to have had more freedom than the countrymen of Burns. It was not until 1800 that Scotland lost its own hereditary serfs, the colliers, bound to their masters by an Act of the old Scottish Parliament.

Investment in the future was not limited to land. Thomas Telford regarded his great programme of Highland road, canal and harbour building in the 1800s 'in the light of a working academy from which eight hundred men have annually gone forth improved workmen'. The idea of education as a suture which bound industry to the estates was shared by academics, in the application of theory to industrial problems and in the movement for educational extension. The collaboration between Joseph Black and James Watt at Glasgow provided a precedent for a continuing strength of the Scottish universities. Their friend John Anderson was to endow in Glasgow one of Europe's first and most successful technical colleges. Scottish secondary and higher education didn't always reach its own high claims, but it was, in terms of access and relevance, much superior to the non-system south of the border. The Royal Commission on secondary education reported in 1868 that one Scot in every 140 was attending a secondary school, and one in every 1,000 a university; the equivalent proportions in England were one in 1,300 and one in 5,800. The subjects taught were, moreover, more attuned to the needs of a changing society. Lyon Playfair, scientific adviser to several Victorian governments and a member of an important Scots academic dynasty, observed in 1889:

The old English universities have not the same function as the Scottish and Irish universities. The former teach men how to spend a thousand a year with dignity and intelligence, while the latter aim at showing men how to make a thousand a year under the same conditions.

Men trained in universities, technical colleges and apprenticeships sustained Scottish industrialisation through its numerous crises. During a long tenure of the chair of natural philosophy at Glasgow Lord Kelvin was both academic and industrial magnate. Anderson's foundation, later the Royal Technical College and finally Strathclyde University, employed George Birkbeck, the founder of the mechanics' institutes, and Andrew Ure, the most notorious apologist for unchecked industrialism, and produced, besides several generations of engineers and metallurgists, James Beaumont Neilson, 'the Arkwright of the iron industry', David Livingstone and Lyon Playfair himself. But industry itself remained the great 'working academy'; the workshops which supplied the mines and cotton mills produced the pioneers of the marine engineering and locomotive-building industries.

Watt had pioneered his condensing steam engine in Scotland in the 1760s, but needed the capital and market of the west Midlands. The steamship, on the other hand, was a native achievement. Scots engineers like the Napier brothers dominated the paddle-steamer era when the narrow seas and the mail routes were conquered, and it was the Clyde again, in the 1850s and 1860s, which made the technical breakthroughs – the compound engine and the surface condenser – that enabled the long-distance freight steamer to oust the sailing ship. Initially the growth of the Lanarkshire iron industry aided this. The town chamberlain of Greenock commented in 1852 that:

Our superiority in producing engines has hitherto been the cause of these potentates preferring the work of our artisans to that of any others. But, now that iron is superseding timber and becoming the principal component, not of the engine only, but also of the hull, our power to excel is vastly increased.

By the 1880s, however, matters were the other way around. The survival of the Scottish iron industry, and its conversion to steel production, depended on the market provided by the heavy industries of the Clyde, where shipbuilding had been joined by locomotive building and structural engineering. Resources and markets were now finite: the economy had evolved in such a way that it had created a dictatorship as rigid as that once enjoyed by the Dundases in Scottish politics.

William Cobbett anathematised 'improved' Scotland, as he rode through it in the 1830s. The great farms of the Lothians were 'factories for making corn and meat chiefly by means of horses and machinery'. Their workers lived in barrack-like rows of steadings or, if unmarried, in the squalor of shared bothies. The agricultural villages had the harsh symmetry of little industrial towns. Cobbett, never a man for the measured judgement, had recognised the other face of the Scots Enlightenment. A society which extended equality of opportunity and eased recruitment into the elite could be callous to those who could not, or would not, co-operate. Professor T. C. Smout has argued that Scotland lacked the popular, secular, radical literature of the sort provided by Wilkes, Cartwright, Spence and Cobbett. The only possible candidates, Burns and James Mackintosh, were famous for their politic recantations. Reform agitation was largely controlled by Whigs, by English or French missionaries, or even fomented by *agents provocateurs*. Edward Thompson has written that 'it is possible, at least until the 1820s, to regard the English and Scottish experiences as distinct', yet what made them so was not a national issue and the pressure of organised labour, but the weakness of both.

In 1841 a government report on distress among the hand-loom weavers commented, anent Glasgow, that 'the lowest districts of other places, both here and on the continent, never presented anything half so bad, either in intensity of pestilence, physical and moral, or in extent proportioned to the population'. Even in 1900, after fifty years of energetic and expensive public health reform, over 60 per cent of the city's population was living in one- and two-roomed houses, overcrowding was five times worse than in England and the urban death rate was very high. 'If the mid-Victorian years were a gloomy age in the social life of the English poor,' according to Eric Hobsbawm, 'they were a black one in Scotland.' But Scottish working-class activity, mild and conciliatory, acquiesced in a very raw deal. Why?

Political radicalism lacked even the degree of representation it had in English 'popular' constituencies like Westminster. Working-class leaders could be co-opted into the elite or bought by it, like the weavers' leader Alexander Richmond. During the difficult 1810s and 1820s, Dr Hamish Fraser has shown, the Court of Session bought off discontent by fixing wages. Where expectations were high, emigration was always a possibility; where life was already miserable, in a hovel on Skye or in Donegal, the city, slums and all, offered a way out. In Europe, even in Cobbett's England, nationalism, the memory of a *volkish* golden age, focused the resentments of the new industrial population, and created expectations of a new social order. Both right and left could subsequently draw on it. In Scotland, on the other hand, industrialisation had been swift and ruthless *because* of an alliance between a resourceful middle class and a flexible aristocracy with its control over Kirk, law, education and poor relief which were all undeniably Scottish. As it ran into trouble in the 1830s, its victims could not look to national solidarity for relief. Scots Liberals were thoroughly *laissez-faire*, and Scots Tories, after their efforts at management collapsed, used the big stick. Sheriff Archibald Alison's obliteration of the Glasgow spinners' union in 1838 put the cause of Scottish trade unionism back for a generation.

DISRUPTIONS

In the half-century after 1789, 'semi-independent' Scotland maimed itself. Economic tendencies were towards integration anyway, but the post-Union conventions lost their strength and Scots of both parties relied increasingly on Westminster. The 'Dundas despotism' pitched into the Jacobins; the Moderates ditched their intellectual liberalism; public docility was enforced by police spies, state trials, and patronage. Otherwise the old order was in poor repair, and politics was polarising on southern lines. The Dundases, more clumsy than savage, were wrong-footed by smart young Whigs in the Edinburgh courts. After 1832 the latter quickly dismantled management, their leader Francis Jeffrey, former editor of the *Edinburgh Review* and now Lord Advocate, glorying 'that no shred or rag, no jot or tittle, of the old system will be left'.

Jeffrey's lieutenant, Henry Cockburn, subsequently the historian of early nineteenth-century Scotland, enthusiastically concurred. 'The Reform Bill,' he announced, 'is giving us a political constitution for the first time.' Indeed, the years from 1832 to 1835 saw an extension of political rights in Scotland far more drastic than the French Revolution of 1830, which had sent a bemused Charles X into exile at Holyroodhouse. The French electorate had increased from 90,000 to 166,000; the Scottish electorate from about 4,500 to 65,000. In 1833 the Scottish Burgh Reform Act, which preceded the equivalent English measure by two years, vested the control of the towns in the £10 ratepayers. The millennium of the Whig intellectuals was ushered in.

Yet it was a flawed paradise. Jeffrey blundered badly in his drafting, leaving, through ignorance of Scots feudal law, loopholes whereby landowners could continue to create 'faggot votes'. This, and the coercion of their tenants, lasted until 1884. The incompetence of the Whigs reflected an absorption in reform politics which distanced them from the real problems of Scottish government. 'Strange,' one of them mused, 'how little one knows of the real condition of the society about one till something leads one to examine it.' Cockburn was more sensitive, regarding a Scottish minister as an '*absolute necessity*'. Yet he thought that assimilation was too strong to turn back: 'Our associations and experience make us jealous of anything resembling provincial government.'

It was under the eyes of a weak Scottish administration that the 'ten years' conflict' was played out. The events which led to the Disruption of 1843 came close to being the religious equivalent of the political revolution. The Kirk, now reinforced by evangelicalism, was a pendant to parliamentarianism: the vehicle for Scottish social and cultural politics. If in 1832 middle-class and professional society opted for parliamentary assimilation, they still wanted a self-governing Kirk to function under their control as the most important *national* estate. But patronage, which had obsessed Davie Deans and the eighteenth-century seceders, had to be destroyed.

Ironically, the institution which Adam Smith thought encouraged liberal thought and market economics was to be attacked by an enthusiast for *laissez-faire*. Thomas Chalmers was the most formidable Scottish churchman since Knox, sharing his gifts as a preacher, ideologist and politician. As a young minister he had almost fallen, like many Moderates, into the pit of deism, but in 1810 he experienced conversion and became probably the greatest evangelical orator of his age, capable of reducing someone as unpromising as George Canning to tears. In the course of seven years' ministry in central Glasgow, he set himself to bring the Kirk abreast of new developments in science and economics while restating its claims, as an established church, to superintend, in Cockburn's words, 'the whole Christian and civic economy of our population'. He believed the Kirk's control of education and poor relief should remain and, in the case of poor relief, be tightened. He set out to prove that the Kirk could relieve poverty through its own collections and the counselling of its elders, without the need for a poor rate and – for a time – succeeded. In fact, what he claimed for the Kirk was semi-sovereign status. When, in 1834, the evangelicals at last ousted the Moderates from the control of the General Assembly, the stage seemed set for a revival of the theocratic nationalism of the Reformation.

The language of the conflict seems totally alien to that of our own day. Yet the evangelicals' contention that, despite the Patronage Act of 1712, a congregation had the right to veto a patron's nominee raised a national issue. Was the Kirk, as a corporation, in partnership with Parliament or subordinate to it? By passing the Veto Act of 1834, the General Assembly insisted on the Kirk's autonomy. By upholding the rights of patrons, the Court of Session and Parliament insisted on its subordination. Only Parliament could break this constraint, but the two parties were unwilling to move, the Whigs because English dissenters wanted all establishments abandoned, and anti-Catholic Scottish evangelicals were against their conciliatory Irish policy, the Tories because of their ties with the patrons, and their interest in nominating to the 30 per cent of 'government' parishes.

The latter took power in 1841, and, with few Scottish MPs, their attitude to the Kirk was more robust than diplomatic. In 1841, after a campaign by Professor W. P. Alison, brother of the Sheriff, Sir Robert Peel launched a Royal Commission on Scottish poor relief, the heart of Chalmers's theocratic ideal. The following year he brusquely dismissed the Kirk's 'Claim of Right', hoping that a hard line would force waverers back to the Moderate side. The evangelical response came at the General Assembly of 1843. Over a third of the Kirk's ministers withdrew, processed to a neighbouring hall, and constituted themselves the Free Church of Scotland, under Chalmers's leadership. Within a year they took about 40 per cent of the Kirk's communicants with them, mainly from the Highlands and the growing industrial towns.

In the short term the Disruption abated conflict between the Free Churchmen, still pledged to the principle of establishment, and older secessionist bodies. Politically, it boosted the Liberals, especially in the towns. Between 1832 and 1885 the Tories won only seven burgh contests. But the Kirk's supervision of much of Scottish government rapidly faded, now that it only represented a minority. Sectarian brawling destroyed any hope of a Scottish consensus and gave an indifferent Westminster the initiative. English precedents were followed not out of conviction, but out of exhaustion. In 1845, after the report of the Royal Commission, poor relief was transferred to ratepayer-elected parochial boards under a Board of Supervision in Edinburgh; in 1855 religious tests were abolished at the Scottish universities; in 1861 school inspection was transferred from the Kirk to the universities; and in 1872 elected school boards were set up in every parish, under the Scotch Education Department, based in London. In 1874 a Tory government abolished patronage, but by then the gesture was meaningless, as in 1887 the Free Church joined the 'seceders' in getting the Liberals to back disestablishment. Religious politics had shifted from defending the unique role of the Kirk in Scottish life to a campaign similar to that of the dissenters in England, which gained in acrimony what it lost in relevance.

Chalmers died in 1847, leaving a thriving church but an altogether narrower religious ideal. His successor as spokesman for dissent in Scotland, the Liberal MP Duncan McLaren, did nothing to broaden it. A draper, provost of Edinburgh and

brother-in-law of John Bright, McLaren stood for sectarian individualism at its narrowest. His domination of Scottish Liberal
politics began with the Anti-Corn Law League in the 1840s and
for backsliding on this issue he had Macaulay ejected from his
Edinburgh seat in 1847, 'notwithstanding the charm of his oratory and his world-wide reputation as a man of letters'. For a
further thirty years the 'member for Scotland' imposed a
narrow, rancorous pietism, devoid of imagination, personality
or social sympathy. Scottish MPs, A. V. Dicey noted in 1867,
were the *delegates* of the aristocracy and middle class, reflecting
the prejudices of their masters. When their standard rose, as it
did after 1880, it was through an influx of carpet-bagging
Englishmen and Anglo-Scots, Gladstone being the most
famous.

On top of the demise of management and the collapse of the
Kirk came the communications revolution. In 1848 central
Scotland was connected to London by two main railways; by
1851 the tracks had reached Aberdeen. In 1707 an overland
journey to London took a fortnight; road improvements had
reduced this to forty-three hours by 1836, and a similar time
could be achieved by steamer. But rail cut this to seventeen
hours, and by 1876 to nine. Almost as important, the electric
telegraph arrived only months after the railway. Instantaneous
communication now meant that government or private business
in Scotland could frequently be conducted from London and an
age of minimal government had little time for regional agencies.
These new utilities were financed from Scotland as much as
from London. Although several railways were built to a distinct
'Scotch Gauge' of 4 feet 6 inches, the Railway Mania lines drew
on English capital and used (mercifully) the English standard
gauge of 4 feet 8½ inches. The character of the five separate
railway companies (which survived until 1923) was almost
aggressively Scottish; long-suffering English shareholders
usually deferred to their Scottish managers; but endemic economic weakness always inhibited rationalisation of an unsatisfac-
tory system and ultimately, in the 1920s, prevented the
formation of a unified Scottish railway authority.

Improved communications created commercial Scottishness.
As well as cutting journey times, the railway reduced costs by
up to 80 per cent and enabled the scenery, sporting facilities
and romantic history of Scotland to be marketed to the

middle classes of industrial Britain. Thomas Cook and David MacBrayne completed the work that Scott, Mendelssohn and George IV had begun. Hotels, hydros, houses for summer letting and golf-links followed the railway and the steamer into the Highlands. In counties where eviction and emigration were emptying the glens, towns like Inverness doubled in size between 1851 and 1891 while Oban on the west coast had a threefold increase. Tourism detracted from political nationalism in two ways: it enhanced the sentimental, tartan and Kailyard image that later nationalists were to spend so much time denouncing; and by making Scottish holidays a part of British upper-class life it fostered the illusion that integration was a two-way process. Queen Victoria visited Ireland only four times and Wales once, but after 1848 spent every autumn at Prince Albert's Scoto-Teutonic Balmoral, dragging attendant politicians northwards with her. Disraeli counted himself fortunate to escape with two visits, but Balmorality was a victory for a tidied-up Tory Jacobitism. Gladstone, obsessed with Ireland for his last fifteen years, visited it only once, but was in Scotland regularly. Before 1914 government was virtually conducted each summer from the country houses of Balfour, Campbell-Bannerman and Asquith, from the grouse moors and salmon rivers of Relugas and Strathconon, or the links of St Andrews or North Berwick.

The Scottish Rights Association of the 1850s was an understandable reaction to this headlong Anglicisation. Even its opponents – Cockburn or the *Scotsman* – acknowledged that Scottish affairs were ineptly handled at Westminster. Yet nationalism could not agitate from strength. It had been identified with Toryism before 1832, and with the liberties of the Kirk before 1843. Both causes failed. Scottish Liberalism lacked a leader like O'Connell, bold and generous-spirited enough to unite the classes that 'improvement' and industrialisation had separated. Chartism's prudent leaders remained oriented towards a British reform. By the 1860s even integrationists admitted that the Scottish cause was being pushed from the scene, while a radical nationalism, owing much to Carlyle, was being adopted by the confraternity of European liberal exiles. Mazzini may have misunderstood Irish nationalism; despite his friendship with Carlyle he knew nothing of Scottish nationalism.

Yet Anglicisation was never more than partial. A popular and political Scottish culture flourished below the party level. Dr William Donaldson's reading in the rapidly expanding weekly press has shown how radical this was, when conveyed in the racy vernacular of William Latta, William Alexander and James Leatham. Scots law was still distinct, so there were always controversies about applying British reforms to Scotland, and an increasing academic interest in its traditions, and relationships with history, anthropology and politics. Religious conflict created, besides its obsessions, a complex structure of parochial and voluntary bodies, from choirs and sisterhoods to the Boys' Brigade. But industrial development added dangerous dependence on the heavy industries to bad living conditions and high emigration. Tackling its problems was complicated by the preoccupation of Scottish entrepreneurs with voluntary local government work and Westminster politics, but the case and the resources for legislative devolution persisted. A local Parliament could have allowed the country's human and intellectual resources to develope social and regional planning, and 'co-order' (Matthew Arnold's word) that literary class whose indifference contrasted with Kierkegaard, Ibsen, Brandes, Bjornson and Strindberg in nineteenth-century Scandinavia. Devolution was too important to be left to the clutch of eccentrics who advocated it.

SCOTUS VIATOR

Offensiveness in the manner, or in the extent of the swamping ought to be blamed or checked, but it is vain, and though practicable would be absurd, to proclaim anything hurtful to the good interest of the Empire, merely because it is either Scotch, or Irish, or English.

Henry Cockburn, dismissing the Scottish Rights agitation of the 1850s admitted that nationalism had a rival, whose attractions forestalled the 'condition of Scotland question'. Opportunity was no longer confined to Scotland *as such*: her partnership with the Empire was reaching its zenith. To ask a middle-class Scot to concern himself with his country was to tell him to stay at home and let his business go hang. For one Chairman of the SNP, Andrew Dewar Gibb, writing in the 1930s, Union and Empire were virtually synonymous:

The existence of the Empire has been the most important factor in deciding the relationship of Scotland and England in the last three centuries . . . a share in the trade of the nascent English Empire was offered to the Scottish Commissioners for the Union of the Parliaments. The bait was taken and the partnership began. For its beginning and for its duration the Empire is largely responsible.

If Gibb had his doubts there were, by the time he wrote, four emigrants, or descendants of emigrants, in the Empire and the United States – Tom Johnston's 'nation of twenty millions' – for every resident Scot. And the wandering Scot had done well. 'He was in the habit of alluding to his Scotch connections,' says Marlow of the crooked financier De Barral in Joseph Conrad's *Chance*, 'but every great man has done that.' Sir Charles Dilke, in his apotheosis of British colonisation, *Greater Britain* (1868), was more explicit:

> The Scotch are not more successful in Adelaide than every-where in the known world. Half the most prominent among the statesmen of the Canadian Confederation, of Victoria, and of Queensland, are born Scots, and all the great merchants of India are of the same nation. Whether it be that the Scotch emigrants are for the most part men of better education than those of other nationalities, of whose citizens only the poorest and most ignorant are known to emigrate, or whether the Scotchman owes his uniform success in every climate to his perseverance or his shrewd-ness, the fact remains, that wherever abroad you come across a Scotchman, you usually find him prosperous and respected.
>
> The Scotch emigrant is a man who leaves Scotland be-cause he wishes to rise faster and higher than he can at home, whereas the emigrant Irishman quits Galway or County Cork only because there is no longer food or shelter for him there. The Scotchman crosses the seas in calculating contentment; the Irishman in sorrow and despair.

Dilke may have exaggerated, but his picture was more accu-rate than that of the emigrant as homeless crofter, driven by factor and shepherd to the Canadian boat. The Scots who went abroad were mainly from the Lowlands, time-served craftsmen, clerks, weavers with their savings taken from the penny bank. They were concerned to get on, and they created an emigration ideology to justify their move:

> Mark you what the proverb says
> Of Scotsmen, rats and lice;
> The whole world over take your ways
> You'll find them still, I guess.

The wandering Scot – merchant, cleric, mercenary or scholar – was already familiar in Europe when that was written in fourteenth-century France. The Auld Alliance with France, the Church and the universities provided the prospect of success in the traditional professions of Christendom. If the Reformation curtailed this internationalism, the wars it provoked offered even greater prospects for the aggressive, whose compatriots were only too anxious to see them employed elsewhere. At one time or another during the seventeenth century there may have been as many as 100,000 Scotsmen in Europe, usually fighting. In addition, the Stuarts started planting Ulster with Scots presbyterians. This Irish province, Gaelic-speaking and Catholic, had acted as a bridge between the Irish and the equally troublesome Highlanders. After 1609 the zealots of the Lowlands and Borders moved in, removing an endemic cause of friction between England and Scotland. By 1650 some 50,000 Scots had taken so enthusiastically to colonisation that government had to curb their expansion. For the next two centuries the Scots-Irish were equally adept at colonising the New World. By 1772 there were 150,000 of them in America, compared with only 50,000 from Scotland itself. They, and not the more recent immigrants from the mainland, provided much of the manpower for the revolutionary armies in the war with Britain.

Until the 1780s government and the landed classes were hostile to emigration, but after 1815 government opinion changed. Population expansion and economic uncertainty made the Highland problem intractable; in the aftermath of war a restless new industrial population posed a constant threat to social stability; wages-fund economics and Malthusian theories of population asserted that only by reducing their numbers would working people improve their living standards. Emigration rapidly gained intellectual and imaginative sanction.

The Earl of Selkirk, whose grasp of Scottish social development was commended by his friend Scott in *Waverley*, advocated and practised the systematic settlement of Canada, where many Scots 'loyalists' had ended up after the American War of Independence. John Galt was similarly active as a government agent and publicist. Before long, Carlyle had elevated emigration into a philosophy of life, a new world where:

> Canadian forests stand unfelled, boundless plains and prairies unbroken with the plough; and on the west and on the east green desert spaces never yet made white with corn: and to the overcrowded little western nook of Europe, our territorial planet, nine-tenths of it yet vacant or tenanted by nomads, is still crying – come and till me, come and reap me!

Between 1815 and 1905 some 13 million emigrants left British ports: 8.2 million sailed for the United States, 2.1 million for Canada, 1.7 million for Australia and 0.7 million for New Zealand and South Africa. Records of country of origin were not kept until late in the century, so arriving at ratios of settlers from Scotland, England and Ireland involves some back-projection from early twentieth-century statistics. Using those in Gordon Donaldson's *The Scots Overseas* (1966) we find that, at a rough estimate, for every 10 Americans of Scots birth or descent, there were 30 of English and 50 of Irish birth or descent. The ratios for other settlement areas are shown in Table 1.

Table 1

	Scots	English	Irish
Canada	10	12	13
Australia	10	35	14
New Zealand	10	22	9
South Africa	10	30	5

Numerically, English and Irish emigrants predominated over the Scots. But since the proportion of Scots to English in Britain was never greater than 1:7, the contribution of the Scots to overseas settlement was disproportionately large, particularly in the Empire, and in Canada it was almost equal to that of

England. Their political and commercial success was thus based on numerical advantage, and the fact that as a whole they were of higher status than those from England and Ireland.

Scotland was unique among European nations in combining an emigration rate of about 4 per cent per decade with an industrial economy. In some ways her situation was closer to that of the seaboard industrialised regions of the New World, from which emigrants moved to a steadily advancing frontier. Frederick Jackson Turner's 1890s thesis about the values of American society being shaped on the frontier and then transmitted back to the east coast was relevant here. Eighteenth-century Scotland had been a frontier society. Its intellectuals and practical men, with their stress on 'improvement', had created values and techniques for overseas settlement, together with reserves of technical competence, skilled labour and professional (notably medical) training.

There was always a pull as well as a push: the promise of high pay, of support from friends and kindred already established. This owed something to the clan tradition and Highland habits of interdependence which had migrated to the Lowlands; it was enhanced by university and apprenticeship relations, Masonic membership, commercial partnerships and religious affiliations, many of which had been forged in the new industrial society. The 'emigration ideology' lacked the official sanction which made the Turner thesis an article of faith in early twentieth-century America. But it altered the Scots' idea of what their country was or ought to be.

PROFESSING IMPERIALISM

Middle-class emigration and the maintenance of links with the mother country were common enough. Many European emigrants were talented professionals, driven abroad by political persecution; the resentment of the Irish exiles was channelled into a movement to resist British rule at home. The Scots conformed to neither pattern, but established themselves in activities which provided two-way linkages with the home country, inhibiting nationalism, while restricting Anglicisation. The more important of these, in myth and reality, were government service, missions, trade and investment.

Scottish militarism gave the soldier a status he did not enjoy in England, where 'going for a soldier' implied a sort of social suicide. Kipling, who did so much to rehabilitate 'Tommy Atkins', rarely mentions Scottish soldiers, although he was partly Scots himself. The veterans who bragged to the young Alexander Somerville of their heroics in the Napoleonic Wars were descended from mercenaries who would have bragged about the Thirty Years War. Most Scottish soldiers could write, and helped create a persuasive martial literature. 'It was the *writing*,' wrote Somerville, 'quite as much as the *fighting* of the Scottish regiments that distinguished them.' The raising of twenty-seven Highland regiments after the Forty-five brought the further glamour of claymore, pipes and kilt, and stories of settlement in the New World to set beside the booty of Frankfurt and Mainz. Over two centuries, from Quebec in 1759 to Aden in 1967, the Scottish infantry, 'the ladies from hell', personified the nation at its most aggressive. Each war produced its heroes: Moore at Corunna, Ensign Ewart at Waterloo, the 'Thin Red Line' of the 93rd Highlanders at Balaclava, Sir Colin Campbell in the Indian Mutiny, the 9th Highland Division at Loos, the 51st Highland Division in North Africa and Italy.

The Scots may appear close to the Croats and Cossacks – 'militant' retainers of a conservative Empire – which Marx saw as a menace to bourgeois nationalism. In fact, the proportion of Scots in the Victorian army was never higher than 1:7 and steadily dropped until it was about 1:14. In half the Scots regiments officers and men were predominantly English or Irish. But recruiting to the Volunteers of 1859 at twice the British average confirms what Hanham has called the 'liberal militarism' element of 'civic humanism'. The reputation put about in bar-rooms by Somerville and his successors was of Scottish bravery and intelligence compensating for the incompetence or cowardice of English officers. Empire thus restated class and national loyalties.

The success of Scots in imperial administration had a similar combination of boldness, competence and lack of caste, along with the less inspirational motive power of patronage. The Nabob, the Indian official who had done well, was a familiar – if not exactly lovable – feature of eighteenth-century society, not just in Scotland. Many of Jane Austen's more horrid characters have meaningfully Scots names. After 1707 the East India Company mollified the Scots, still smarting over Darien. The mercenary spirit did well in the roughhouse of Clive's conquest of French India, although its less savoury side later emerged. The governorship of the Skye minister's son Sir John MacPherson was described in 1784 by his successor Cornwallis as 'a system of the dirtiest jobbery'. But Cornwallis's reforms, separating political from commercial control and Europeanising the services, really opened India to the Scots, especially as the the new Board of Control in London was under Henry Dundas. For twenty years the latter promoted tranquillity in Scotland by transferring much of the country's talent to the Indian army and administration. Scots administrators – Mountstuart Elphinstone, Sir John Malcolm, Jonathan Duncan and Lord Dalhousie – presided over the great epoch of utilitarian reform, in which the sub-continent was treated as a laboratory for financial, legal and educational experiment. Through them, and through the direction of the London office of the Company after 1818 by James Mill, the disciple of Bentham and Dugald Stewart and historian (at a safe distance) of British India, this process became a practical demonstration of the social speculations of the Scots Enlightenment.

Ironically, the full working-out of this policy, with the introduction of the Indian Civil Service in 1852, penalised the Scots. Competitive examination gave advantages to the two old English universities, where examinations had been the business end of reform since the beginning of the century. The attempts of the Scottish universities to produce suitable candidates led them to copy the English norm. Although one Scot, Allan Octavian Hume, founded the Indian National Congress in 1885, and another, Patrick Geddes, was to inspire the independence movement's greatest statesman, Jawaharlal Nehru, reputations continued to be made in Indian administration right up to 1947. Lord Reith regretted that he was never 'fully stretched' by being made Viceroy in 1941; the job had already been offered to, and turned down by, Tom Johnston. The age of Scots domination had passed, and that restless reformer's priorities were different.

By the time the scramble for 'underdeveloped' territories got under way, after 1870, the Colonial Service reflected the impact of several conflicting ideologies, some with a Scots background. The idea of trusteeship for the natives was associated with Sir James Stephen, 'Mr Mother Country', permanent head of the colonial service, 1834–47, of that Forfarshire tribe which later colonised Bloomsbury. This humanitarianism frequently collided with a robust and democratic, but also intolerant and racialist notion of 'settler liberty' of Scots provenance, while the latter also contributed to the more 'scientific' racialism associated with the 'new imperialism' and in particular with Alfred Milner, Governor-General of South Africa, 1897–1905.

About half of Milner's close associates – John Buchan, Philip Kerr, Patrick Duncan, Starr Jameson, F. S. Oliver – were Scots, and their attitudes were moulded in part by the 'conservative utilitarianism' of Fitzjames Stephen (Sir James's son) and Henry Maine, also of Scots descent, which combined an appreciation of native institutions with the neo-Darwinian view of the genetic inferiority of the native. But to read the throwaway racial remarks in John Buchan's *Prester John* (1910) is to realise a distinct moral and intellectual decline since James Mill wrote his *History of India*. Mill's assumption that the Indians could only govern themselves if they became good utilitarians has been replaced with a series of racial gradations; the enemy is the educated native, the very man whom Mill strove to create.

Should *Prester John*'s Africa be taken as a fantasy world? There might be truth in this. Kipling, politically a much nastier animal than Buchan, wrote sympathetically about real Indians whom he knew; Buchan wrote insensitively about imaginary Africans. But Buchan comes alive when he describes his settler David Crawfurd 'getting on'. He celebrated the trustee, but he wrote for the settler, with his indifference to the native population. Such was the persuasiveness of imperial print capitalism.

Buchan shouldn't be judged by this money-spinning early work. He ended his career as an enlightened Governor-General of Canada, appreciative of all the country's races, but aware that its very identity was the triumph of its Scots settlers. The Dundee-born radical William Lyon Mackenzie in 1836 started the disturbances which brought about the report of Lord Durham's Commission and the concession of representative government; the Glasgow-born Conservative Sir John A. Macdonald accomplished the diplomacy which led to the founding of the federal Dominion in 1867. From then until his death in 1891 he dominated Canadian politics and carried through, with the aid of the Banffshire cousins John A. Smith and George Stephen, later Lords Strathcona and Mountstephen, the construction of the Canadian Pacific Railway, which gave the Dominion a physical unity. Given their numbers, national *qualities* were scarcely required – although one of Macdonald's liberal opponents, the former Oxford professor Goldwin Smith, an obsessive anti-Semite, got worried about the Hebraic appearance of the Highlanders. But the Scots could always call on a relatively homogeneous community, focused on church and school, to produce the degree of organisation and literacy that politics in a new country require. The same thing went for Australia and New Zealand, which by 1900 had produced a dozen or so Scots-born colonial premiers. The Scottish people, denied authority by nobility and plutocracy, now had the chance of power. Alexander Mackenzie, a Perthshire stonemason, beat Macdonald to become Prime Minister of Canada in 1873 (the trouble was, Goldwin Smith observed, that he didn't stop being a stonemason); in 1884 Robert Stout, an Orkney teacher and freethinker, became Prime Minister of New Zealand; in 1908 in Australia Andrew Fisher, an Ayrshire miner, became the first Labour Prime Minister in the world.

For the Scots working man emigration realised the libertarianism of Burns, himself a near-emigrant. It was in the settlements, not in Scotland, that the aggressive individualism of his 'Jolly Beggars' was celebrated, for example by the Renfrewshire weaver John Barr, who went to New Zealand in the 1850s:

> Nae mair the laird comes for his rent,
>   When I hae nocht to pay, sirs.
> Nae mair he'll tak me aff the loom,
> Wi hanging lip and pooches toom,
> To touch my hat, and boo to him,
>   The like was never kent, sir

> At my door-cheeks there's bread and cheese,
> I work or no', just as I please,
> I'm fairly settled at my ease,
>   And that's the way o't noo, sirs.

The Maoris who were, in the same colony, ruthlessly dispossessed by Sir Donald McLean, the Tiree tacksman's son who ran the Land Purchase Department, could reflect on the consequences of the belief that 'courts for cowards were erected'. In other colonies natives and less astute settlers suffered similarly.

'Ten times Scotch are the highlanders', wrote a prospector from the Australian diggings in 1839. 'Poor as rats at home they are as rapacious as rats abroad.'

Settler patriotism was as ambiguous as settler liberty. The Scots were quick to set up Caledonian Societies and Burns Clubs and Highland Gatherings, often before such institutions were founded in Scotland. They also sent back a lively if rather eccentric clutch of nationalist agitators, from the Australians T. D. Wanliss and Theodore Napier to the New Zealander Sidney Goodsir Smith and the South African Wendy Wood. Yet their support of nationalism was rarely significant. They were either nostalgic – Jacobitism flourished in Australia and America until the end of the nineteenth century – or else straightforwardly radical, with little time for tradition. Andrew Carnegie, an ambivalent practitioner of 'triumphant democracy', brusquely rejected an appeal to subscribe to a monument to Robert Bruce: 'A King is an insult to every other man in the land.' The settler usually integrated at the level his talents carried him to, adopting new social mores and class distinctions. The National Party of Scotland found this out the hard way in the 1930s. Arthur Donaldson, later Chairman of the SNP, attempting to raise funds in America, wrote back, disillusioned, to Roland Muirhead:

> Trade had been bad here and still is. It has hit our people hard because so many of them are wage-earners and many of them were not provident during their prosperity. The Scots who do have money are either of the second generation or else have been here for very long periods and they are not interested in our movement – will not be, I am afraid, until it becomes internationally interesting . . . I have come to the conclusion that we should not appeal further for members in the United States and the Dominions.

The 'nation of twenty millions' was an important myth. It preserved, within the imperial experience, a cultural continuity that ultimately survived it. It both endorsed the Union, which made colonisation possible, and called it into question: why could Scots govern colonies, but not Scotland? And, in grimmer days, between the wars: without the Union, would emigration have been necessary? The ethics of colonisation were divisive.

Some Scotsmen would go along with Dilke's notion that they were bound in time to extinguish the 'lower races' whose land they occupied. Others drew on Scotland's experience of internal migration to argue for the coexistence of cultures. As colonisation was joined by the scramble for 'underdeveloped' territory, a new myth emerged which sanctioned the Scots' role in that – the myth of the missionary. Even today, if one Scots schoolchild knows who Sir John Macdonald was, ten know about Mary Slessor – the Dundee mill-girl who became a missionary in Calabar – and a hundred about David Livingstone.

Missionary activity peaked between 1874 and 1914 when no Scots congregation could fail to be aware of the hundreds of clergymen and evangelists sustained by the three main Scottish churches. Yet the reality was more complex. The Kirk's main mission at Blantyre in the Shire Highlands of Nyasaland had a long struggle to survive against indifference at home and much the same was true of the Free Church missions. Missions in fact came late to the Kirk, and gained most success when working closely with imperial government. It was not until 1829, nearly forty years after the first foreign mission societies had been formed in England, that the Kirk sent its first missionary, Alexander Duff, to India. When the idea had been mooted in 1796, the Moderates compared missionaries to Jacobin agitators, one remarking that:

> to spread abroad the knowledge of the Gospel among barbarous and heathen nations seems highly preposterous, in so far as it anticipates, it even reverses, the law of nature.

The law of nature, which, according to Lord Monboddo, a Moderate judge with anthropological leanings, placed the Negro close to the orang-utan, won out over the word of God. When Scots missionaries went abroad, they went, like Robert Moffat and his future son-in-law David Livingstone, as agents of the London Missionary Society. The Kirk's decision to start was the work of Chalmers and the Evangelicals, but it was far from being an emotional response. Duff planned a co-ordinated educational system for the Indian upper classes, undertaken in collaboration with government. Macaulay's 1835 prescription for the recasting of Indian education on Western lines, suited his purposes exactly, and the Kirk's colleges became a recognised part of the government system. Despite a setback in 1843, when the missionaries to a man left the Kirk for the Free Church, the momentum was not lost.

The Free Church had missionaries but no missions; the Kirk missions but no missionaries. In some ways the financial problems of both stemmed from this enforced doubling of effort, as the Kirk, through a lay association, set out to recover the ground it had lost. The Free Church was imperially conscious, and joined Edward Gibbon Wakefield in promoting planned colonisation in Otago in New Zealand in 1848. Leaving his Indian educational colleges to the Kirk, Duff established new ones under Free Church auspices, and the Free Church also expanded black education in southern Africa through patronage of the Lovedale seminary established by the Glasgow Missionary Society in 1824. With the contribution of medical missions, in which the university of Edinburgh took a leading role, missionary activity was largely a broadening of the 'stream of social education'. But the personality that was stamped on it after the middle of the nineteenth century was that of Livingstone, and the combination of exploration and evangelicalism that he represented. As a dissenter, Livingstone stood on the fringes of Scottish religious life, and it was the Congregationalist London Missionary Society and the Anglican Universities' Mission which involved themselves most in his explorations. But his memory provided the impulse that established the Central African missions of the two churches in the 1870s, and involved them directly in the scramble for Africa.

The Free Church established its mission station at Livingstonia on Lake Nyasa in 1874, followed by the Kirk's Blantyre in 1876. Several hundred Scots settlers followed, and shortly found themselves in conflict with the slavers and the Portuguese whom Livingstone had fought. Following the settlers came the African Lakes Trading Corporation, largely promoted in Scotland, which turned the conflict into a small but persistent war which lasted from 1885 to 1896. It was almost like a replay of Darien, with the difference that imperial support, in the shape of Cecil Rhodes, Frederick Lugard and Harry Johnston, was thrown behind the Scots, and success ultimately guaranteed. For the next eighty years Nyasaland was effectively a sort of Scots colony, whose internal affairs remained, at

67

successive General Assemblies, a concern of Scottish politics until the mid-1960s.

Against the settler ideology, the missionaries tried to protect and work with the native population. Attitudes could vary from the respect and equality with which Livingstone treated his African allies to the condescension of many self-proclaimed 'trustees'. But the Livingstone tradition ensured that no missionary coming from a Lanarkshire mill village – or, for that matter, from the Highlands – would go on about the superiority of European society. The fight against slavery and disease counterbalanced 'banjo Christianity' and enabled the Scots to exploit their distance from the slave trade and their excellent medical education.

Frontier-like, the missionary impulse impinged on, and modernised, domestic religion. Livingstone's death in 1873 coincided with the great Scottish revival conducted by the American evangelists Dwight Moody and Ira Sankey between 1873 and 1875. After nearly forty years of sectarian battling, this was remarkably ecumenical activity, and a leading role was taken by a young Scots scientist, Henry Drummond, who became a fervent promoter of missions, settlement and colonial trade, and the sort of welfare policies which would facilitate them. Drummond, a post-Darwinian Hugh Miller, tried to square scientific advance with an evangelism founded on the 'modernist' theology of such as Robertson Smith. This provided a popular ideology for the Liberal Imperialism which, advocated by politicians like Rosebery and R. B. Haldane (whose grandfather had pioneered Scottish foreign missions), became important in late Victorian Scotland.

Running in harness with imperialism was trade, one of the main Scots motives for Union, as the Earl of Roxburghe had observed. Commerce with France and north Europe declined as legal and illegal trading with England and her possessions increased. Darien showed the impossibility of a small nation trying to compete with the great European powers, so the prospect of being lifted to prosperity on the backs of the English appealed. Success, when it came, owed much to Scotland's situation. Her western coasts were out of range of French privateers; the winds blew fair from Clyde to Chesapeake, and for the southern passage back. A ship could make two voyages a year from Port Glasgow against one from the Thames. By 1770

Glasgow was rivalling Liverpool and Bristol as an entrepôt for American and West Indian goods, and was handling more than half the tobacco imported to Britain. Through the leaders of its commerce, the 'tobacco lords', Defoe's 'beautiful little city' attempted to rival what Adam Smith considered the ceremonious vices of its scruffy Gothic neighbour. But such men created commercially resilient institutions in the joint-stock banks, and along with the Board of Manufacturers they stimulated the linen industry. When, after the American War of Independence, the tobacco trade collapsed, a new trade and new manufacture – cotton – found an environment ready to receive it.

Scots traders looked across the Atlantic because, apart from coastal traffic and the 'triangle' trade to West Africa and the Americas, the East India Company dominated external trade. The Scots compensated for their exclusion as independent traders from the half of the world that it controlled by moving into its administration, and on the Atlantic they perfected the combination of technological alertness, commercial flexibility and shrewd collaboration with government that they later applied elsewhere. The end of the French wars in 1815 might have meant a shift of trade to the south; instead it led to the breaking of the East India monopoly by Kirkman Finlay, the great Glasgow cotton spinner and warehouseman, in 1816. Three years later Dr William Jardine left the East India Company to start trading, with another young Scot, at Canton. Within two decades Jardine, Matheson and Company, a conglomerate with interests in shipping, textiles, tea and – most important – opium, had become the greatest European trader in China, on whose behalf Palmerston fought the Opium War. Jardine, Matheson's home trade was mostly with London or Liverpool. Important though the Clyde remained, it never regained the significance it had enjoyed before the American revolt. Finlay died a wealthy man, but his friends and compatriots Sir John Gladstone and William Ewart, who traded from Liverpool, left fortunes three times as great. The Liverpool Scots – 'an alien group, prosperous and conspicuous' in S. G. Checkland's words – had their parallels in Melbourne and Calcutta. The coming of the steamer reinforced their distinctiveness, but if the Cunard packets were built on the Clyde they sailed from England, where their market lay.

By 1900 the mainstream of Scottish capital was flowing not into industry or trade, but into foreign investment. In October 1884 a writer in *Blackwood's Magazine* observed:

Whether this vast exportation of our surplus wealth be wise or unwise, Scotland is to a large extent responsible for it. In proportion to her size and the number of her population, she furnishes far more of it than either of the sister kingdoms. England gives sparingly and Ireland hardly any, but Scotland revels in foreign investment.

By 1914 the United Kingdom had about £4,000 million invested abroad, an average of about £90 per head of population. Scots investors accounted for £500 million, an average of nearly £110. In the 1870s they had pioneered investment trusts which poured money into land, mines and railways in the United States, Australasia and Asia, sometimes judiciously and sometimes disastrously. In the 1880s Scots investors were said to provide two-thirds of the capital for cattle ranching in the American West. You could not, a correspondent of the London *Statist* wrote in 1885, talk to any reasonably well-off man in the streets of Aberdeen, Edinburgh or Dundee, without railroads and prairies coming up. Just when the bawbee-minding Scot was becoming a music-hall turn, the Scots bourgeois was throwing his money about with a flamboyance the Scots aristocracy had never managed.

The result was close to the 'economic interpretation of imperialism' which J. A. Hobson advanced at the time of the Boer War. The low wages of the proletariat depressed the home market through under-consumption, and the surplus profits of the capitalists consequently had to be invested in 'underdeveloped' or colonial territories. Hobson's theory was in several points wide of the mark – capital in fact shunned the colonies for the USA – but Lenin used it to prove backward Russia's entanglement in a global capitalist crisis in 1917, thus justifying the Bolshevik revolution. In Scotland, too, it was peculiarly relevant. Living standards were lower, which created problems for the consumer goods industries, while contacts with the English-speaking world and the colonial Empire were well developed. In the thirty years before 1914 the line of least resistance for Scottish enterprise was not to stay at home, nor even to migrate south, but to go abroad.

As in Turner's thesis, the frontier of Greater Scotland transformed the attitudes of the core community. In particular it strengthened loyalties that were neither nationalist nor integrationist: the identities of the cities in which about 40 per cent of the population lived by 1900, and in particular that of Glasgow, which accounted for 25 per cent. Urban, rather than national, identity was the central fact of late nineteenth-century Scotland. Yet, as Geoffrey Best has remarked, Scottish cities were socially and culturally distinct from English cities. Aberdeen and Edinburgh, whose growth was modest, remained regional centres, reflecting traditional values in their caste systems and civic culture. Dundee was tied to the Empire through the jute industry and its enormous foreign investments. And Glasgow was already in 1885 being called the Scottish Chicago. It had its American counterpart's protean capacity for demolition and rebuilding; its buildings were experimental, steel-framed and concrete; its artists and patrons took their taste from the continent. It hosted the world at three lavish exhibitions, and its public utilities – tramways, electric and hydraulic power, water supply and sewage disposal – were internationally famous as examples of municipal socialism. Overcrowding remained, but the working class had been contained, disciplined, and provided with a level of social welfare which was, in the circumstances, remarkable for being adequate. For the 20 per cent or so of its inhabitants who were middle-class, Glasgow provided collective opulence on an unprecedented scale: libraries, concert halls, clubs, elaborate suburban railways, tea-rooms which were the wonder of the age, orchestras, golf-courses and, above all, the huge playground of the Clyde, with its yachts and pleasure-steamers, its quiet resorts with their piers and Italianate villas. In its way, it was as symmetrical an 'improved' society as the late eighteenth century had seen: an independent city-state and its *contado*, closer to Europe or America than to England, or, for that matter, to Edinburgh. But it was an improvement founded on the narrow base of the heavy industries. While trading by the 'Iron Ring' on the Glasgow Exchange set the world standard for pig iron-prices, while Scottish marine and railway engineers in Singapore and Johannesburg offices sent orders back to the works in which they had served their time, Glasgow continued to flourish. But its competitors in Germany and America were already flexing their muscles.

After 1815 semi-independent Scotland had been absorbed effortlessly into 'British' expansion. Scottish nationalism was pre-empted by British liberalism. Later on, as the second wave of 'peasant' nationalism broke on Europe, imperialism created a further identity, compensating for the weakening of the national institutions. In this, some prehensile myths, like that of military prowess, could still breed reality. And Greater Scotland was underwritten by the fact of success in settlement, administration, trade and investment: more substantial than the pretensions of nationalist eccentrics, and no less Scots. Defensive nationalism gained importance only when difficulties in the balance which underlay Greater Scotland coincided with structural tensions in British politics. This happened in the 1850s, and was paralleled by the Britain-wide attack on 'centralisation' which destroyed supervisory bodies like Chadwick's General Board of Health in 1854. It happened again in the 1880s, when the financial difficulties of Scottish investors, and the Highland agitation, were matched by the Chamberlainite radicals' challenge to property and entrenched political power. In both cases the gains to nationalism were negligible, though how negligible was only to become apparent after 1914.

'THAT DEPRESSED REGION'

For Adam Ferguson the society of the small *polis* was where man realised himself. Emile Durkheim and the post-industrial sociologists gave the nation-state this responsibility for directing individual egos otherwise disoriented by the impact of industrialism and the division of labour. The alternative was anomie, in which individual wills either conflicted destructively with each other, or drifted into undirected apathy. Scotland, before 1914, lacked the apparatus of the nation-state, but the functional linkage of industrial growth, emigration and imperial involvement provided both practical contexts and plausible myths for Scots fulfilment during a period of revolutionary social transformation. During World War I this came to an end.

Describing this cessation of industrial growth, and the jolt given to relations with the rest of Britain, Principal Rait of Glasgow University came up with something close to anomie:

Like other portions of the Empire, Scotland has, since the

end of 1918, suffered from the weariness produced by stupendous effort and from a consequent restlessness and impatience which has found vent in industrial disputes and in an eager adoption by some of the youth, of new social ideals, in which the influence of Russian Bolshevik experiments and propaganda has been conspicuous.

Reintegration through nationalism was faced with the weakness of the nationalist movement. Rait's belief that disruption would be quieted by 'the restoration of commercial and industrial prosperity' turned out equally false. Between the wars, Scotland was a disoriented society.

This was not just the result of the war itself, but of the political ideologies it validated. Economically, the war took a heavy toll of Scots manpower. The militarist myth had fused with panic about economic breakdown to make the Scots enlist enthusiastically – 26.8 per cent of the miners joined up in the first year – and a disproportionately high number were killed. War also swelled the heavy industries, just when some belated attempts were being made to broaden the industrial base into cars and diesel engines. So, dependence on railway equipment and steamers increased, despite the challenge of new technologies, scarcely represented in Scotland. After the war competition and excess capacity took their toll; once a short boom had sopped up wartime losses and fulfilled demand backlogs, industry tipped into sustained decline. Unemployment had been 1.8 per cent of the insured work-force (on the whole skilled men) in 1913 (the figure for London was 8.7 per cent), it rose between 1920 and 1931 to a minimum of 10 per cent, and in 1931–3 to over 25 per cent. This was not simply the result of Scots economic problems: the international impact of the depression shut off emigration, which had peaked between 1911 and 1931, when as many people left as had left in the period 1871–1911. But a larger – and consequently cheaper – work-force did nothing for economic development. In 1908 Scots industry had provided 12.5 per cent of UK production; by 1930 this had fallen to 9.6 per cent.

Contrasts between the prosperity of 1913 and the problems of subsequent years still feature in conference speeches. Yet the weaknesses were largely the result of decisions taken in Scotland by Scotsmen while the economy was still prosperous and relatively autonomous. Nationalist writers – or at any rate some of them – were aware of this. In *Caledonia, or the Future of the Scots* (1926) George Malcolm Thomson, a journalist in the Beaverbrook entourage, was scathing:

> Scotland is already a land of working men and petty tradesmen, a land, that is, in which both work and trade are destined to wither. She is sinking slowly in an economic and racial quagmire . . . She is an annex, half-industrial, half-sporting, of English civilisation, and tomorrow she will be a proletarian state, blind, resentful and submerged, populated by a nation of machine-minders doing the bidding of foreign capitalists . . . There is no intellectual community capable of producing the friction of minds from which ideas are generated. It is a land of second-hand thoughts and second-rate minds, inapt to improvise or experiment, an addict to the queue habit in the world of ideas, and woefully unaware of the time-lag that makes a visit to it a voyage in time as well as in space for most West Europeans.

Thomson's assault was timely if somewhat paranoid. Assimilation was as sweeping as a century earlier. In 1928 Scottish government was put under the London Civil Service. In 1929 the Free Church and Auld Kirk, whose brawling had permeated national affairs for almost a century, quietly amalgamated, and without any prior investigation, Scottish local government was drastically reorganised. The parish councils, the first institutions of local democracy in rural Scotland, were abolished after scarcely thirty years, to the dismay of radicals in the Labour Party as well as traditionalists in the Convention of Royal Burghs. The tendency had been summed up by one Labour MP, William Adamson, in 1924:

> We believe that government policy is to subordinate Scottish administration to Whitehall to a far greater extent than has ever been the case, and to remove from Scotland practically the last vestige of independent government and nationhood and to have its centre in London.

Equally depressingly, it was a Labour government that he attacked.

The younger men who had survived the war, like Thomson and MacDiarmid, wanted to bury the old order, but still had to create a nationalist alternative. Nationalism was not just divided between left and right; on the left, where it was potentially strongest, there was a new challenge. Wartime production demands on the industries of the Clyde Valley, with their depleted labour force, strong craft unionism, and antiquated management structure, had produced a temporary but powerful alliance between craftsmen and socialist militants. 'Red Clydeside' was more legend than reality, but after the war its activists dominated the founding of the Communist Party of Great Britain. The revolutionaries were articulate and able, the first Scottish working men to rationalise an effective politics out of their own experience. Where the Chartists had adopted middle-class self-improvement, and Keir Hardie moved south, they canvassed drastic remedies for the multiple ills of the Scottish industrial belt. But the programme of the Comintern meant integrating Scottish socialism with world revolution. Temperamentally and organisationally, William Gallagher, J. R. Campbell, Arthur MacManus and Harry McShane echoed the religious millenarianism – Calvinist or ultramontane Catholic – in which they had been reared. Once again, religion frustrated nationalism.

Between the wars the left had little success in Scotland anyway. If there was a consistent electoral trend, it was rightwards. In 1922 – the year the 'red Clydeside' travelled to London – only 13 Unionists were elected in Scotland, against 27 Liberals and 29 Labour. By 1935 there were 43 Unionists, only 3 Liberals, 20 Labour and 5 Independent Labour MPs. Labour's early impact was due largely to two things: the wartime growth of the trade unions, and the migration of the well-disciplined Irish Nationalist vote, which the rise of Sinn Fein had left orphaned, from the Liberal Party. This owed more to the organisational gifts of Catholic Labour politicians like John Wheatley and Patrick Dollan than to any mass conversion to socialism, as the government of Glasgow has demonstrated down to the present day. Wheatley laid the foundation of the council housing programme which was indelibly to mark Scottish society in later years, but its scale was not yet sufficient to enable Labour to fill the vacuum left by the collapse of the Liberals.

'Aristocratic and socially conservative', the Scottish Liberal leaders looked back to the days when they had given their party its majority in Westminster. Neglecting the collectivist remedies offered by Lloyd George, most of them drifted quietly into local alliances with the Unionists, and in 1931 imparted to the National coalition, which enjoyed a staggering 64–7 majority over Labour, a markedly antique appearance. In 1910 business-men and lawyers had dominated Scots representation; in 1931, assailed everywhere by industrial problems, Scots MPs were largely lawyers, landowners and military men.

The deterioration of political Conservatism reflected the weakness of Scottish business leadership. If the inter-war British economy was strait-jacketed by financial orthodoxy, the pos-ition in Scotland was worse: magnates and family dynasties from the old staple industries were keener to protect their own status and power than to experiment in new fields. The Census of Production of 1935 found that, in the growth industries of cars and electrical engineering, under 2 per cent of the work-force was employed in Scotland. Bodies formed to promote industry, like the Scottish Development Council and the Scottish Economic Committee, were hampered by dissension between the old industrialists and the new. Only in 1937 did government policy switch from encouraging the unemployed to move south, to creating jobs in Scotland itself. The Scottish Industrial Estates Corporation, set up with a capital of £4 million to build an industrial estate at Hillington outside Glasgow, created 15,000 jobs. But armaments orders placed on the Clyde totalled £80 million, bearing out the Clydesdale Bank's ominous remark of February 1938: 'what building was to English recov-ery, rearmament has been to Scottish'. When war broke out, the economic problems of Scotland seemed as intractable as ever.

The problem was as much one of diagnosis as of prescription. Scotland shared the malaise of the British economy, but suffered from its own structural weaknesses, the lack of institutions, individuals and concepts capable of defining the sorts of reform needed. The devolved departments were now situated in Scotland, but lacked experience or authority in economic policy and physical planning. The universities, which were to provide almost a surfeit of prescriptions for the economy in the post-war period, were silent. The intellectuals were preoccupied with Marx or social credit, both apocalyptic rather than remedial. Southern control could have been extended, had the National government bothered itself. But if it moved, it was gently in the opposite direction. The Scottish National Development Council

(SNDC) was set up with bipartisan backing in 1930. Four years later the Secretary of State, the publisher and former Liberal Sir Godfrey Collins, created a commissioner for the Scottish Special Area, and funds from his budget subsidised the SNDC and its Scottish Economic Committee. By 1938 it was recommending a development agency for the Highlands and a substantial devolution of economic power. Enlightened Tories such as Walter Elliot ensured that 'planning' with a regional component was put before the influential Barlow Committee at the end of the 1930s, although it was in the circumstances of war that the new orthodoxy of a state-guided economy, formulated by J. M. Keynes, took effect.

By this time the men and ideas were available to give state planning a Scottish dimension. The men of Greater Scotland had come back to a nationality that they had ignored for nearly a century. In the course of his dynamic Secretaryship (1941–5) Thomas Johnston drew on his experience on the Empire Marketing Board and took the Tennessee Valley Authority and the Ontario Power Company as precedents for his North of Scotland Hydro-Electric Board. In 1939 James Bowie, Director of the Dundee School of Economics, set up by an industrialist in 1931 to remedy the deficiency in economics teaching in the land of Adam Smith, applied Keynesian remedies directly to Scottish problems in his book *The Future of Scotland*. Bowie had spent most of his career teaching in America and his remedies smacked of the New Deal. Recognising that the resources of Scotland lay primarily in its people, and the importance of retaining them in their communities, he wanted a state-financed Scottish Development Commission to plan the economy, control the heavy industries, and assist the growth of light industries. His aims were only partially secured by Johnston's Scottish Council on Industry in 1942, but they were given widespread publicity by nationalist and left-wing organisations. Through Johnston's efforts, powers that might have gone south stayed in the north, and the authority of the Secretary of State was extended into new areas like physical planning and industrial development. The centralisation implied by post-war planning schemes would at least meet a countervailing force and a countervailing hope. In Bowie's words:

The best way to make Scotland a powerful partner in the

Empire is to treat her as we have treated our dominions and to grant her successive instalments of power to set her own house in order. The present tendency to decentralise should be accelerated, and the next step is to give Scotland an effective instrument of diagnosis and prescription.

3

THE INTELLECTUALS, 1707–1945

The deepest result of this complex involvement in British society was that the provincial's view of the world was discontinuous. Two forces, two magnets, affected his efforts to find adequate standards and styles: the values associated with the simplicity and purity (real or imagined) of nativism and those to be found in cosmopolitan sophistication. Those who could take entire satisfaction in either could maintain a consistent position. But for provincials, exposed to both, an exclusive concentration of either kind was too narrow. It meant a rootlessness, an alienation either from the higher sources of culture or from the familiar local environment that had formed the personality. Few whose conceptions surpassed local boundaries rested content with a simple, consistent image of themselves or of the world. Provincial culture in eighteenth-century Scotland was formed in a mingling of these visions.

John Clive, 'The Social Background', in
Scotland in the Age of Improvement (1970)

MARXISM AND THE DEMOCRATIC INTELLECT

'The national leaders fought with intellectual weapons, and for intellectual prizes.' A. J. P. Taylor observed that the Habsburgs were more troubled by compilers of linguistic dictionaries than by socialist revolutionaries. Had he lived, Marx would probably have agreed. He had assumed that intellectuals alienated from capitalism – 'a portion of the bourgeois ideologists, who have raised themselves to the level of comprehending theoretically the historical movement as a whole' – would mobilise the industrial proletariat, the nation-state simply providing their 'historic' political framework. But after 1848 anticipations of an industrial – or at least literate – society gave them the chance to confront or even divert the forces of economic change. They became the ideologues of the second wave of nationalism, when peasant societies, challenged by literacy, industry and centralised government, looked for a new national *Geist*, an 'imagined community' which could contain the shock of social change. As educational reformers, philological researchers and cultural revivalists they were backed by conservatives, trying to confound 'scientific materialism', and by radicals, trying to fuse it to the atavistic force of national loyalty. They helped fashion the institutions which promoted industrialisation and mass politics; they also established at their heart the ethnic, religious and cultural components of a potent 'false consciousness'.

Marx derived his model from England, where the social framework for capitalist industry was established by a 'pre-nationalist' struggle for legislative supremacy between King and Parliament. But England's apparent typicality masked a distinctive national evolution: of great territorial wealth moulding both legislature and executive, allying with bourgeois forces and, where need be, calling on its power-bases in the periphery. After 1870 this structure was to be challenged by the 'second wave': intellectual-directed nationalism in Wales, where the political nation had long been in abeyance, and in Ireland, where land and language issues in a peasant society helped shift nationalist rhetoric into the intransigent mould of Sinn Fein. Intelligentsias might remedy the lack of institutions by making their collective imagination serve as a surrogate nation. Not in Scotland. Despite the semi-independent estates, a good case for legislative devolution, a command of press and public opinion, the Scots seemed only to contribute a decorative nostalgia. Even in the 1970s, after the literary renaissance and amid a political crisis, commentators such as Neal Ascherson were struck by the fact that the political and cultural inputs of the national movement simply were not synchronised.

But for most of the time after 1707 nationalism was not the only, or the most important, option for the Scottish intelligentsia. Its loyalty was a dual one, and only its weaker element concerned the home country. The other loyalty was as powerful and protean as the achievement of 'Greater Scotland'.

MacDiarmid aptly claimed *Moby Dick* as the great Scottish novel; it has nothing to do with Scotland in any respect save its theme of a man's obsessive pursuit of his own destiny, an ego unconstrained by community or God; an intellectual ambition as huge and arrogant as the political wilfulness MacDiarmid applauded in the reluctance of the Scots to behave like any other nation. Ahab was Prometheus or Christ or Nietzsche's Superman. But this heroic view of missionary Scottishness had to coexist with the means to the desired end: the fact that prosperity, materially and intellectually, required collaboration with the English, however unendurable their comfortable self-satisfaction. 'I hope you in Oxford don't think we hate you,' John Stuart Blackie asked Benjamin Jowett in 1866. 'We don't think about you,' was the reply. Blackie, classicist and Celticist, a Scoto-Germanic eccentric, was a useful irritant, and did his bit for Highland land reform; such originality as Jowett had (not a lot) was as a 'moderate' of the Scots Enlightenment. Yet his Balliol was one of the main channels through which ambitious Scots made their way.

The internal tensions involved were only fitfully visible to Hugh Miller's 'unthinking Saxons'. What, for instance, did they make of James Bryce, who praised the traditional Scots university course to Gilbert Murray as the best possible, yet who disparaged the provincial English universities (on the whole following in the Scots tradition) as 'Lilliputian' and exalted the values of Oxford? Was the Anglo-Scottish tradition only a range of institutions to be exploited and thereafter regarded only with nostalgia?

In 1809 the *Edinburgh Review*'s Francis Jeffrey, whom Walter Scott regarded as an unrepentant assimilationist, sketched the apparently anodyne picture of the country that the successful Anglo-Scot retained:

> It is connected in their imagination not only with that olden time which is uniformly conceived as more pure, lofty and simple than the present, but also with all the soft and bright colours of remembered childhood and domestic affection. All its pleasures conjure up images of schoolday innocence, and sports, and friendships which have no part in succeeding years.

'That olden time' wasn't simply 'temps perdu'; it was also Adam

Ferguson's image of a community glued together by non-commercial values, whose subversion by 'commerce' would not lead to 'improvement'. Over a century later Neil Gunn, in his political allegory *The Green Isle of the Great Deep* (1944) offered 'the human familiarity, the life-warmth' of the Highland boy Art as the antidote to the subtle and insidious tyranny of a modern totalitarian state:

> 'The later phase of life on earth has tended to destroy the wholeness of the child mind at a very early stage. The intensive pursuit of what is called education has also tended to disintegrate the young mind.'
>
> 'In what way does the boy Art differ?'
>
> 'In that he was still the complete boy. The country community he came out of was to him a complete and familiar community. Old Hector – and this is what some of us were slow to grasp – was his natural friend. The boy's simplicity was found again in the old man's – and the old man's was the simplicity refined out of experience. Added to that was the background of what they call Nature. Which means that the subconscious responses had a natural field of action . . .'

This was more than a longing for Tir-na-nOg – the Land of Eternal Youth, closer to Gunn's friend and publisher T. S. Eliot's idea, 'to arrive where we started / And know the place for the first time': a complicated meditation on intuition and experience which retained a positive identity for beleaguered modern man.

This dualism, torn between cosmopolitan opportunism and demotic roots calcified into nostalgia, is directly relevant to the present, for it has been largely since the war that it has been rationally appraised. This has involved inverting the usual approaches to the intellectual history of nationalism. Notions of a continuum or of a consistent evolution have to be left on the margin. The question why Scotland developed no orthodox national intelligentsia is now seen as far more important. The maturity of contemporary nationalism is that it has faced up to this, while the decay of the United Kingdom consensus has driven some of the most corrosive critics of Scottish nationalism to endorse it.

Most nationalist intelligentsias see themselves as the servants of a national *Geist*. They do not court metropolitan recognition;

indeed, given their usual language loyalties, they cannot. Welsh Eisteddfod rituals started *in* London, they were never *of* the place. The Scots have, by contrast, an ambiguous relationship to the metropolis: a desire to exploit it in the only way open to a provincial – by understanding and mastering its ideology – and an enduring suspicion that (a) this path might be blocked by a socially selective clique, and (b) that once the door is levered open or smashed in, there might be nothing there.

Metropolitan culture might, or might not, be a sham; native culture might, or might not, be genuine. The enduring characteristic of the Scottish intellect since the Reformation has been cultural insecurity at one pole or the other. The existential remedy has traditionally lain in the energy and acumen of individuals, and the openness of the Scottish estates to intellectual innovation – often against orthodox nationalist opposition. The significance of the present crisis is that it has occurred at both poles: political nationalism in Scotland has coincided with the intellectual and political atrophy of the British elite. Europeanisation, the modernisation of higher education, and the communications revolution have made the Scots intelligentsia acutely aware of the break-up, not only of the unitary state, but of monolithic theories of social change.

In 1977 I wrote that the most critical of these developments was the reappraisal of Marxism. This invites the riposte that Marxism has not so much been reappraised as buried. But stay awhile. In Eastern Europe the jury is still out on 'market reforms' which have brought rampant inequality and social collapse; in China an authoritarian communism has outperformed, and been applauded by, its capitalist rivals; it is healthier to be ruled by Italian communists in Bologna than to be ruled by Italian Christian Democrats in Palermo. In the years after 1956 the left was critical of East European Stalinism, while Western bankers kept it alive by pumping loans into it. In this practical sense, Scotland's unfashionable commitment to 'socialism with a human face' seems prescient rather than archaic.

The components are, however, more complex than the original *démarche* associated with the New Left in the 1950s, the overthrow of the crude Marxian notion of governmental and cultural institutions being a 'superstructure' erected on an economic base. Historians and political writers such as E. P. Thompson, Eric Hobsbawm, Victor Kiernan and Raymond

Williams disaggregated 'the British way' into specific experiences, and in so doing they implied that the separate identity of Scotland, Ireland and Wales was to be respected if not (at this stage, at any rate) explained. A statement like Hobsbawm's in *Industry and Empire*:

> Scotland and Wales are socially, and by their history, traditions, and sometimes institutions, entirely distinct from England, and cannot therefore be simply subsumed under English history or (as is more common) neglected

wouldn't have occurred to a Marxist thirty years earlier. It certainly didn't occur to Marx himself.

Ideas mattered; were not just projections of the self-interest of economic groups. This affirmed the importance of political transaction *à la* Lewis Namier, but also the role of ideology in moulding the conventions that sanctioned it. It is in this perspective that the Scottish tradition – George Davie's 'democratic intellectualism' – loses its inscrutably idealist qualities and begins to show the mutual influences of 'philosophic' discourses – logic, theology, anthropology, jurisprudence – on one hand, and of a distinctive politics on the other.

GRANDEURS AND MISERIES OF CALVINISM

The crisis of authority in early modern Scotland produced a situation in which ideology rather than social status determined the role of the intellectual in society; and a range of political relationships could be activated to ensure that it continued to do so. In this way the intellectuals, in David Caute's definition those who 'tend to apply theoretical arguments to the solution of practical problems or, conversely, search for the principles and symbols embodied in concrete instances', were given a preemptive role in society that they lacked elsewhere in Britain. Their professions changed, from priest to lawyer and scholar, novelist to administrator and technologist but they were able, for nearly four centuries, to recruit and to market their talents on their own terms – which coexisted with the growth and development of the United Kingdom and its Empire.

The Reformation was the critical discontinuity, through its dramatic adoption of a religious ideology – Calvinism – associated with advanced urban commercial communities. Intellectual

84

and commercial connections with Europe were strong; monarchic authority, which rapidly imposed Lutheranism on Scandinavia, was weak. George Buchanan was representative, as the greatist Latinist of his day and a fierce opponent of divine right, of a new clerisy negotiating its way between competing political groups – the nobility, the Kirk, the towns, the English. But success only came after 130 years of struggle, which absorbed energies that at other times could have humanised the community. Gramsci would later marvel at how the 'traditional intelligentsia' of the British professions had pre-empted the role of the 'organic intelligentsia' of industrial capitalism. In Scotland this process was telescoped: the Calvinist elite anticipated the 'organic intelligentsia'. All that was missing was capitalism.

The aims of Knox and Buchanan were only partly achieved, but between 1560 and 1690 materially and morally the Kirk became, in R. H. Tawney's words, 'the real State in Scotland', creating institutions and attitudes which the Union was to vitalise. Calvinism stressed an autonomous and capricious God who

> Sends ane to heaven an' ten to hell,
> A' for thy glory.
> An no' for any gude or ill,
> They've done before thee.

This liberated and imprisoned. On the whole it led to a practical stoicism. Predestination recognised the same sort of lottery in life as in death. Over this pit, Calvinism constructed rules to keep civil society together. As James Hogg showed in *Confessions of a Justified Sinner* (1823), it could mask tendencies far darker than those Burns caricatured in 'Holy Willie's Prayer', but it provided the hard-and-fast rules a frontier society needed. Areas of collective responsibility which the English state contracted out to the aristocracy or forgot about, in Scotland passed into the hands of the Kirk: notably education and poor relief, where Calvinist values were expressed at their most emphatic. English empiricism tranquilly reflected existing hierarchies; in Scotland ideology fretted to reconstruct them. It forced the intellectual to act, continually launched him on a country which frustrated or redirected his efforts.

The seventeenth century presented the Scots with the option of Calvinism in one country, or the export of revolution. The latter, during the Civil War,led to direct rule by Cromwell and a counter-attack by the episcopalians, until in 1688 the Kirk was confirmed, and after 1707 the clerisy was tied to a Union whose terms actually enjoined the persecution of episcopalians and Jacobites, the latter being thicker on the ground in Oxford than in the Scottish universities. The way was at last clear along which the Kirk could lead society towards improvement.

This premature religious revolution sent the wandering Scot off in search of a community that could contain his ambitions. A trauma altogether too severe to justify even the intellectual and material triumphs of post-Calvinist Scotland? Four centuries later, amid the debris of the achieving society, Neil Gunn and Edwin Muir looked back on the Reformation as a pre-industrial assault on community, which made it much more difficult to cope with this challenge when it came. In the words of George Mackay Brown, a pupil of Muir and a Catholic convert:

> It was then that the old heraldry began to crack, that the idea of 'progress' took root in men's minds. What was broken, irremediably, in the 16th century was the fullness of life in a community, its simple interwoven identity. In earlier times the temporal and the eternal, the story and the fable, were not divorced, as they came to be after Knox: they used the same language and imagery, so that the whole of life was illuminated . . . Innocence gave place to a dark brooding awareness . . . From that time, too, the old music and poetry died out, because the single vision which is the source of all art had been choked. Poets followed priests into the darkness.

This was overdriven. But when the struggle between Coleridge's 'civilisation and cultivation' was joined in Europe and England in the nineteenth century, one result was the reclaiming of the traditional community as the nation, an organism which could supposedly sustain 'the fullness of life' in the industrial age. In Scotland, however, its time was long past.

IMPROVEMENT

Kirk and law were central to Scottish intellectual life after 1707. The Kirk rapidly shifted from near-heresy to an established centre of authority, under the control of such as William

Robertson the historian, Adam Ferguson the social scientist and Thomas Reid the philosopher. More than any other group the Moderates – the archetypal red Scots – made possible the Scottish Enlightenment (a late Victorian coinage), which gave the country a reputation rivalling that of London, Paris and Vienna, not least in the eyes of savants like Voltaire and Jefferson. As the latter put it in 1789, where science was concerned, 'no place in the World can pretend to a competition with Edinburgh'.

The Moderates were far removed from the passions of early presbyterianism. But if Ferguson and Robertson regarded John Knox as a boor, their notion of a civil society mindful of the status quo still gave a role to the Kirk and its courts as national institutions, however much qualified by landed patronage. The literati drew the wrath of later generations for their agnosticism about nationality. Carlyle, in his essay on Burns (1828), was scathing:

> Never perhaps was there a class of writers so clear and well ordered, yet so totally destitute, to all appearance, of any patriotic affection, nay, of any human affection whatever.

But this was more true of Hume and Smith, who despaired of the future of the small *polis* in the epoch of the nation-state, than of Hutcheson, Reid or Ferguson. The vitality of the Enlightenment depended on semi-independence, conscious decisions by men working within the estates, who realised their strengths and weaknesses, and the need to control the drive to integration. Edinburgh, whose carefully planned New Town of 1767 imported metropolitan amenities, was a substitute London, not an imitation, a centre for otherwise unsettled professional men and their clients: landowners not wealthy enough to move south, lawyers dependent on them for their briefs, merchants and manufacturers who still traded in a local market, ministers and teachers who had risen in the Scottish universities but could never buy their way into the English professions.

The rise of Edinburgh would be remarkable enough without the paraphernalia of nationalism. Yet, interestingly enough, much of this emerged: the romanticism unleashed by 'Ossian' MacPherson in the 1760s, the folklorism of Allan Ramsay, Burns, Grose and Scott; the idea of community as something more than an aggregate of men in Ferguson and John Millar.

Ferguson stressed the aggression and touchiness that community required; the problem was that the old Scots order displayed these in ways which split the state. Against this the specialised estates and the 'British' orientation of semi-independence offered a stable basis for 'improvement'.

Yet an important element of the pre-industrial community underwrote the Enlightenment: a network of collaborative, voluntary bodies which created a politics of mutual reinforcement. The Edinburgh Speculative Society of 1764 is exemplary. Its members later included Scott, Henry Brougham, Jeffrey and Cockburn – at daggers drawn in their politics but still prepared to spend their Wednesday evenings drinking and talking around the fire at the university. Both the condition for and the result of this was a remarkable versatility: ministers wrote plays; Law Lords and publishers discoursed on the descent of man; Charles MacLaren edited both the *Scotsman* and the *Encyclopaedia Britannica* (itself an Edinburgh project). When Adam Ferguson, minister and sometime infantryman, found that gaining the Edinburgh chair of philosophy meant that he had to teach physics and not ethics, he set to and kept himself a fortnight ahead of his class. Polymathy was not a curiosity in eighteenth-century Scotland, it was a condition of survival.

'There appears in the genius of the Scottish people – fostered no doubt by the abstract metaphysical speculations of their universities – a power of reducing human actions to formulas or principles.' Walter Bagehot's observation was just. The essentially deductive foundations of the Enlightenment were posited on the notion of an innate 'consciousness', 'conscience' or 'common sense' from which the individual could intuitively recognise his social nature. This was an essentially conservative position, in that such an innate quality was unchanging: Enlightenment thinkers often thought more in terms of decadence than of progress. But their social vision contributed to one of the Enlightenment's main achievements – and the one which bound it tightly to industrial development – the systematic collection and dissemination of knowledge. The *Encyclopaedia Britannica* was joined by the *Statistical Accounts*, a parish-by-parish social survey compiled by ministers to a pattern devised by the agricultural improver Sir John Sinclair of Ulster. The Ordnance Survey had its beginnings in Scotland, and what C. R. Fay called 'the stream of social education' was forced along in the early nineteenth century by the 'monitorial' system of Dr Andrew Bell, which Dickens savaged as M'Choakumchild's Academy in *Hard Times*:

> He knew all about the Water Sheds of all the world (whatever they are), and all the histories of all the peoples, and all the names of all the rivers and mountains, and all the productions, manners, and customs of all the countries, and all their boundaries and bearings on the two-and-thirty points of the compass. Ah, rather overdone, M'Choakumchild. If he had only learnt a little less, how infinitely better he might have taught much more!

The excesses of the enlightened Scot drew the fire of Peacock and Cobbett as well as Dickens, but did not lead to Anglo-Scottish friction. However distinctive its origin, a society concerned to instruct and improve saw no boundaries to its efforts, and imposed no barrier to those wanting to join it. Eighteenth-century Scotland owed much to its English immigrants, to the surgeon-chemist John Roebuck, who helped found the great Carron Ironworks and patronised James Watt, to the iron and cotton magnates Dixon and Houldsworth, and to the protean Welshman Robert Owen who drew the crowned heads of Europe to his social laboratory at New Lanark. In turn, improvement opened the road to the south. Were the Scots too apologetic about their provincial accents in polite English society? Possibly, but has enough been said about the new, harsh lingua franca of calculation and organisation that they helped impose? The relationships that underpinned the golden age, retaining the talented without risking them developing into an intellectual proletariat, could not endure. But an unusually potent range of intellectual and educational investments had been created.

The stream of social education was broad rather than deep. The obverse of polymathy and systematisation was a certain slapdash quality in Scottish intellectual life which increasingly began to irk not only those writers who sought a wider audience, but also those who wanted to preserve an organic community. Such discontents underlay the foundation of the Edinburgh Academy to offer a strict classical education on English lines in 1824, and the attempt to reform the Scottish universities two years later. This created the paradox that just at the time when nationality became significant in Europe, and explicit in Scotland, the impulses that propelled it were absorbed into the movement for further integration. This was particularly important in the cases of Scott and Carlyle.

WIZARDRY

In 1807, in a debate at the Faculty of Advocates in Edinburgh, Walter Scott attacked proposed changes in the Court of Session as violations of the Treaty of Union. Afterwards he turned on Francis Jeffrey: 'Little by little, whatever your wishes may be,' he said, with tears in his eyes, 'you will destroy and undermine until nothing of what makes Scotland Scotland shall remain.' Parliamentary and legal reform, not the Union of 1707, would quiet the old song. Scott was a Tory partisan, and a fairly comprehensive reactionary, but he spoke with authority. As a novelist and folklorist, he was the precursor of those reconstructors of historic identity who propelled European nationalism. As a politician and lawyer he stood at the fulcrum of semi-independent Scotland. As an historian, in the tradition of Hume and Robertson, his perception of the evolution of the state since the Union of the Crowns was critical. No less so was his ambiguous engagement with contemporary reality.

In that great sequence of novels, from *Old Mortality* via *The Heart of Midlothian*, *Waverley*, and *Redgauntlet*, to *The Antiquary*, Scott spanned the century following the Restoration as sociologist as much as romancer. Carlyle in the nineteenth and Georg Lukács in the twentieth century congratulated him on filling the past with 'living men, not by protocols, state papers, controversies and abstractions of men'. He dramatised the Enlightenment's preoccupation with the structure of society, setting carefully delineated characters against complex and mutable environments. These moulded freedom of action, so there were few tragic heroes, but a continuing reappraisal of moral worth in the light of social change. The nation progressed from conflicting statuses and religions to contract and 'improvement'. Armed dialecticians mutated into litigious citizens or picturesque bandits.

Scott's preference for social description over plot made him treat great events obliquely. The Union and the rebellions do not dominate; they are fitted into the milieu. *The Heart of Midlothian* is about the consequences of the Union, although the Act itself is scarcely mentioned. By a mixture of meticulous research and sympathetic caricature Scott recreates the unsettled mood of pre-Athenian Edinburgh, its citizens scunnered at the absence of 'their' Parliament. Yet the pre-Union period is also seen as one of bigotry and bad law. The Scottish Parliament, after all, had passed the statute of hanging for child-murder under which Effie Deans was condemned. (It had also reimposed serfdom in the mines and salt-works.) The virtues which triumph are, indeed, those of the seventeenth century – Jeannie Deans's moral conviction and the Duke of Argyll's political grasp – but stripped of fanaticism and opportunism thanks to the security and wider horizons granted by the Union. Jeannie transmutes the hair-splitting pietism of her Covenanting father into sound morality; Argyll transmutes chieftainship into statesmanship and improving landlordism. In the sociological language of the Victorians, both personify the change from a militant to an industrial mode of society, in which social relationships – and morality – will be founded on calculation. Even the novel's unsatisfying ending, an odd combination of pastoral and melodrama, is significant. Staunton and Donacha slaughter one another among pastures, once Highland, now made rich by the husbandry of Douce Davie Deans: the men of violence perish irrelevantly in the landscape of improvement.

The juxtaposition of fanaticism and traditional authority with legality, rationalism and social change became commonplace in the British novel, especially when dealing with industrialisation and the extension of European influence. Scott started the literary tradition which led to Conrad and Forster. But – after a tantalising jeté in *The Chronicles of the Canongate* – he fell silent before the new confrontation between landed society and capitalism, industrialisation and democracy. He viewed this with pathological gloom, yet his disciple, Balzac, equally conservative, revelled in dissecting it. Even Scott's able contemporaries John Galt and James Hogg, who described their society and religion with equal insight, lacked successors. Why?

Not just through failure of individual inspiration. Economics mattered. Capitalism wasn't just there to be observed: it penetrated the literary world and made historic Scotland marketable. Scott's ascendancy coincided with Scottish publishers breaking into the London book trade and the rule of the 'Scotch reviewers'. Constable, Black, Chambers and Blackwood were followed by Macmillan, Collins, Nelson and Blackie: publishing, not writing, built the Abbotsfords of the nineteenth century. As editors and popularisers George Gilfillan, Robert Chambers, George Lillie Craik and John Douglas Cook were ephemeral, but influential. Not for nothing did Ezra Pound's Mr Nixon advise Mauberley to pay attention to the strictures of Dr Dundas. Such literary entrepreneurs dictated the sort of Scotland that would be written about, more or less the same Scotland that middle-class tourists came north by steamer and train to see. The 'Scotch novel' in its intermittent vogues, provided the new industrial society with recreation, not self-analysis.

After 1830 the Whigs were in office. Scott died, fighting them to the last, but the ruling elite they represented was, in his sense, recognisably 'British'. Prominent Englishmen – Lord John Russell, Sydney Smith, Lords Palmerston and Brougham – had savoured the late Enlightenment when barred from the continent by the Napoleonic Wars. If Jeffrey and Cockburn proved broken reeds, such families like the Stephens and Macaulays contributed to the evangelically minded 'intellectual aristocracy' of public service. Rightly believing himself superior to anyone he had so far met there, Carlyle took the London coach in 1834. With foresight. After the Ten Years' Conflict and the Kirk schism of 1843, the tide set to the south.

'British social and cultural thought' – and for most of the nineteenth century the phrase is justified – as much as adminis-tration or technology, was to be dominated by men of Scottish birth or descent: Ruskin, Mill, Gladstone, T. B. Macaulay, Leslie Stephen. The dividend on past educational and social invest-ment was impressive. But how unsettling the implications were for Scotland is shown by the case of Thomas Carlyle.

CARLYLE'S EMPIRE

'There is no sight half as impressive as a Scotsman on the make.' In 1908 J. M. Barrie struck at an awkward truth, relevant to more than his own success – itself disfigured by the tragedy he anticipated in *Tommy and Grizel* – and the careerism of his Kailyard contemporaries. The pursuit of success denominated red and black Scot alike. They were organisers, activists, publi-cists, their eyes on the main chance as well as the reality of their society. Did this make for profundity? Carlyle in 'Signs of the Times' (1829) had his doubts:

> Not the external and physical alone is now managed by machinery, but the internal and spiritual also . . . Instruction, that mysterious communing of Wisdom with Ignorance, is no longer an indefinable tentative process, requiring a study of individual aptitudes, and a perpetual variation of means and methods, to attain the same ends; but a secure, universal, straightforward business, to be conducted in the gross, by proper mechanism, with such intellect as comes to hand.

The sage did not have to torment himself: the machine was ready to project suitable material. Carlyle saw, and said to his contemporaries and successors, where he was going. The impact of this on English culture was salutary: Carlyle stands behind that stunning triumph which the realist novel – Dickens, Trollope, Mrs Gaskell, George Eliot, Meredith – enjoyed between 1840 and 1880. But in their success as public preachers the sages sacrificed much of the analytical intellect and practical social engagement of the Enlightenment. By the 1870s it was easier for Marx to carry on its traditions than it was for the Scots themselves.

In the north, religious repression appeared compounded with pseudo-science. Phrenology, centred among Duncan MacLaren's radical friends in Edinburgh, was no improvement on Monboddo's speculations on evolution and language; Robert Knox on *The Races of Man* (1850) was a disturbing regression. Samuel Smiles's equation of economic progress with a simple set of moral injunctions was scarcely an adequate successor to the work of Adam Smith. H. T. Buckle in 1861 condemned Edinburgh for lapsing into a credulous medievalism, thanks to the deductive methods of Scots philosophy; in 1865 John Stuart Mill settled accounts with the school's last great man, Sir William Hamilton. Even Matthew Arnold, trying to do something for the Celts, pushed them firmly into a commercialised twilight. By the 1880s, as the reformed English universities were gaining momentum in scholarship and research, the Free Kirk was persecuting Robertson Smith, its greatest theologian and a pioneer of social anthropology, for heresy. His move to Cambridge in 1885 seemed a capitulation. A year later the radical and secularist J. M. Robertson wrote of the country in terms which seem to anticipate the *mise-en-scène* of George Douglas Brown's horrific farewell to the century *The House with the Green Shutters* (1901):

> Austerity and joyless gloom on the one hand produce their natural corrective in dissolute mirth and defiant licence on the other. . . . A moral duality, so to speak, runs through past Scottish life in a way that seems at times perplexing.

If the absence of a national focus is critical here, Carlyle should have supplied it, and did not. In his indictment of mechanism he paraphrased Schiller's words, written in 1796:

> That polypus nature of the Greek states, where each individual enjoyed an independent existence, and in case of need, could act with the whole, now gives place to an ingenious engineering, in which a mechanical life forms itself as a whole, from the patchwork of innumerable but lifeless parts. The State and Church laws and customs, are now rent asunder; enjoyment is now separated from labour, the means from the end, exertion from recompense.

German writers had seen nationalism as a means of reconstituting individuality in the age of industrialisation and rationalism. Carlyle agreed with them. His contempt for the detachment of the literati was as scathing as his assault on the economists. Witness his essay on Burns. Yet although his remedies were nationalist – in their authoritarianism and Anglo-Saxonism they prefigured imperialism, possibly even Fascism – the nationalism was transferred. Where to? Profoundly Scots in speech, the 'greatest talker in London' had a style more *outré* than anything the Scots had produced in the eighteenth century. He considered himself, for a time, an Englishman; until, finding the race unserious, he courted Prussia. But he was accepted as the arbiter of the English language's integrity in its struggle with the new industrial society. English served and was served by Carlyle and the other emigrants. It spelt integration, when the dual culture of Scotland was in decay; it had also to be protected from perversion by the new social order. Carlyle or Mill or Ruskin was concerned with defining progress, liberty, representation or economics: something distinctively Scots. Outsiders from a provincial culture under pressure were testing the currency of a metropolitan elitism and, if it rang true, enlisting in it.

It wasn't surprising that Carlyle was reverenced by Disraeli – the sentiments were not reciprocated – because what Carlyle was up to paralleled the contemporary incorporation of the Jews within European, and particularly German, culture. 'Alienated from a Judaism which they regarded as parochial,' as Frank Field has written, they were attracted by 'the single-mindedness and relentless moral seriousness . . . which had profound affinities with that of the Jews themselves'. Theoreticians of this literary and scientific medium, Jewish intellectuals from Heine and Marx to Freud and Karl Kraus gave it the *gravitas* their fathers gave their own culture. The founders of the Pan-German Party in the Austrian Empire were Jews. Zionism only came with racial rejection and anti-Semitic propaganda. As the Scots never suffered from this, their integration into imperial Britain was dramatic and painless.

When the Oxbridge intelligentsia campaigned for democratic reform in the 1860s in *Essays on Reform* (1867) they demanded 'a more national spirit in our politics'. Their arguments might be drawn from Mazzini, and almost half of them were either Scots or partly Scots, but the vessel for the ambitions released by Calvinism and improvement was 'Britain' – not a Cobbettite rural equilibrium but a restless part of the 'emigration ideology' Carlyle helped create. Foreign involvement, what A. J. P. Taylor called 'trouble-making', and some aspects of imperialism satisfied this drive. One or two writers were bold enough to provide intellectual justifications. John Davidson, the disciple of Nietzsche, saw the work of the empire-builder as the destiny of the race:

> I broke your slothful dream of folded wings,
> Of work achieved and empire circumscribed,
> Dispelled the treacherous flatteries of peace,
> And thrust upon you in your dull despite
> The one thing needful, half a continent
> Of habitable land! The English Hell
> For ever crowds upon the English Heaven.
> Secure your birthright; set the world at naught;
> Confront your fate; regard the naked deed;

Enlarge your Hell; preserve it in repair;
Only a splendid Hell keeps Heaven fair.

This Promethean element was tangled up with and morally justified by the concept of trusteeship, exemplified by Indian administrators, soldiers and missionaries: the respect shown Livingstone by the Africans he protected and the Arabs he fought. It even penetrated movements which were ostensibly anti-imperial. The agitation about Turkish brutality and misgovernment in the late 1870s, in which the ageing Carlyle featured and which reached its peak in Gladstone's Midlothian campaign, was explicitly directed against Disraeli's 'imperialism', yet it also hoisted the values of Protestantism, and Scottish Protestantism in particular, over the Turk, the Catholic and the Jew. It was a prelude to the energetic imperialism of such Scottish Liberals as Lord Rosebery in the 1890s. More complex yet was the case of R. W. Seton-Watson who, as 'Scotus Viator', set himself to lead the Slavs out of the bondage of the Habsburg Empire – with considerable success. An excess of such 'severitas' probably helped bring about the collapse of the balance of power on which the new liberties depended. But 'Scotus Viator' could not have existed in a non-imperial Britain.

At the very least imperialism provided a set of injunctions to which the individual could relate. Emile Durkheim connected the ultimate social breakdown of suicide with the degree to which society imposed its demands on the individual, 'a bolt that might snap if the nut of society held it too tightly or too loosely'. For the Scots the parish was choking, the intermediate level of the nation-state unavailable. The 'emigration ideology' offered a structure which might hold – 'severitas' at the cost of imagination and sensitivity. Conrad, alert to the impact of imperialism on the European consciousness, drew this mind-set in the deliberacy of MacWhirr, the Ulster-Scot captain of the stricken *Nan-Shan* in *Typhoon*. Kipling echoed him in the lines he gave engineer MacAndrew:

But – average fifteen hunder souls safe-borne fra' port to
    port –
I *am* o' service to my kind. Ye wadna blame the thought?
Maybe they steam from Grace to Wrath – to sin by folly
    led –

It isna mine to judge their path – their lives are on my
  head.

To opt out, to make one's own rules, to try to achieve something significant *in* Scotland, was risky. It was done – often
impressively – at a local level. We know this from William
Donaldson's work on the weekly press and the muscular,
ingenious, intelligent poetry anthologised in Tom Leonard's
Radical Renfrew (1991). The language retained its power and
radicalism. But the political mechanisms didn't exist to enable
such writers to play 'national' roles. Instead, the country was
fitfully illuminated by remarkable figures, teetering between
inspiration and destruction: Edward Irving trying to unify all the
Christian churches, Carlyle and Ruskin driving themselves into
dementia with their rage against the cash-nexus, Hugh Miller,
alive so richly in his autobiography *My Schools and Schoolmasters*,
trapped between Genesis and geology and ending by shooting
himself, Charles Rennie Mackintosh, the finest architect of his
day, forced out of Scotland by neglect and professional jealousy.
Originality, if unconstrained by Empire, nationality or community, seemed programmed to self-destruct.

Such tragedies, foregrounded against a powerful nationalist
movement, could resonate. Parnell's martyrdom in 1891 at the
hands of the bishops and his party created a symbol which
moulded a younger generation of Irish writers, from Yeats to
Sean O'Faolain. Most 'uncanny Scots' vanished into the dark.
Davidson, whose ambitions were the greatest, whose influence
ran from MacDiarmid to T. S. Eliot, walked into the sea in 1909,
to be remembered by MacDiarmid as 'A bullet-hole through a
great scene's beauty, God through the wrong end of a tele-
scope.' The imperial experience highlights the crucial Scots
anomaly: development failed to coincide with nationalism. The
estates which elsewhere provided the matrix for industrialisation, class society and a socialised intelligentsia, halted at their
eighteenth-century limits or regressed. The Kirk split, the law
was marginalised by the commercial acumen of the south; by
the 1870s moderately gifted Oxford graduates were taking chairs
at Scottish universities. But Scotland remained distinctive, and
the red Scots as its beneficiaries kept it that way, as a means of
recruiting a metropolitan and imperial elite, free from aristocratic and professional privilege. Meanwhile the vacuum of

nationalist *expectation* was filled by the treacly effluent of the Kailyard.

KAILYARD

The Kailyard had both a specific and a general identity. Historically it was a clutch of novelists and short-story writers who emerged in the 1880s and 1890s around William Robertson Nicoll, Free Churchman, editor and confidant of Lloyd George, and J. M. Barrie. They specialised in sentimental tales of rural Scotland and cunningly contrived to scoop a large market both in Britain and among the emigrants in North America. When he died of pneumonia in Mount Pleasant, Iowa in 1907, while on an American lecture tour, the Reverend John Watson, 'Ian Maclaren', had already sold several million copies of books like *Beside the Bonnie Briar Bush* and *The Days of Auld Langsyne* on both sides of the Atlantic. The Reverend S. R. Crockett did almost as well with *The Stickit Minster* and *The Lilac Sunbonnet*. There were others – less characteristic and thus more durable – like Neil Munro and J. J. Bell, whose comic stories related to the urban lives of most Scots, but on the whole the formula provided a commercial escape route to the nirvana of a rural past.

The ideas planted in the Kailyard – Lallans for kitchen garden – were already widespread and quite complex. The Robertson Nicoll tribe came late. Burns, Scott, Galt and Hogg could lapse into sentimentality, though their countryside was real enough. The Kailyard was deliberate. Dismissing the Scottish Rights Association in the 1850s, Henry Cockburn wrote:

> The memory of Old Scotland . . . can only live in the character of its people, in its native literature, and in its picturesque and delightful language. The gradual disappearance of the Scotch accent and dialect is a national calamity which not even this magniloquent association can arrest.

Was this its inaugural address? In 1857 Edward Ramsay, episcopalian Dean of Edinburgh, published his *Reminiscences of Scottish Life and Character*, which had run through twenty-two editions by his death in 1872. While Cockburn's anecdotes illuminated *his* 'theoretical history', Ramsay made the community a harmless and heart-warming entertainment for an age which had forsworn such pernicious authors as Richardson and Fielding. The ideas of Watson and company were more interesting: the social reforming Hegelianism of T. H. Green and Edward Caird, the religious modernism of Henry Drummond and Robertson Smith. A mild didacticism was going on. But the real intellectual energy of the writers covered in our own day by Donaldson and Leonard was being diluted by the mass production of pawky characters for a middle-class market at home and abroad which wished to be reminded of a wholesome Scotland, untainted by urban and industrial problems.

These stereotypes influenced even hostile authors. George Douglas Brown's *The House with the Green Shutters* and J. MacDougall Hay's *Gillespie* can be seen as a Kailyard inverted: small towns whose inhabitants do each other down and kill each other off. Both books are much more than satires on a genre; but their obsessions diverted Scots literature from an inquiry into individual consciousness and social change. Scott was at F. R. Leavis's 'most conscious point of the race in his time'; so were Galt's 'theoretical histories' of land and politics in the Scotland of Dundas. But no Dickens or Bennett wrote in the shadow of the Scottish cities; William Alexander recorded the commercialisation of the land, and the experience of urbanisation, for the people of the north-east – but it was left to the Wessex Hardy to pin down the Kailyard Scot himself, sentimental and astute, in Donald Farfrae in *The Mayor of Casterbridge*.

Why did realism fail? It was hard to follow Scott, who cast a long shadow, or to write honestly about the moral ambiguity of the 'emigration ideology' and imperialism, while benefiting from both. Yet the central constraint lay where Scott was at his weakest: in probing individuality. Hogg and Galt had shown that this was possible. But there experimentation stopped, checked by religious puritanism and its inherent hypocrisy. A society beset with terrifying social problems was *threatened* by realism. The customary targets of religious condemnation – alcoholism and promiscuity – were merely reflexes of the deep-seated and intractable evils of poverty and overcrowding. To expose these would be revolutionary; it would also break the discipline of puritanism by mentioning the unmentionable. The Kirk enforced silence out of conviction, the middle classes out of fear. The bogus community of the Kailyard was an alternative to the horror of the real thing. Although expatriates such as Thomas Common and William Archer, the first translators of Nietzsche and Ibsen, attempted to cope with intellectual change, the predicament of Scotland, as Robert Louis Stevenson found, was a schizoid state which could only be suggested by allegory. Dr Jekyll and Mr Hyde remain the most potent symbols Victorian Scotland produced.

Social escapism affected areas where standards were high enough to attain international recognition. If *fin-de-siècle* Scottish literature is forgettable, *fin-de-siècle* Scottish art and architecture is not. The 'Glasgow Boys' – W. Y. MacGregor, E. A. Walton, John Lavery – domesticated the techniques of Whistler and the French realists; William MacTaggart's west-coast impressionism was *sui generis*; the art nouveau designers and architects around Rennie Mackintosh, the arts and crafts revivalism of Robert Lorimer and the structural innovation of J. J. Burnet: all were bold and original, as 1890s flats and villas – elegant, convenient and manageable – still bear witness. But, as far as artists and architects were concerned, industrial Scotland did not exist. The painters' subject-matter was drawn from the land, from the small towns, from the seaboard. If they abandoned the folksiness of Sir David Wilkie and the deference of Sir Henry Raeburn, they also abandoned Wilkie's absorption with his society and Raeburn's delineation of the character of a ruling class. Apart from Muirhead Bone, an excellent architectural draughtsman rather than a painter, and John Quinton Pringle, a talented amateur, the artists totally ignored Glasgow, its industries and its slums. There was no Scottish Daumier or Van Gogh (although Scottish patrons and dealers bought both), not even an equivalent of Sickert and the Camden school. Even the breakthrough in photography made by Hill and Adamson in the 1840s, which could have led to innovation in style and subject-matter – as in France – was never followed up. Talent and skill did not generate a creative discomfort.

The same went for the architects. The best of them, like Burnet, created a functionalism from the factories and engine-shops of the industrial revolution – impressive, urban, comparable with the Chicago school. In the 1870s and 1880s architects looked to take the lead in social reform, with several bold experiments in workers' housing, employing standard modules. Given the huge output of 'functional' ships and railway equipment, architectural innovation seemed almost inevitable. But it didn't happen: architecture in 1914 had changed little over forty years. Burnet had set out to conquer new territory in London; Mackintosh, deserted by all but a few patrons, took to water-colours; Robert Lorimer built meticulous reconstructions of seventeenth-century castles for millionaires; the Glasgow people went on living in their one- and two-roomed flats.

There was one dissenting voice: a throwback to the universal intellect of the Enlightenment. Patrick Geddes, biologist, sociologist, architect, town planner and socialist, established in 1892 at the Outlook Tower, at the top of Edinburgh's picturesque and squalid Royal Mile, a community hall which was to become a pioneer sociological research institute. Geddes, the pupil of Huxley, Haeckel and Reclus, used concepts derived from biology to argue for an organic balance – an ecology – of the sexual, social and political life, which could become a goal for community planning. In the 1890s he took up the theme that Carlyle had voiced sixty years before:

> Everything I have done has been biocentric; for and in terms of life, both individual and collective; whereas all the machinery of state, public instruction, finance and industry ignores life when indeed it does not destroy it.

Geddes's fate was peculiar, but characteristic enough of red Scotland. He had no lack of patrons. He projected fifty town planning schemes in India and the Middle East, established a considerable reputation in America, chiefly through his disciples Victor Branford and Lewis Mumford, and in 1924 founded and settled at the Scots College at Montpellier in France where, in 1930, he received a knighthood from Ramsay MacDonald. His influence on social planning in the twentieth century has been incalculable if not wholly beneficial, as his ecological idealism discounted less inspirational factors like politics and economics. In present-day town planning, his name is often used to mask commercial calculation. But in turn-of-the-century Scotland he was a resilient outsider. His pioneer town plan for Dunfermline, commissioned by the Carnegie Trust, was turned down by the council. The few schemes which bore fruit on his native soil were far outnumbered by the opportunities provided by Empire.

RENAISSANCE

Geddes was one of the first to recognise the Scottish literary renaissance of the 1920s. Indeed, thirty years earlier he had tried to incubate something of the sort as a publisher at the Outlook Tower. It resembled the contemporary Irish movement, but without Yeats: 'Fiona MacLeod', if mysterious, was no substitute for an arrogant and learned man who knew double-entry book-keeping. The 1920s certainly generated more talent: Neil Gunn, Edwin Muir, Lewis Grassic Gibbon, James Bridie, Compton Mackenzie, Eric Linklater; and it had in MacDiarmid a figure comparable to Yeats and Joyce. It has been a continuing influence, important though also complex, on the post-war nationalist movement. But during a depression which compounded all the problems of industrial Scotland, it was scarcely more influential than political nationalism.

MacDiarmid proclaimed himself the central figure of the Scottish renaissance. With justice. As an artist and literary entrepreneur, he stated the predicament of the national intelligentsia. His aim was vast: to pull red and black Scotland, thesis and antithesis, into confrontation, creating out of perpetual debate a continuing, vital culture. This was not achieved by any logical process; but logic and consistency figured nowhere in MacDiarmid's programme. Aristocrat and democrat, nationalist and cosmopolitan, communist and social creditor, urbane conversationalist and soap-box ranter, he set out, with all the energy of Carlyle, to comprehend everything:

> I'll hae nae hauf-way hoose, but aye be whaur
> Extremes meet – it's the only way I ken
> To dodge the curst conceit o' bein' right
> That damns the vast majority o' men.

Thus his manifesto of 1926 *A Drunk Man Looks at the Thistle*. Yet he also wrote to Muirhead in 1928 to say that it would be over twenty years before his work would take effect. He was realistic. Only after World War II, and in particular from the late 1950s, was the scope of his ambition – and the size of his achievement – recognised. He could then compliment the country on its intellectual maturity.

But why, after producing poetry, political and lyrical, of rare insight, wit and beauty, and challenging criticism, was he neglected by a society crying out for such activism? MacDiarmid in his prime in the 1920s and 1930s shifted the intelligentsia some way along his road, but then both stuck. An attempt to move south and edit a radio weekly in London ended in traumatic disaster. Ogre and martyr, MacDiarmid went into a literal wilderness, his work circulating almost in 'samizdat' form. By 1945 he was creatively burnt out; as Norman MacCaig put it, he kept his genius but lost his talent. He was sometimes appreciated for the wrong reasons, even for the wrong poems (an inveterate quoter, some of his borrowings became attributed to him). On the whole, he was regarded as a gifted vernacular lyric poet, with a taste for axe-grinding. Not least because of his own complex personality. Not everyone wanted the old tradition of 'flyting' – arguing politics, literature and music for twelve hours at a stretch – and drinking (though MacDiarmid's sexual and alcoholic stamina was less than he boasted about). Yet this tension between private conviviality and public aggressiveness was matched, intellectually, by the tension between his Scottish loyalties and his universal ambitions.

MacDiarmid was not affected by the Scottish crisis alone. As a member of the *New Age* avant-garde he was as aware as Yeats, Eliot and Pound of the effects of 'industrialised' war on European civilisation in general and Britain in particular: an empty, 'mechanistic' society had suffered moral and material trauma. These 'provincials' saw the collapse and, still aware of their own involvement with the centre, sought alternatives: Eliot's Anglo-Catholicism, Pound's right-wing revolutionism, Yeats's return to Ireland. MacDiarmid's cosmopolitan nationalism was cognate with this, as was its complement, his Anglophobia. His 'Scotland' was imprecise: in *Albyn* it was 'the old Brythonic kingdom', taking in England down to the Humber and the Mersey, a synthetic construct, an idealist antithesis of 'England'. His friends and allies, Denis Saurat, Pound, K. S. Sorabji, Sean O'Casey, were an international *Sezession*, whose mission – to use the small nation to redeem civilisation – was drawn from the dubious but stimulating source of Spengler's *Decline of the West* (1922).

Neither this heterogeneity nor his own uneven output bothered a man who called himself a volcano: 'producing heat and light and also a great deal of rubbish' – Carlyle on the French Revolution over again. The trouble was that the correspondence between the European breakdown and the Scottish opportunity was far from exact. The Scottish literary movement had no ideological homogeneity. It was an *ad hoc* defensive coalition – a sideways glance at Ireland, a worry about the break-up of Scottish society. Lacking the Irish literary movement's links between mass organisation, academic activity and official patronage, this lash-up between ex-home rulers (backed up by journalists, Kailyarders and Anglo-Scots) and root-and-branch separatists (backed up by revolutionaries and linguistic revivalists) could not be expected to last. But for the moment the use of the vernacular by MacDiarmid's generation gained general approval from both sides, as a means of conserving national distinctiveness. Much play was made with the development of *Landsmaal* (rural Norwegian) in Norway and the survival of Frisian in North Germany and Holland. 'Lallans', or Lowland Scots, was still strong enough in working-class talk to provide a linguistic line to be held against 'creeping Anglicisation', although Erskine of Mar wanted to restore the Gaelic. But Lallans was the rock on which the literary movement foundered.

Vernacular poetry continued after Burns, and even expanded with the growth of the local press. Sixteen dreadful volumes of *Modern Scottish Poets*, exhumed from newspaper back-files for the most part, were published in the 1880s and 1890s:

> Frae mony a but and ben,
> By muirland, holm and glen,
>   They cam' an hour to spen' on the greenwood sward;
> But lang hae lad an' lass
> Been lying 'neth the grass,
> The green, green grass o'Traquair kirkyard.

Not Harry Lauder but an Oxford professor of poetry in demotic mood: Principal Shairp's 'The Bush aboon Traquair' shows the thinness of the tradition; Swinburne and Kipling, who were not Scots, could, and did, do better. But, MacDiarmid believed, with a properly exploited traditional vocabulary, Lallans could handle a wide range of subject-matter with greater force and subtlety than standard English. His model in this was James Joyce, who in *Ulysses* (1922) had used a reworked language, and the peculiar discomfort of the Irish literary and political experience, as a springboard for a complex and subtle exploration of human consciousness.

Lallans was rich in words and idioms denoting action, physical shape, destruction and disorganisation, and abuse of all sorts, while it could retain the dignified cadences of the Makars, the medieval court poets. MacDiarmid took full advantage of this in his greatest poems, ranging from knockabout to cosmic speculation to images of the fulfilment of body and mind. *A Drunk Man Looks at the Thistle* is a statement about the relationship of the individual to culture, community and the life of the intellect comparable in scope to the contemporary extended poems of Yeats, Eliot and Pound. This is not the place to attempt comparisons of quality, but 'this lurching, inebriate's progress from Milne's Bar to the Absolute Idea and back again', as Tom Nairn has called it, carries tremendous power, not simply because of its ambitions, but because argument and deflating wit continually burst in to bring the poet back to the reality he has to vitalise:

> Sae God retracts in endless stage
> Through angel, devil, age on age,
> Until at last his infinite natur'
> Walks on earth a human cratur'
> (Or less than human as to my een
> The people are in Aiberdeen);
> Sae man returns in endless growth
> Till God in him again his scouth.

The thistle, mutating throughout the drunk man's vision, is not a symbol of nationalism: it is the eternal negation of man's present state, on which his mind must act, as thesis on antithesis, to secure his liberation. The nation, on the other hand, is a human construct, a necessary matrix of traditions and institutions, which can be, indeed has to be, used to cope with and homogenise this process:

> Thou, Dostoevski, understood,
> Wha had your ain land in your bluid,
> And into it as in a mould
> The passion o' your bein' rolled,
> Inherited in turn frae Heaven
> Or sources fer abune it even.

Is Scotland big enough to be
A symbol o' that force in me,
In wha's divine inebriety
A sicht abune contempt I'll see?

For a' that's Scottish is in me,
As a' things Russian were in thee,
And I in turn 'ud be an action
To pit in a concrete abstraction
My country's contrair qualities,
And mak' a unity o' these
Till my love owre its history dwells,
As owretone to a peal o' bells.

And in this heicher stratosphere
As bairn at giant at thee I peer . . .

MacDiarmid's intentions for Lallans went far beyond the liberal-minded *Gemeinschaft* ideals of most vernacular revivalists. In political poems written around 1930 – the first two 'Hymns to Lenin' and 'The Seamless Garment' – he used it to communicate directly with working people to promote communism and political mobilisation:

Hundreds to the inch the threids lie in
Like the men in a communist cell
There's a play o' licht frae the factory windas.
Could you no' mak' mair yoursel?
Mony a loom mair alive than the weaver seems
For the sun's still nearer than Rilke's dreams.

MacDiarmid's experiments with language, both Lallans and his later 'scientific' idiom, place him alongside those writers whose cultural bearings were reoriented by World War I. His real political commitment made him a much more important socialist poet than the public school radicals of the 1930s. He is the 'red Scottish' inheritor of Scott and Carlyle, but his relations with nationalism seem as ambivalent. Yeats and Joyce were similarly placed. But to a much greater extent even than Yeats, he suffered from 'the day's war with every dolt' that organising a national movement implied. Yeats was at least given, by his Ascendancy and American patrons, a theatre in which to transform the mob into a nation, and a stage from which to berate it when it backslided. MacDiarmid, among journalists and popularisers, found that an apparent unanimity about the plight of Scotland masked a general hostility to his own goals and standards.

STONY LIMITS

For MacDiarmid, Lallans was a vehicle for national differentiation and political mobilisation. The idea of preserving the old community was secondary, although Langholm, his boyhood home in the Scottish Borders, continued to supply symbols for his later work – 'the ground-plan of my mind' – and his dislike of cities led him to spend most of his life in the country. 'Community' was more powerful in the other writers of the renaissance, in Gunn, Linklater and Muir. Gunn rarely strayed out of the Highlands, and couched his political and philosophical allegories in terms of its natural and social life. To the Orcadians Linklater and Muir, the communities of the northern islands were always an alternative to the brittle and changing relationships of the south. But the opposition of community and progress was seen at its most intense in the work of James Leslie Mitchell, 'Lewis Grassic Gibbon', whose achievement as a novelist came close to MacDiarmid's as a poet. In three novels written in an arresting vernacular prose-poetry, *Sunset Song* (1933), *Cloud Howe* (1938), and *Grey Granite* (1934), collectively called *A Scots Quair*, Gibbon described the decline and dispersal of an east-coast farming community under the pressure of war and industrialisation. The novels, strongly influenced by Marxism and diffusionist anthropology, move from the passivity of the crofters in the face of the destruction of war to the conversion of the heroine's son, in the final novel, to 'a faith that will cut like a knife' and a role in the militant labour movement of the Scots cities.

That was the programme. In fact the intensity and lyricism of the writing, the sensual apprehension of the land and its people, shifted the whole impact until the reader feels with the young crofter, Ewan Tavendale, sensing the futility of the war, and walking away from the front to his inevitable execution:

> it was the wind that came with the sun, I minded Blawearie, I seemed to wake up smelling that smell. And I couldn't believe it

was me that stood in that trench, it was just daft to be there. So I turned and got out of it.

Ewan's wife, Chris Guthrie, who moves through this enforced social evolution, completes the circle by returning to the land, symbolising Gibbon's other, near-mystical faith in 'the great, green international' which links peasant communities throughout the world and in other ages, back to the men who reared the megalith circles which loom over the parks of Kinraddie. Between traditional community and international revolution, Gibbon found no place for Scottish nationalism, which appears in the *Quair* only to be ridiculed. Although he joined MacDiarmid in attacking bourgeois Scotland in *The Scottish Scene*, published just before his tragically early death in 1935, he had little sympathy with the compromises involved in his friend's nationalist projects.

The literary revival was political in the sense that its cohesion had to be maintained by continual balance and negotiation. MacDiarmid was – almost by his own definition – no politician. But he had acted for so long as the arbiter of the literary movement that he became identified with it. His discomfort actually increased as it became more political, as its journalists and Anglo-Scots didn't share his revolutionary views, or even those of the National Party he had helped found in 1928. The moderate Scottish Party was more to their taste, and when amalgamation of two parties loomed in 1933, the left wing of the Nationalists was purged and MacDiarmid went. He had made intellectual concessions to promote the political movement; it rejected him for the conservative establishment. The political nationalists soon found that consensus did not pay off, and were left with the enduring stigma of being hostile to the intellectuals.

This attack was pressed home in 1936 by Edwin Muir in *Scott and Scotland*, written, ironically, in response to a commission from MacDiarmid. Muir was scarcely a lesser figure and, as a nationalist, socialist and social creditor, shared several of MacDiarmid's political enthusiasms. An Orkneyman who had migrated in poverty to Glasgow, he had been, in fact, more deeply scarred by industrial society. He had struggled out of it via the ILP and socialist journalism, settled in Europe, and gained an international reputation – at that time more as the translator of Kafka and Rilke than as a poet. Although he had sympathised with the Lallans movement in the 1920s, he saw Scotland in the following decade as the casualty of its own offspring: industrialisation and repressive puritanism. His remedies were socialism and a regenerated community, in comparison with which nationalist politics and the vernacular revival threatened to cut Scotland off, permanently, from the European cultural mainstream. Muir was no provincial. Life in Germany and Czechoslovakia in the 1920s and 1930s had led to sympathy with the new European nations; but he had also become aware of the totalitarian threat. His cosmopolitanism was as great as MacDiarmid's but the gap between community and nationalism was real enough. Moreover, he reflected the regrouping of the European intelligentsia in the face of Fascism, which had succeeded the centrifugal tendencies of the 1920s. Scottish nationalism of MacDiarmid's militant variety seemed to him to divide, where unity was needed.

Muir's stance was, however, marginal to the Scottish intellectual predicament. To blame Scotland's problems on the Reformation was to neglect the achievements of Calvinism and the Enlightenment, and the persistence of a unique form of Scottish, if not national, consciousness in both. So, not surprisingly, he misinterpreted as parochial MacDiarmid's programme, which was anything but:

> To prove my saul is Scots I maun begin
> Wi' what's still deemed Scots and the folk expect,
> And spire up syne by visible degrees
> To heichts whereo' the fules ha'e never recked.

On the other hand, various of the lesser talents in the MacDiarmid convoy were easy meat. Political poetry is the great soft option for cultural critics with more opinions than evidence. MacDiarmid the politician, already thrown over by the nationalists, rounded on Muir and attacked him without mercy and without any vestige of political nous. At a time when personality counted in establishing the credentials of the vernacular revival, MacDiarmid appeared an unhelpful amalgam of Calvinist ranter and Stalinist commissar, persecuting the diffident and gentle Muir. At the same time he forsook Lallans for the elaborate quasi-scientific vocabulary of his later work, with a grand Carlylean curse:

The idiom of which constructive thought avails itself
Is unintelligible save to a small minority
And all the rest wallow in exploded fallacies
And cherish for immortal souls their gross stupidity.

He had intended the revival to be promoted by continual dialectic; but it wasn't strong enough for this.

The 1930s was a decade of eclipse as much for MacDiarmid, assailed by personal and money problems, as for literary nationalism. Despite his radicalism, he fared no better with the Communists than he had with the National Party. Its membership and leadership included a large number of Scots, but the Communist Party had always looked to the south, when not fixated by Moscow. In the 'popular front' atmosphere it was, moreover, eager to court the anti-Fascist establishment, notably the Labour Party, and even the moderate SNP. The Scots who fought for the International Brigade in Spain evoked great sympathy; the Scottish Tories even produced an anti-Fascist aristocrat in the shape of the Duchess of Atholl; pacifist, internationalist and left-wing causes were strongly backed at the universities, hitherto the stronghold of nationalism. In 1936 the Reverend Dick Sheppard, founder of the Peace Pledge Union, was elected Rector of Glasgow in a campaign which attracted national attention, soundly beating Winston Churchill. In fact, in terms of the liberal-left dissent which dominated the decade, the red Scots found (as it happened for the last time) that they were well served by the United Kingdom. Lord Reith was telling the masses what they ought to hear, John Grierson what they ought to look at, Boyd Orr what they ought to eat, and J. B. S. Haldane what they ought to think.

Reith's prescriptions didn't include letting the Scottish renaissance anywhere near a microphone, as Moray Maclaren and David Cleghorn Thomson found out to their cost at BBC Scotland. By World War II literary nationalism had made only limited progress among the Scottish intelligentsia, whose definitions of 'Scottishness' within the Union still seemed valid. The ideology of the national estates was intact, as were the channels for promotion by merit within the United Kingdom and the Empire. The economic component of the Union had cracked, but its political and intellectual components had held, and so had ensured that economic remedies would be unionist, whether from right or left. While the wartime devolution of authority boosted nationalism of a ceremonial sort – the *Scots Independent* applauded the fact that St Andrew's Day in November 1944 was celebrated by the government and the BBC on an unprecedented scale – this threatened to resurrect the Kailyard, something so innocuous that it almost aided integration. 'Actually, I'm a bit of a Scottish nationalist' conveyed a vague centrism, more acceptable than socialism or even, in an age of waning faith, profound religious conviction.

But seeds had been sown. Younger poets, such as Sidney Goodsir Smith, Douglas Young and Robert Garioch, writing in Lallans, or Norman McCaig, George Bruce and Edwin Morgan, writing in English, inherited MacDiarmid's rigour, his internationalism, and his conviction that real creativity was possible in Scotland. From the Highlands, the Skye schoolmaster Sorley Maclean and George Campbell Hay, son of the author of *Gillespie*, wrote lyrics in Gaelic of a quality unknown since the eighteenth century. The great treasury of song and ballad created by tinkers and fisherfolk, farm labourers, crofters and textile workers waited to be opened up by such left-wingers as Hamish Henderson and Norman Buchan, following the popular culture initiatives of Roosevelt's New Deal. Research began for two dictionaries of the vernacular in 1931 and in the schools younger teachers – Bruce and McCaig and Hector MacIver at the Royal High School in Edinburgh – were convincing the next generation that the Scottish revival was important within the European tradition. Whatever their metropolitan ambitions, the red Scots now felt that the renaissance could no longer be dismissed as a parochial outburst, that MacDiarmid, Gibbon and Muir, whatever their differences, were speaking with their accents. They had isolated problems about the relationship of culture and society which the more hierarchical tradition of English social criticism had neglected. At this stage the feeling might only express itself in a mixture of guilt and irritation when others used the old stereotypes of black Scotland. But it existed.

Part II

4

LEADERS TO NO SURE LAND
Unionist Scotland, 1945–1979

Consider these, for we have condemned them;
Leaders to no sure land . . .

C. Day Lewis

SCOTLAND: NEW AND UNKNOWN

In 1936 a visit to Motherwell decided Edwin Muir to write his
Scottish Journey. The sprawling, silent steel-manufacturing town
seemed to him to exemplify, in its total subordination of com
munity to material development, the fatal impact of industrialisation on Scotland. With the slump it had ceased both to work
and to exist as a community. It, and the hundreds of industrial
settlements like it in the Scottish central belt, were simply
accumulations of buildings and people, whose only reason for
existence was their contribution to the organisation of capitalism. Capitalism, wielded by Scots against Scots, not the dep-
redations of the English, was the spectre that had to be
exorcised before any valid community could be re-established.

Nine years later Motherwell gave the SNP its first election
victory, and fifty-seven years later it remains a paradigm of the
Scottish predicament. Few of the houses of 1936 still stand. New
housing schemes and multi-storey blocks, a new civic centre, a
new station, have opened. The Clyde Valley is now a huge
recreation park; the Duke of Hamilton's stables at Chatelherault
a baroque belvedere where the locals hold their wedding recep-
tions. A town has been created which Muir would hardly recognise, a town that is strange to me, and I was born and brought
up in it between 1944 and 1949. But the Ravenscraig steelworks,
opened in 1961 to replace the disused plants of 1936, has lain

115

derelict since June 1992 – awaiting demolition and a rumoured rebirth in Indonesia.

The critical factor was in one generation capitalism, in another government; then capitalism again, but of international dimensions. In 1936 the vast majority of the working population was employed by several large privately owned steel and heavy engineering companies, and rented its houses from private landlords. In the 1970s the state-owned British Steel Corporation was the main employer, and Motherwell and Wishaw District Council the landlord of 83 per cent of the households. Policy decisions aimed at preserving employment and population had kept in being a settlement originally established for industrial convenience. What would happen to it when a globalised industry found it surplus to requirements?

What is true for Motherwell applies to the other settlements of the Scottish central belt, from the former colliery villages of Ayrshire to the textile towns of Strathmore. A combination of policies to attract work to areas of unemployment and to disperse the congested population of the Glasgow conurbation has created a new Scotland, neither urban nor rural, which straggles westwards from the fringes of the Firth of Forth to the lower Clyde. It is this unknown Scotland, not in the guidebooks, away from the motorway, seen fleetingly from the express, that holds the key to the modern politics of the country.

After the war government action became critical at national and local level, joining the old dialectic between autonomy and integration. Both tendencies grew, and competed, so it was no longer easy to identify gains and losses. The decline or takeover of a traditional industry could lead to Scottish initiatives to attract substitute industries, or the granting of new powers to St Andrew's House. Conscious or unconscious, these responses changed Scottish politics from being determined by economic performance, institutional conservatism and intellectual abstention, to a dependence on personalities and political initiatives. People now expected that a Scottish response would be made to economic difficulties. At the same time, the Labour councillors who took over local government in most of industrial Scotland were preoccupied with urban reconstruction, attracting industry and the highly political business of allocating council housing, rather than with any long-term assessment of the future of their communities.

FROM TENDENCY TO TRANSACTION

1945 was the line of division, the hinge. Before then, Scottish politics was reasonably predictable, thereafter it grew more unstable, more dependent on actions and reactions. The change was partly one of consciousness: tendencies emerged which became distinct only long afterwards. Nationalism, if marginal, was persistent. Integration was different to assimilation. Intellectual 'transferred nationalism' was shifting back to give the Scots a new sense of their own experience. All these forces made the post-war British political establishment define its position *vis-à-vis* nationalism, something it had not done for a century. Would the wartime nationalist challenge continue? In British society the central state loomed larger, but the rules had changed: a Scottish society detached from party politics was no longer possible. Activists had to use such devolution as existed to secure reforms in the interest of specific social groups. Nationalists were only one such group, but they could become an interest to be appeased.

This enhanced the distinctiveness of Scottish government. Westminster used to be insensitive out of ignorance; now sins of commission were also involved. Despite a 'neutral' rhetoric, some ministers' decisions inevitably hurt Scottish interests, but politics now gave the resulting resentment a cutting 'national' edge. The rise of the SNP was not itself inevitable. The other parties could have pre-empted it. They failed to do so partly because they regarded Scotland as 'marginal', but also because failures of leadership deflected Scottish politics on to a course they were unable to cope with.

Post-war politics in Scotland hinged on two factors. The first was internal: power passed from the owners of the economy in alliance with the estates to political and administrative groups concerned to provide collective social remedies, with or without external assistance. The second stemmed from the economic aims of post-war British governments. They either had to combine sophisticated planning with adequate finance and consultation, or risk a revolution of rising, but continually frustrated, expectations. Lacking this, Scottish politics after the late 1950s became increasingly unpredictable.

ADMINISTRATIVE DEVOLUTION

No simple economic substructure, responsive to fiscal controls, underlay political behaviour; the Scottish economy was the product of substantial, if not always sensitive or successful, political intervention. The behaviour of Scottish electors and power groups both depended on and influenced these trans-actions, something remote from the relatively simple equations between economics, class and politics used by the 'behaviourist' political scientists and psephologists who provided the market research for the manipulations of the social democrat consensus. The failure of this consensus to come to terms with Scottish politics, or to solve the country's economic problems, gave the SNP its chance.

Scottish government was functional. Despite Johnston's inno-vations no statutory bodies existed to discuss and plan for future social changes. Labour created a Scottish Economic Conference to continue the work of Johnston's Council on Industry. Dismissed by practically everyone as a talking shop, it met a few times but was already moribund when Labour left office in 1951. 1945 had been a victory for the reformist politicians and admi-nistrators of the centre-left who had advocated economic plan-ning before the war, and now perpetuated it into peacetime. As well as a new ideology, a new elite had taken over, an academic oligarchy drawn from the two old English universities. The gains Scottish autonomy had made had to be set against this, and against the fact that a relative decline in population had weakened regional bargaining power.

The formal recognition of Scottish distinctiveness by central government became more pronounced. The French Canadian politician René Levesque, soon to be the driving force of the province's reconstruction, told a conference in Edinburgh in 1975 that when he had been stationed in Scotland during the war, government had emphasised its 'Britishness'. Now, even without constitutional change, it stressed its 'Scottishness'. He contrasted this with Canada, where in a federation the power and self-confidence of the Ottawa government seemed to be continuously deployed against the nominal sovereignty of the states. This shrewd perception reflected the expansion of the devolved administration. In 1937 the Secretary of State super-vised, along with one parliamentary under-secretary, 2,400 civil servants. Johnston secured another under-secretary in 1941, and ten years later the Conservatives added a third, along with a Minister of State of Cabinet rank. By 1970 Labour had added a second Minister of State. Six political heads, and two law officers, supervised 8,300 civil servants. Even after thirteen years of Thatcher and Major this figure had risen to 10,700 in 1992 (if legal and other personnel were added, 13,500). At the same time the competence of the Scottish Office was steadily extended. It took over electricity in 1954 and roads in 1956, created the Scottish Development Department in 1962, and the Highlands and Islands Development Board in 1969. After the 1950s the pace of growth increased; the chronology of Scottish administration and legislation was crammed with boards, commissions, inquiries, plans and bills.

This devolution was not grounded in logic. It was the result of two mutually opposed philosophies: socialist planning and Conservative hostility to it. The growth of the Scottish Office in the early 1950s stemmed from Churchill's promises of decentralisation which, in appealing to Scottish nationalism, almost sounded like his father 'playing the Orange card' in Belfast sixty-four years earlier:

> The principle of centralisation of government in Whitchall and Westminster is emphasised in a manner not hitherto experienced or contemplated in the Act of Union. The supervision, interference and control in the ordinary details of Scottish life and business by the Parliament at Westminster has not hitherto been foreseen, and I frankly admit that it raises new issues between the two nations. . . . I do not therefore wonder that the question of Scottish home rule and all this movement of Scottish nationalism has gained in step with the growth of socialist authority and ambitions in England. I should never adopt the view that Scotland should be forced into the serfdom of socialism as the result of a vote in the House of Commons.

Churchill's rhetoric, like his election promises of 'a senior member of the Cabinet to be constantly in Scotland' – a Viceroy? – and the return of the Scottish university MPs, *was* the nationalism of noisy inaction, but the ministerial team was strengthened. By contrast, the next major accession of authority, in the mid-1960s, was carried out by a Labour government committed to centralised planning and (at least until 1968) eloquent against legislative devolution of any kind.

Despite this ambiguous process, St Andrew's House, and its newly built hideous satellites, had become by the late 1960s the terminus for an increasing amount of Scottish business. Its civil servants were 'much more accessible to the general public than those in Whitehall' and thought of their careers 'almost entirely in Scottish terms'. Professor H. J. Hanham, a critic of its continued subservience to the south, wrote that 'the creation of a Scottish Parliament appears on the face of things to be the only way of revivifying the present administrative machine'. This was not, in 1969, likely to provoke much dissent in St Andrew's House itself.

The relative independent-mindedness of the Scottish administration was not something that any government, whether Labour or Conservative, had premeditated. It was the outcome of frustration when the functional role it had been promised was, through economic circumstances, denied it. Had the Labour government's ambitious planning strategy worked, the Scottish Office would have continued to fulfil its role within the traditional administrative structure. Yet the economic problems it had to face seemed constantly to swell beyond its own capacities. The problem was that it was attempting to fill a role which, before World War II, had not been performed by government at all, but by the most powerful of the traditional Scottish institutions, the business community.

BUSINESS BLUES

The only major business reputations made in post-war Scotland were those of the retailers Sir Hugh Fraser (Lord Fraser) and Sir Isaac Wolfson (Lord Wolfson). Before the war, on the other hand, the leaders of the Scottish heavy industries played a major role as representatives of British as well as Scottish capitalism, and as senior government advisers and (in times of emergency) executives. Sir James Lithgow, the owner of the largest shipyard on the Clyde, also dominated the Federation of British Industry and the National Shipbuilders' Security Corporation, which 'rationalised' the industry in the 1930s. Sir William Weir (Viscount Weir), another Clydeside engineering magnate, took charge of aircraft production during World War I, set up the electricity grid and the beet sugar industry in the 1920s, and replanned the transatlantic steamer services in the next decade. Sir Andrew Duncan ran the Central Electricity Board and later the British Iron and Steel Federation. Lords Maclay and Inverforth dominated merchant shipping, and Lord Macgowan ICI, while Sir Robert Horne headed the Great Western, and William Whitelaw the London and North Eastern Railways. These men represented the old school of business: the heavy industries. Their markets were export-dominated, their solution to economic difficulties was wage reductions, their attitude to new manufacturing options such as radios or electrical goods was conveyed by the tone in which they delivered the epithet: 'sheltered industries'.

They were realistic about the role of the state, and made admirable administrators of state or semi-state industries; they were also capable of quirky acts of goodwill to unorthodox bodies (Linlithgow financed the Iona Community, run by the outspoken left-winger George MacLeod). But their Cobdenite economics alienated them from the left, and their Unionism was fervent. In 1932 Scottish industrialists organised an energetic attack on the infant nationalist movement, which provided them with a secure place in its demonology. In the government of Britain, the victory of the centre-left in the early years of the war meant their departure from the right hand of the politicians, while in Scotland they appeared doubly damned as the architects of the country's dependence on heavy industry. Deprived of power, their survivors and their sons sulked. They cold-shouldered such bodies as the Scottish Council: Development and Industry, which was bankrolled by largely Labour-controlled local authorities in the early post-war years. But neither it, nor the civil servants, could restore the link that had bound Scottish industry to central government.

Yet the legacy of the heavy industries remained critically important. When the economics department of Glasgow University carried out a pioneer inquiry into the Scottish economy in the early 1950s it found that 'dependence on heavy industry has grown rather than diminished'. The gloomy forecasts of the 1930s were not borne out. Unlike World War I, World War II left the shipyards of Germany and Japan in ruins, while Scottish yards suffered very lightly and were in a strong competitive position. The inquiry editor, Professor (Sir) Alexander Cairncross, noted:

> it is neither surprising nor inappropriate that the product by which Scotland is best known abroad and of which she is proudest are the great liners that have been launched on the narrow Clyde.

'Liners' and 'narrow' took on an ominous timbre within very few years, especially when combined with Cairncross's other observation about 'the comparative indifference of Scottish industry to new equipment, new knowledge, and new opportunities for development'.

Four years later, the *Third Statistical Account* volume on *Glasgow* could still regard 50,000 tons as the upper limit of size for a freighter (the average size of a Clyde-built ship being 6,000 tons), and conclude that, all things considered, 'there is no fear of competition from the air' for the passenger liner. So, to take the *Queen Mary II* 'doon the watter' in the mid-1950s was to pass through a world that had changed little for half a century. The twenty-odd yards still employed 27,000 men, as many as they had employed in 1900. The old dynasties were still in control – Stephens, Yarrows, Lithgows – just as the old shipowners whose handsome freighters lined the Clyde stuck to their traditional routes and their traditional liveries: black and red funnels for the Clan lines, black and buff for the 'Hungry Hogarths'. The Irish steamers still loaded at Anderston Quay, the MacBrayne coasters at Kingston Dock, Robertson's little puffers still butted down the Firth to Crinan and the beaches of the Outer Isles. The supertanker, the container ship, the vehicle ferry, the Boeing 707, seemed far away. They were not. State-financed or state-subsidised yards in Europe and Japan and factories in America were already building them, with modern equipment, efficient management and a flexible labour force – and often advice from Clydeside entrepreneurs. On the Clyde purchases of new equipment made up barely half of annual depreciation; management was only equalled in conservatism by the unions. When nemesis came, it came fast. Between 1950 and 1954 Scotland's share of world shipbuilding output was 12 per cent; by 1968 it was 1.3 per cent. Only seven yards were still in production and of these only two were economically viable. When the *Queen Elizabeth II* steamed down the Firth on a maiden voyage which completed the disasters that had punctuated its construction, it left a river only marginally more lively than the Styx.

The collapse of the railway engineering industry was even more spectacular. In the early 1950s it employed about 10,000 men in Glasgow, Motherwell and Kilmarnock. With 5,000 workers and three plants, the North British Locomotive Company was the second-largest of its kind in the world, with a near-monopoly position in several Commonwealth countries. Practically every week a huge truck crawled down the streets from Springburn, bearing a gleaming locomotive to the great crane on Lancefield Quay which would swing it like a toy into the hold of some Singapore- or Durban-bound ship. Nearly all these locomotives were steam: the technology of diesels and electrics was alien to Springburn, closer to that of the motor industry. And the market for steam locomotives was shrinking fast. Springburn tried to compete, taking advantage of the huge British Railways modernisation programme of 1955, but its products were disastrous. By 1960 the company, ironically under the chairmanship of Lord Reith, was moribund. By 1963 only one wagon-works at Wishaw and a small locomotive works at Kilmarnock, together employing less than 1,000 men, remained. Twenty years later the last large merchant shipyard on the Clyde was owned by Norway, the last locomotive works by Austria.

The rapidity of heavy industrial decline was unexpected, but, by the intervention of government, new and at the time exciting industries were coaxed north to fill the vacuum. The Wiggins Teape group built a pulp and paper mill near Fort William, on a railway threatened with closure. In 1962 the British Motor Corporation announced a truck plant at Bathgate in West Lothian, and the Rootes Group a car plant near Paisley, promising a total of 11,000 jobs. To serve these the government loaned the steelmaking firm of Colvilles £50 million to build a strip mill at Motherwell, after a decision-making exercise characterised, in the words of an authoritative commentary, by 'secretiveness and lack of candour . . . [and] deliberate withholding of information'. In such inauspicious circumstances did Scotland move into the new age of growth industries and regional economic policy.

The northward march of the motor industry was the result of government pressure. The other major growth sector of the

Scottish economy owed much to pressure from Scottish bodies, notably the Scottish Council. This was the expansion of foreign-owned factories, mainly American. Such concerns were not new to Scotland. During the nineteenth century, while massive capital exports flooded from Scotland to America, there was a fairly strong counter-flow, bringing over the Singer sewing-machine factory at Clydebank, the North British Rubber Company in Edinburgh, and Babcock and Wilcox, 'the largest boilermaking works in the world', at Dumbarton and Renfrew. Dundee, which only a few decades earlier had been the fountainhead of investment in the American West, began the new wave by attracting National Cash Register in 1946. An energetic public relations campaign was aimed – by the legendary expatriate David Ogilvie of Ogilvie, Mather, among others – at American firms worried about being excluded from European markets. The result was that in 1973 148 plants employing 14.9 per cent of the Scottish manufacturing work-force were American-owned. Of all American firms established in the United Kingdom since the war, over a third found sites in Scotland, creating 30 per cent of new jobs between 1958 and 1968.

The Scots found a quick affinity with the Americans – often themselves of Scots descent – and their easygoing, demotic directness. Even trade unionists were prepared to overlook non-recognition, provided the incomers didn't go for cheap labour contracts. This 'Fordist' expansion sustained prosperity in several areas otherwise threatened with mass unemployment, but created numerous structural disadvantages. 'American' industries – business machines or electronics – were well adapted to female labour, demanding high manual dexterity rather than craft specialism. They were set up in areas like Dundee where the run-down of the traditional textile industries provided them with an inexpensive and adaptable work-force. The female labour force increased, while the male labour force continued to decline. Whatever this did to overall employment statistics, the absence of jobs for heads of families helped promote growing emigration during the 1950s and 1960s. Further, by importing managers, research and marketing personnel (or carrying out these functions elsewhere) American firms restricted upward mobility and graduate recruitment. Although they employed 87,730 in 1973, they took on only 250 graduates between 1965 and 1969. The industrial continuity which their

high technology promised masked an essentially colonial relationship in which decisions were 'taken' at head offices in
New York or Chicago instead of being 'made' in Scotland.

CONSENSUS COLLECTIVISM

In the 1950s Scottish manufacturing industry (about a third of
GNP) was still largely privately and Scottish-owned, and market
responsive. The role of government was marginal. Elsewhere,
however, state action proved critical in creating frameworks for
economic and social change. Agricultural subsidies enabled the
modernisation of farming on a scale unparalleled since the
eighteenth century, but cut the farm labour force between 1951
and 1971 by over 70 per cent. The effect on the countryside of
the Lowlands, the Borders and the north-east was profound, as
the activities of local centres declined, bus and train services
became uneconomic, cinemas, halls and schools closed. Farm
steadings, tidied up for weekend visits by urban professionals,
belied a clearance as drastic as that of the nineteenth century.
Rural Scotland was becoming a country of the old.

In the Highlands and Islands, by contrast, past intervention
by government had a quite different effect on agricultural
efficiency. The 1884 Crofters' Act had granted the crofters security of tenure, but its main intention, to produce holdings of
viable size, was realised only in the Orkneys and Shetlands.
Elsewhere, the demoralisation bred of a century of eviction and
emigration, and the continued indifference of landlords, sustained the slow dissolution of a society which seemed not to care
much about achieving anything at all:

> O that the peats would cut themselves,
>   the fish chump on the shore,
> that we might lie intil our beds,
>   for ever and evermore!

North and west of Oban and Dingwall an altogether different
time-scale and logic seemed to take over. The roads became
single-track, trains, buses and steamers infrequent; crofting
communities seemed to combine Sabbatarianism, reliance on
subsidy and whisky drinking with a way of life somehow magi-
cally protected from the attentions of economists or anyone
concerned with getting a return on investment. The prudent

tourist travelled by motor coach or the elderly SS *Killarney*, which cruised up the western coast in summer. Motoring from southern Scotland to the north-west took days rather than hours. The Highland frontier still held, but only just.

Throughout the Highlands the traveller would encounter the dams and pylons of the North of Scotland Hydro-Electric Board, the major achievement of Johnston's Secretaryship, which he now headed. By the time he retired in 1959, £50 million had been spent on them, yet despite the powers the Board had to 'collaborate in the carrying out of any measures for the economic development and social improvement of the North of Scotland' there had been none of the Tennessee Valley sort of industrial development that its proponents had hoped for and its opponents had feared. The only heavily capitalised industrial plants in the Highlands were the distilleries and three aluminium works which had built their own hydro-electric schemes, while the withdrawal of the navy from its northern bases was actually diminishing the industrial element. By the 1960s the hope that cheap hydro-electric power would aid the Scottish economy seemed increasingly forlorn. At the limit of its development, in 1963, hydro-electricity provided under 30 per cent of Scotland's generating capacity; by 1973 this had dropped to 18 per cent. Could the money spent on Johnston's great vision not have been better employed re-equipping the Clyde shipyards and engineering works?

In a way the Hydro Board symbolised the relationship of government and the economy in the 1950s. Its purposes were vaguely nationalist and vaguely socialist. It served a myth, that of the Highland way of life. Its elegant power stations commemorated an autonomy respected by a Conservative government. The Conservatives, in fact, intervened only gingerly in Scottish affairs and respected the other great shibboleth of the Scottish left, the provision of subsidised housing. Although in 1961 42 per cent of Scottish households rented from local authorities, and in 1971 51 per cent – more than double the proportion in England – rents were on average less than half those in the south. This situation had existed since World War I, and no attempt had been made to change it, despite the fact that losses on the housing accounts of Scottish burghs and counties were made good by the ratepayers, who could pay up to 25 per cent more than their southern counterparts. The low-rent policy of

Scottish Labour councils was the nearest they came to imposing the 'dictatorship of the proletariat', and led to a direct political cleavage along owner-occupier/tenant lines. Edinburgh alone of the four cities had an owner-occupier majority, and Edinburgh alone was controlled by the right wing. Low rents were frequently gained by sacrificing amenities on housing estates: Billy Connolly's description of Glasgow's Easterhouse as 'a desert wi' windaes' is all too true of estates the size of Perth with one pub, a post office, and a street of battered shops. The arcane regulations whereby housing was allocated also impeded mobility of labour, while the resulting high rates penalised commerce and industry. Yet the Conservatives retreated from confrontation, despite the fact that low rents had been shown to contribute little to solving the problem of the slums.

If the economic politics of Scotland was the politics of illusion, then illusions ended in the slump of 1957–8. The Glasgow economists had warned in 1954 of 'an industrial economy that shows signs of lagging behind the rest of the country'; by 1959 even the usually euphoric Scottish Council was announcing that 'the short term prospects for industry and employment in Scotland are not good'. The heavy industries were now showing signs of terminal disease and the slump checked American investment. In October the Scottish electorate anounced to Prime Minister Macmillan that it had had it better, and the Conservatives lost five seats. Thereafter Scotland began to figure more prominently, if not always consistently, in the thinking of both government and opposition.

THE PLANNER'S VISION

The year 1960 saw Conservative policy shift in the direction of planning, and regional planning in particular. Macmillan, the friend and publisher of Keynes, had been MP for Stockton during the depression and knew the problems of the older industrial areas. This awareness was increased when Cairncross came south as chief economic adviser in 1961. (Macmillan had a predilection for Scots economists; Allan Young had helped draft his 'Middle Way' policies in the 1930s.) Conservative regional policy was at its most spectacular in north-east England, whither Lord Hailsham, cloth-capped, was sent to liaise with the equally ambiguous socialist magnate T. Dan Smith. In

Scotland, besides extending local employment assistance, the government set up a planning group to work on West Central Scotland and gave assistance to the Scottish Council in preparing an authoritative report on the economy.

The *Inquiry into the Scottish Economy* which reported in November 1961 was chaired by (Sir) John Toothill, the English-born managing director of Ferrantis. Toothill had been closely involved with the Scottish Council since 1946, and Ferrantis was one of the few new industries with heavy research and development investment in Scotland. The Toothill Report was neither a detailed plan nor a statistical investigation, but a straightforward statement of the requirements of new industry and the value judgements underlying these. Its conclusion was that a major shift in policy, away from palliating unemployment in the older industries to stimulating a totally new industrial structure, was vital:

A given industry may be expected to adapt itself to change provided the change is not too drastic in terms of the industry's technology and trading practices. Successful shift is less likely where there is a fundamental change in the nature of production and in the marketing relationships. The newer growth industries have been of kinds which would have meant just such a shift or adaptation in Scottish industry and this – not any sudden or general collapse of entrepreneurial calibre – is the basic reason why it has not in the main diversified itself.

The Toothill Report had little to say about the heavy industries, and less about devolution. Yet although it stressed better transport links with the south, such integrationist ideas were countered by the argument that this would enhance Scots control of Scots industry, as it would no longer be a remote province. To this end it supported the decentralisation of research, development and physical planning, and large-scale investment in education at all levels. A new industrial structure had to be created, as well as a new and adaptable labour force and a new managerial and technocrat class, and the responsibility for this was placed firmly on government.

Government responded. The Science Ministry was set up, the Scottish Development Department created, the Robbins

Committee into higher education and the Brunton Committee into Scottish secondary education promised wide-reaching reforms; the Buchanan Report not only sanctioned massive urban redevelopment but called for the creation of powerful regional authorities; the Beeching reorganisation of the railways provided fast passenger and freight connections with the south. An approach was also made to the Highland problem, in a style far different to that of Johnston. A partnership between the Glasgow retailer Sir Hugh Fraser, various commercial concerns and the Scottish Office was set up to build an 'integrated tourist complex' at the railway junction of Aviemore in the Grampians; nearby ski-runs would supplement the summer trade and provide all-the-year-round business. Fraser's architect – for a project of surpassing vulgarity – was the well-connected Yorkshireman John Poulson; his government liaison man was the senior civil servant 'Gorgeous George' Pottinger. Much was subsequently to be heard of both.

'The white heat of the technological revolution' was appropriated by Harold Wilson as a Labour slogan in October 1963, but it was in fact common to both parties. The opposition, however, reserved the right to make what capital it could out of those social groups the new consensus rejected, and to minister to the faithful who found their cherished myths tossed aside. Labour, headed in Scotland by William Ross, a former Ayrshire schoolmaster with a Knoxian line in invective, exploited these options for all they were worth. Pit and shipyard closures were hurled at the government, the discontent of every organised group in Scotland was channelled by Labour MPs and activists to arrive on the doorstep of Michael Noble, the innocuous and reasonably progressive Conservative Secretary of State. The Liberal revival, which had centred on Edinburgh University, where David Steel and Russell Johnston had secured the election of Jo Grimond as Rector in 1960, also contributed, especially in the Highlands, which were threatened by Beeching's intention to close down most of their railways and by a landlord-backed campaign against the Hydro Board. Despite the radicalism of his government's policies, the appearances of Macmillan in the north, like someone out of P. G. Wodehouse, suggested that the Tories still viewed Scotland as a huge sporting estate, and were doing their best to keep it that way. Images were important, and when the Earl of Home, one of the country's largest landowners, was 'evolved' into Macmillan's place, reality seemed to have caught up with them.

Sir Alec, as he rapidly became, got into Parliament in a by-election straight out of John Buchan's *Castle Gay*, fought in the mountains and bars of Kinross and West Perthshire. The Liberals hoped for Tory rebellions, Labour slung in its right-wing cohorts from the Glasgow University Union, including a young John Smith; the veteran Arthur Donaldson stood for the SNP, infecting Paul Johnson of the *New Statesman* with 'a totally new kind of boredom'. Hugh MacDiarmid was astounded to discover there were 123 other communists concealed in this Landseer landscape. Convoyed by retired colonels (the constituency held some sort of record for Old Etonians per square mile), Sir Alec was displayed, icon-like, to the villagers. Everyone declaimed against the Beeching cuts (which shortly removed about half of the constituency's railways); Labour promised a Highland Development Board. To no avail. Sir Alec was returned with an absolute majority, because many Scots still liked being ruled by a laird. The age of heart-failure-inducing by-elections had yet to dawn.

Nevertheless, the defeat of the Conservatives a year later, when their MPs fell from 31 to 24, owed much to the archaic nature of the party. Despite a high level of support, it had never, as in England, digested the fragments of the Liberal Party and established itself in the business community. The continuance of some sort of Liberal loyalty split the 'radical' vote, which would otherwise have gone to Labour, but the Scottish Tories remained dominated by landowners, farmers and professional men, and severed from urban right-wingers, who had their own independent Progressive or Moderate parties. Paradoxically, the majority of Conservative Secretaries of State after 1932 were drawn from commercial or industrial backgrounds. Sir Godfrey Collins, 1932–5, headed the publishing concern; Walter Elliot, 1935–8, came from an auctioneering family and was a distinguished scientist in his own right; John Colville, Lord Clydesmuir, 1938–40, was from a Motherwell steel firm; John S. Maclay, Viscount Muirsheil, 1957–62, was the son of Lord Maclay, shipping magnate and shipping controller in both world wars; while Michael Noble, 1962–4, came from the dynasty which had run Armstong-Whitworths. Yet they seemed content to be custodians of a museum whose exhibits –

Clydeside reds and grousemoor lairds alike – were to be cherished rather than challenged.

WHITE HEAT TO RED FACE

Labour's return in October 1964 set the seal on the regional planning consensus. Through Johnston's initiatives and under Labour's Town and Country Planning Act of 1947, development plans had been drawn up for the main cities and regions of Scotland, mainly by the disciples of Patrick Geddes. Pigeonholed for over a decade, these were now to be used as the basis for an interlocking system of national and regional planning, directed from London by the new Department of Economic Affairs. Throughout Britain Regional Economic Planning Boards (of civil servants) were set up, advised by Regional Economic Planning Councils (comprising business interests, trade unions and local authorities). In Scotland these were further supplemented by the Regional Development Division of the Scottish Office. The first two years of William Ross's Secretaryship were as energetic as he had promised they would be. In 1965 he carried legislation to set up a Highlands and Islands Development Board – an executive as well as a planning body – against Tory grumblings of 'undiluted Marxism', established a permanent Law Reform Commission under Lord Kilbrandon, and issued a circular to local authorities requiring the reorganisation of education on comprehensive lines. In the following year the Scottish Plan appeared, along with a White Paper on Social Work, while a Royal Commission under Lord Wheatley began to examine the reform of local government. The groundwork for a new Scotland seemed well advanced.

When the Highland Development Board was set up the *New Statesman* described it (appreciatively) as 'an almost perfect example of Voltairean enlightened despotism'. The socialist new order wasn't democratic; indeed with Ross dispensing some 400 posts the eighteenth-century parallel was only too apposite. As for Labour's attitude to nationalism, the *Scotsman* commented in 1976 that it had prepared the soil 'in which the seeds of nationalism could take root', yet this was more evident in Wales, where it raised the Welsh Secretary to the Cabinet and established the Welsh Office. Many of Ross's reforms either paralleled similar

131

legislation in England, or were intended to 'bring Scotland level'. Comprehensive education was always seen thus, unfairly, as Ross, for all his 'dominie' manner, was radical about education, and the Scottish system was better adapted to the change. But the growth of regional planning, with its stress on city-regions and car-commuting, suggested that nation might shrink to region. With some mid-1960s plans suggesting a new cross-border region centred on Carlisle, Sir Walter Scott's expectation that Scotland might end up being run like Northumberland – if not by Northumberland – seemed far from fantastic.

Assimilation through a dynamic policy of regional development might have worked. George Brown's raid on Clydeside in the autumn of 1965 – which saved the Fairfield shipyard from closure, placing it under the tripartite control of private industry, government and the unions – was widely praised, although it effectively placed under state control a hitherto Scottish-owned firm. The *Plan for Scotland*, when it came out in January 1966, was not just qualitatively more advanced than the *National Plan* of October 1965, but aimed to remove Scotland's high emigration and unemployment and low wages – elements of national distinctiveness no one was proud of – through direction of industry and preferential grants. The initiative appeared to rest securely with Labour, which in the March election pushed its total of seats to 46. In ten years, the number of Tory MPs had declined from 36 to 20.

Labour's exultation did not last. The seamen's strike, which aroused the well-publicised complaint of the island communities that their plight was being neglected by Westminster, was followed by the economic crisis which brought the fight for supremacy between the Department of Economic Affairs and the Treasury to a head. The DEA lost, deflationary policies were brought in, the grand design of a planned, expanding economy was deferred. Retribution came swiftly in England, with by-election reverses unprecedented in peacetime politics. The Tories were the main beneficiaries, but on 12 July 1966 Welsh nationalism scored its first success, when Gwynfor Evans took Carmarthen with a personal poll of 39 per cent. It had been a Lloyd George rather than a Labour seat, but the *Blaid* had polled only 16 per cent at the general election. The precedent was an ominous one for Labour's Scottish fiefs.

The Labour Party in Scotland was not well prepared. Despite its victories in three successive elections, its internal state was parlous. The legend of the red Clyde was just that; Glasgow Labour – right-wing, badly organised and poorly supported – typified most Labour 'fortresses'. Radicalism and enthusiasm were mainly found in marginal or hopelessly Tory constituencies, among students or young professional people, or the numerous ex-communists who had 'come over' in 1956. It was rarely reflected by the elected representatives. The standard of Labour MPs in Scotland was lower than in England; as local government work was unpaid, many party activists were excluded from it and Labour councillors – small businessmen, trade union officials and housewives – had only a primitive level of political consciousness. The key to success in the Labour Party, as one weary left-winger maintained, was 'the law of the rise of the charismatic numskull':

> Go to meetings, become minutes secretary, organise jumble sales, canvass, but don't say anything. Never express a political opinion. Then nobody will know what you stand for and they'll sort out everyone whose line they do know. That way you become an MP, as they can't think of anything against you.

But in 1967, the year of the Pollok and Hamilton by-elections, even the most charismatic of numskulls was in for a very rough time.

Planning hung around Labour's neck like an albatross, big, dead and smelly. Targets had been set which could never now be reached, regional development teams worked on plans which had little hope of fulfilment, inquiries were set up into social problems insoluble without enormous public investment. All of these blew up in Labour's face. The Cullingworth Committee's Report on *Scotland's Older Housing*, published in 1967, found, for example, that 'one in three persons lives in a house considered either substandard or unfit for human habitation'. It placed the blame squarely on central government:

> For, though local authorities by no means come through our examination unscathed, the problem, especially in Glasgow, is of such huge dimensions as to place it beyond

133

the resources of any single authority, even though it be the biggest authority in the country.

Ross was made responsible for the failings of his Conservative predecessors, as well as for the management of Glasgow by Labour (which Cullingworth, in the circumstances, probably let off rather lightly). With the mounting tide of left-wing criticism of Westminster policies in general, he had also to cope with activists who seceded to single-issue groups, and flung the conclusions of inquiries like Cullingworth's back at him. The Highlands and Islands Development Board's new powers went to its head and it began thinking in terms of a city of 300,000 based on Inverness. It ran into accusations of neglecting the Gaelic-speaking west and enriching its own members. In turn it accused the Secretary of State of niggardliness and interference. An imaginative development plan for the Central Borders, an area of high emigration, coincided with the determination of the Ministry of Transport to close the only railway which served the area. At all turns the Secretary of State was blamed for the shortcomings of Scottish local government and Scottish industry, while Treasury constraints checked any initiatives of his own. A lot *was* done. Government expenditure per head was about 20 per cent up on the rest of the UK. But the promises of the planners were a *fata Morgana* hovering ahead of the Scottish voter, and Ross the dominie was not the man to explain tactfully the realities of the situation.

Ross was the greatest Secretary of State, in the sense that he developed the post to the limit of its powers. He used his weight in the Cabinet and kept his civil servants under control, while, in uneasy harness with his Permanent Secretary, Sir Douglas Haddow, he accelerated the transformation of the Scottish Office from an administrative to a planning agency. He knew where power lay in the Scottish Labour movement, and he never lost contact with it. He was a Scottish manager of the classic type, serving the system that he knew well, but he had little knowledge of, and less liking for, those who wanted to change it. Ironically, he had much more in common with many SNP members than with younger Labour people, who were distressed at his aversion to liberal reforms and his Kailyardery. The qualities which made him a good Secretary of State actually made it more difficult for him to meet the challenge of the new

Scottish politics, or, for that matter, to solve the country's worsening economic dilemma.

INTRACTABILITY

The Scottish economy didn't just lag behind the English in terms of aggregate performance. It was a different kind of economy, more dependent on the production of capital goods on the one hand and on the service industries on the other. By definition it was difficult to control by regulating the demand for consumer goods, as the factors which stimulated investment in the capital goods industries were not always the same as those which stimulated consumer demand. The *National Plan* was seen as a means of producing a general identity between the two economies, after which the Scottish economy would respond to the same stimuli as the English. This did not happen. Not only that, but by the end of the 1960s grave doubts were being expressed about whether the exercise ought to have been undertaken in the first place.

Undercapitalised and antique though they were, the heavy industries – shipbuilding, coal, steel, railway and mechanical engineering – had good reason to remain in Scotland. A skilled labour force existed, the universities supplied highly trained technical staff like naval architects and metallurgists; a range of associated concerns manufacturing navigational equipment, machine tools and mining machinery provided its own type of diversified economy. This the new transplants failed to do. The motor industries of Linwood and Bathgate were assembly plants, whose supply industries did not follow them north. As Peter Jay, the *Times* monetarist economic correspondent, told the Scottish Council in 1974, such industries were artificial: if they had non-labour cost advantages equal to those of the traditional industries, they would have been traditional industries as well. They could only have 'taken off' if, as in the German *Wirtschaftswunder*, wages were determined regionally, and were lower in the north – something unthinkable given the power and ideology of a unified trade union movement. Instead 'the initial once-and-for-all penalty of losing traditional industries with comparative international advantages [was] transformed into a perpetual dynamic of decay'.

In 1970 a sub-committee of the Scottish Council produced a

135

report which was diametrically opposed to the Toothill ortho-doxy. *Oceanspan* involved a return to the rationale which had underlain Scotland's growth in the eighteenth century: the nation as entrepôt, with the Common Market supplying the political framework that the Union had then provided. The Clyde, the largest natural harbour on the European Atlantic seaboard, could turn round giant bulk carriers, vessels that could be a menace in the confines of the Channel. Cargoes could be transferred in the Firth and bypass the European ports by using the Channel Tunnel or the river and canal systems of the EEC countries. The mid-Scotland ship canal, which generations of nationalists had urged, came back into prominence. Moreover, the Clyde as a transhipment point would attract industries that would benefit from economies of scale, such as steelmaking, shipbuilding and oil refining. *Oceanspan* meant, in other words, the redevelopment of the Ulster-Scotland 'inland sea' as a mini-Rotterdam, in the interests of the heavy industries.

Behind *Oceanspan* was their last great magnate, Sir William Lithgow, who had inherited the family shipyards at Port Glasgow, amalgamated them with those of Scott's at Greenock, and made the combine the largest and most successful ship-building firm in Scotland. He was as resolute a defender of capitalism as his father, and stood out on his own when other Scottish business leaders made their peace with Labour and planning. *Oceanspan* put this whole consensus in question, but it was over a decade too late. The drilling rigs were already strik-ing oil off the Shetlands, opening up a quite new economic theatre. As the first assault of the SNP ended in failure, opinion about the industrial future of the country was more fragmented and volatile than it had been since the war. Sir William hedged his bets by acting as consultant to Hyundai, the growing Korean shipbuilding and engineering conglomerate. He was a wise man.

5

NOTHING ABIDES
Civil society, 1945–1979

As far as the United Kingdom is concerned, the Scots have
at least some consciousness of their 'Kailyard' as a problem; the English are still largely unaware of having arrived
there.

> Tom Nairn, 'Old Nationalism and New Nationalism',
> in *The Red Paper on Scotland*, 1975

ESTATES AND POLICIES

In 1962 David Keir, editor of the *Edinburgh* volume of the *Third
Statistical Account*, tried to convey the timbre of life in the capital
by dining *chez* Sir Compton Mackenzie in the New Town. His
guests were Anne Redpath, the artist, Sir David Milne, former
Permanent Secretary at St Andrew's House, Lord Cameron,
Dean of the Faculty of Advocates, Alastair Dunnett, editor of
the *Scotsman*, and Sir Compton himself: representative of the
country's douce, semi-nationalist establishment. Their cosy discussion would have provoked a snarl or two from Brownsbank,
the Lanarkshire cottage where, like Yeats in his tower at
Ballylee, MacDiarmid stood guard over the Scottish *Geist*, but it
reflected a society still confident in its distinct institutions, most
of them helpfully centred in Edinburgh. Lord Cameron thought
that Walter Scott's eighteenth-century Edinburghers had a point
about the benefits of a Parliament: 'We could aye peeble them
wi' stanes when they werena gude bairns.' Sir David Milne
warily agreed that Scotland was a political unit of a sort:

> That's because Scotland is the right administrative size. In
> general, this goes for government as well as for running

newpapers, and for a lot of other things . . . it hasn't the remoteness of England, say, as an administrative unit. The contacts and the relations between the centre and the periphery in England are nothing like as close as here.

But as they talked, such certainties were already crumbling, and with them the prestige of the institutions they represented. The light that slanted into Sir Compton's windows faded on the slums and empty slipways of the Clyde, and on the disused shale mines of West Lothian.

Kirk, law, local government and education had traditionally protected the nation, while troubled economic strategies and regional plans made pressure for devolution among civil servants and the electorate grow almost by default. But the estates were at risk through secularisation, collective intervention, and doctrinaire educational prescriptions. In nineteenth-century Europe such a challenge had accelerated the emergence of formal nationalism, strengthening resistance and calling new institutions into play. Overdue by a century, could a cognate process take place in post-war Scotland?

The omens were not good. In 1961 George Davie had celebrated the 'democratic intellect', by which he meant the way that institutions such as Anne Redpath's Royal Scottish Academy *selected* their members, the trained and the talented, from a broad social spectrum. No pluralist society lacks such institutions: Scotland, however, was unique in having, for so long, depended on them for its government. Yet Davie wrote almost elegiacally about Anglicising as a *fait accompli*. Challenged by centralisation, their own enfeeblement, they were at risk. Robin Cook, while a student socialist, argued in 1966 that St Andrew's House impeded socialism and ought to be replaced by direct rule from London. But the failure of planning meant not only the survival of the estates, but the creation of a distinctively Scottish alternative politics.

James Kellas, in *Modern Scotland* (1968), focused attention on the continuing distinctiveness of Scottish civil society, but only 20 of his 230 pages dealt with economics. In 1868 economics would have loomed much larger, although Kirk, law and education then played a much more powerful social role. National development was no longer directed by the entrepreneurs, and the decline of the capital-goods 'imperial' economy paradoxically increased the influence of the estates, as they moved into the vacuum. Scottish local authorities, for example, put up nearly half of the money for the Scottish Council: Development and Industry in 1946, while nearly all the great shipyards and the North British Locomotive Company contributed no more than the basic £3 subscription. The universities took an unprecedented interest in social and economic matters in the 1950s and 1960s. The churches were always ready with prescriptions for the country's social and political ills. As spokesmen for a society whose problems remained obstinate and distinctive, they remained relevant.

PARLIAMENT HOUSE

In 1986, making a documentary about Scottish politics, I found that the leaders of all the political parties – Malcolm Rifkind, Donald Dewar, David Steel and Gordon Wilson – had qualified as lawyers. Of the estates the legal system was the most prehensile. The authority of 'Parliament House' – its own elite of 'writers', solicitors and advocates – was unquestioned. If they could not practise in the English courts, neither could English lawyers practise in Scotland. They were a powerful group, but less patrician than before, quicker to move into commercial businesses such as estate agency and fund management. They were also conscious of the penalties of their anomalous position. Scots law had been threatened by the development of administrative law since the mid nineteenth century, but as there was never a British code – as in France or Germany – an irreducible minimum of legislation had always to be translated into its categories. So any prospect of thorough assimilation could be ruled out. Nationalism was vitiated, however, by the party affiliations of many Scots advocates. Political patronage meant that on any change of government the posts of Lord Advocate, Solicitor-General and the Advocates Depute (crown counsel) would fall vacant. Having stood in some hopeless constituency or being a member of the Fabian Society or Bow Group then came in useful. The judges – Senators of the College of Justice – were political appointments, and many had been Lord Advocates or Solicitors-General. Most were Tories, but the independent Lord Kilbrandon, and the former Labour Lord Advocate Lord Wheatley both figured in the reforms of the mid-1960s. The law faculties of the universities had produced Dewar Gibb in the 1930s. Influenced by Lord Cooper, a Tory but a prickly legal nationalist, and Professor T. B. Smith, they remained deeply immune to southern contagion.

Besides the business of patronage, law had its own surrogate politics. The elaborate and extended cases about 'issues of principle' which punctuate Scottish legal history were often ceremonial assertions of the independence of the Scottish courts. Frequently stemming from disputes between or within the estates, they personified the 'ideology of noisy inaction'. But by the mid-1960s, law and lawyers were a more positive force, giving technical assistance to the government's numerous inquiries and plans, and undertaking renewal through the Scots Law Commission, set up by Labour in 1965. In that year *New Society* marvelled at 'the start of a legal renaissance in Scotland', citing curricula, at Edinburgh and elsewhere, which (eccentrically for Britain) displayed 'an awareness of the social and international implications of the law'. Entering Europe in 1973 meant that the Scots system would no longer be a British freak, but somewhat closer to European jurisprudence than English common law.

There was, indeed, some progress. Legislation on young offenders, which integrated the former juvenile courts with social work departments, meant both a new social conception of law and a reassertion of Chalmersian social counselling. The Land Court, under Harald Leslie, was seen as an instrument of Highland land reform. But did law reform require a devolved legislature? This was the view of Kilbrandon, who had secured the Young Offenders' Act and was Chairman of the Law Commission. In March 1972 Heath made him Chairman of the Commission on the British Constitution. Four years earlier, in October 1968, the law had quietly provided the SNP with its main platform for the 1970s. By the Continental Shelf (Jurisdictional) Order, the activity of extracting oil and gas north of 55° 50' was placed under the Scots courts, giving, in the opinion of some, though not all, lawyers, the Scots their title to this potential wealth. To support this, the SNP was able to produce the Professor of Public Law from Edinburgh University, whose 'legal renaissance' helpfully included much European public and commercial law. Shortly afterwards, another nationalist,

140

Neil MacCormick, the son of 'King John', was appointed to Edinburgh's Regius chair.

Nothing is straightforward, least of all in the law. In the 1980s Scots legal reform took two directions, both easily personified. The urbane debating skills and philosophic mind of MacCormick, the former Fellow of Balliol, were launched at one forlorn SNP candidacy after another; he helped shape the Scottish Constitutional Convention, and then saw the SNP's participation in it torpedoed by perhaps his brightest pupil, Jim Sillars. Out of Parliament House came the mathematician John MacKay, a figure of formidable capability, said to have been offered the Lord Advocacy by Labour before accepting it under the Conservatives. In 1987 he followed Lord Hailsham as Mrs Thatcher's Lord Chancellor. The difference between the two men was total: a caricature clubman (albeit a radical on devolution) followed on to the Woolsack by the Highland elder of a sect of astonishing rigidity, intent on dynamiting the well-fed privileges of the profession he was supposed to lead. In the days of Cockburn and Jeffrey, legal reformers had hoped to integrate *and* retain their dominance in the north. This had not greatly changed, but the question was now: integration with what? For MacKay it meant a London legal establishment purged of its Englishness. For MacCormick, like Kilbrandon before him, it meant Brussels.

THE PASSING OF THE BURGHS

Local government bore even more sensitively on public opinion about nationalism. The abolition of parish councils in 1929 boosted the National Party, as local government was assumed to be guaranteed by the Act of Union. Such changes destroyed traditions while failing to provide an immediate identification with the new unit. 1929 probably accelerated the loss of community Edwin Muir mourned; it cerainly heralded forty years of indifference to local democracy. Municipal polls were low, councillors elderly and dull; issues rarely rose above rates and council-house rents. Labour held on to the larger towns and most authorities in the industrial areas. The Moderates or Progressives (until the late 1960s Conservatives were virtually unknown in local government) held Edinburgh, several medium-sized country towns and suburban burghs around

141

Glasgow. There were still genuine Independents in the Highlands, the east coast and the Borders, surviving industrial change and population migration. 'Small burghs' came as tiny as New Galloway, with scarcely 300 people; Bellshill was a 'village' of 10,000. The Border burghs of Galashiels, Hawick, Selkirk, Jedburgh and Kelso kept their thrawn independence, collaborated little with each other, and less with the northern English. When a speaker at a Langholm Burns Supper sugges-ted that the town might reconcile itself with MacDiarmid, its most distinguished son, there were, that delighted delinquent noted, shouts of 'Nonsense! Nonsense!' and 'Away back to Hawick!' Glasgow's neighbours fought the city's encroach-ments; more remote towns co-operated with it in settling large numbers of 'over-spill' families. Such anomalies were com-pounded by the appearance of five entirely new towns. East Kilbride was designated in 1947, Glenrothes in 1948, Cumbernauld in 1955, Livingston in 1966 and Irvine in 1969. Planned to provide centres for light industry and eventually to house nearly 10 per cent of the country's population, these were an exercise in social 'management' as drastic as that of the improvers' planned villages, and as autocratic. The problems and opportunities they created would contribute to SNP success.

A major overhaul was overdue. The Scottish Office advanced a scheme in 1963, drawn up by George Pottinger, but, largely through Pottinger's own diplomatic failings, this was rejected. In 1965 Ross appointed a Royal Commission under Lord Wheatley to produce a scheme for a wholesale reform. Unlike the Redcliffe-Maud Commission in England (whose regional level never took off) Wheatley's intentions for 'top-tier' authori-ties were from the start ambitious: large regions were seen as a 'rational' alternative to nationalism *and* to Scottish Office bur-eaucracy. Professor John Mackintosh, at this stage Labour's 'lone devolver', regarded an 'all Scotland' top tier as administra-tively efficient and politically attractive. His scheme tackled the main difficulty that beset Wheatley: how to replan the congested central belt while representing the mass of the population who actually lived there.

Wheatley's solution, announced in September 1969, was to create seven large regions: Strathclyde, Lothian and Borders, Highland, Grampian, Tayside, Central, and Dumfries and

Galloway, under which were to be forty-nine district councils. The regions would control transport, town and country planning, social work and education; the districts' housing, the arts, recreation. The Heath government's White Paper of 1971 granted, in response to public controversy, two further regions, Fife and the Borders, and special types 'all-purpose' councils for Orkney, Shetland, and the Outer Isles. Legislation followed quickly, and although the Commission on the Constitution was already in session when Wheatley reported, no attempt was made to co-ordinate the reform of Scottish government with the new regions, nor were the various semi-regional quangos controlling the health service included in the new scheme. Since both governments seemed to regard Crowther/Kilbrandon as a means of deferring devolution *ad infinitum*, this made sense, but the resurrection of the SNP after autumn 1973 meant that the introduction of the new system coincided with the whole principle which underlay it being questioned.

Wheatley got one glancing reference in the 836 pages of Harold Wilson's *The Labour Government, 1964-70*, published in 1971. Crowther/Kilbrandon vanished into some oubliette. Both Labour and Tory doubtless hoped that, once established, regional government would meet SNP charges of 'remote government' and give higher standards of administration through economies of scale. Pressure to implement Kilbrandon removed the first advantage, while inflation after 1973 and the need to compensate employees of the old system removed the second. As well as favouring the SNP by weakening old loyalties, regionalisation gave them the bonus of new grievances to exploit.

Local government, anyhow, had problems enough. Labour councils with their housing debts were condemned by right-wingers who were against spending money on anything. Periodic scandals exposed low standards on both sides. These were often minor – backhanders for granting licences, giving planning permission, or allocating council houses – but with the growth of council expenditure came more disturbing trends. Big corporation contractors moved in on local politics, both as right-wing councillors and as employers of Labour colleagues, who thus gained jobs compatible with the sizeable demands of council work, though not with independence. The amateur tradition now led to the rule of powerful interest groups, as councils undertook the new and expensive business of urban reconstruction.

The Buchanan Report, which appeared in November 1963, called for the almost total replanning of cities to accommodate a constantly rising level of car ownership. The flaws in Sir Colin Buchanan's logic – his neglect of public transport, walking or cycling, his underestimate of regional variations in income and car ownership, and his conviction that there was some sort of causal connection between roadbuilding and economic perform- ance – seem now to make his rise from a relatively humble town planning official to the doyen of his profession in a couple of years one of the more mystifying phenomena of the 1960s. But his report was given the hard sell by its steering committee under Lord Crowther, by the Minister of Transport, Ernest Marples, and by the British Road Federation, and nowhere was its prescription swallowed as enthusiastically as in Glasgow, with a proportion of car ownership in 1966 of 1 car to 11 people (compared with 1 to 4 in Surrey). The resulting destruction removed some slum properties, but also laid waste one of the liveliest and most ingenious European urban landscapes. In the late 1960s a Labour council provided the middle-class motorist with urban motorways and a fine suburban electric railway system, and filed away its working-class electors in thirty-storey blocks of flats. Some observers, like the poet Edwin Morgan, in futurist mood, saw this as protean: the city transfiguring itself like its American counterparts. But the industries displaced by the roads closed down or went away; money was diverted from areas, like housing and social work, where it was already in desperately short supply; the population projected for the city in 1980 fell from 900,000 in 1961 to 750,000 or less in 1973. Like the model aeroplanes that South Sea islands built to induce their gods to bring them Western consumer goods, the great six-lane roads were a sort of cargo-cult. But prosperity did not come.

The entrenched conservatism of Edinburgh, by contrast, saved the city from destruction. The city engineer thought up a grandiose ring road project in 1965, and in 1967 the leaders of the Labour group joined with the right wing to force it through. There was a revolt in both parties and among well-heeled amen- ity societies. A public inquiry prompted the council to reject the scheme, and a variant designed by Buchanan himself, and to come out against big road schemes of any kind. One result of the foray of the SNP into local politics between 1967 and 1969 was to eliminate many dim Labour councillors, and a new graduate generation was more left-wing and more articulate, eager to reappraise policies on housing, health and town planning. Reform even affected Glasgow Corporation, with the jail gates opening for some of the less reliable comrades. But such improvements came when the old councils were facing reorganisation. Innovations were curbed by their extinction.

In 1974, the second, oil-powered, nationalist assault was revving up, and Scottish local government had no real conviction about its status and future role. Socialists looked to the new units to provide a 'good government' alternative to self-government, but had to admit that the past record wasn't helpful. The lesson of the 1960s was that the Scottish administration should intervene more positively in local government affairs, but this would only be possible with some sort of representative government. A Conservative Secretary of State like Gordon Campbell, who represented only the majority party in Westminster, could never hope to take such intiatives.

UNGODLY COMMONWEALTH

In the early 1950s *Sunday Post* readers were entertained or scandalised by the tale of an eccentric painter at work on a vast mural on the ceiling of a Glasgow kirk. The mural had Creation as its theme and was a wondrous blend of the mystic and the scientific. Some of its characters were recognisably of the Glasgow locality. Others had realistic genitals. After oohs and aahs, and problems about payment, work stopped. The kirk shortly fell victim to urban reconstruction.

Alasdair Gray's travails, later fictionalised in *Lanark*, were somehow symbolic of the relation of religion to Scotland. Religion can identify a community but it can also inhibit the sort of imaginative political commitment that progressive nationalism requires. In nineteenth-century Europe secularisation had helped transfer denominational loyalties to the nation. In Scotland the obsession with church affairs during and after the Disruption, and the arrival of a large Irish immigrant community, kept religious affiliations resilient. Even in the 1950s church membership, at 60 per cent of the adult population, was nearly three times as great as in England: 25 per cent of the total population were still members of the Church of Scotland, and 13 per cent of the Catholic Church.

After an inter-war career distinguished by intolerance and indifference to social issues, the Kirk rapidly came abreast of Keynesian economics and the welfare state; its General Assembly's quasi-parliamentary function allowed it to comment widely on British and Commonwealth politics. Authoritarian and conservative, the Catholic hierarchy still loomed over the Labour politics of West Central Scotland. By the mid-1960s, however, a permanent decline in observance and influence had set in. The number of communicants in the Kirk dropped by 1 per cent annually, rising to 2 per cent in the 1970s. Decline in Catholic numbers only began in 1970, but recruitment of religious personnel and teachers shrank.

Various factors lay behind this. City clearance and overspill schemes shifted many people away from established congregations, and broke up the cross-class activism that organised them. Television and the belated impact of materialist and rationalist ideas also took their toll. After the war the Kirk was aware of the challenge, and eager to testify to a new era, but its response was ambiguous. George MacLeod and the Iona Community offered a combination of nationalism, social intervention and psychological insight: effervescent but unstable and, to traditional presbyterians, suspiciously tolerant of ritual. The other approach, American evangelism, had a record going back to Moody and Sankey in 1873–5. The 'Tell Scotland' crusade of the Reverend Tom Allan in 1947 grew in parallel to MacCormick's Covenant movement, rather as Evan Jones's 1905 revival in Wales accompanied the triumph of Lloyd George's Liberals. But personal conversion – at mass rallies – somehow became decoupled from social reform. Tell Scotland's climax came with the Scottish Crusade of Dr Billy Graham in the winter of 1954–5. But where Moody and Sankey had re-created the Godly Commonwealth ideal, and helped end three decades of sectarian conflict, Graham used new technology – radio, television and land-lines to churches and halls throughout the country – to preach a blend of conservative fundamentalism and the material benefits of American individualism. His crusade was a withdrawal from politics, perhaps even a withdrawal from Scotland, as it paralleled a huge emigration to the USA. Even on evangelical terms, personal conversion in the Kelvin

Hall had to be sustained by fresh parochial resources in the new housing schemes. It was not. The Kirk regressed intellectually while making no significant gains in communicants.

The Progressives remained influential if unrepresentative. Under George MacLeod, Geoffrey Shaw and Kenneth MacKenzie, their links with other churches, and their industrial, urban and missions role, was as considerable as their influence in the Labour Party and on anti-colonial and disarmament movements. But their resonance in an increasingly middle-class rank and file was limited. The influence of the left probably rose to a climax in 1960–64 with CND and the crisis of the Central African Federation. But thereafter, as well as suffering from the ebbing of left-wing confidence, the Progressives within the Kirk were disadvantaged by left-wing secularism.

Within the Catholic Church, paradoxically, radicalism was sustained by the rise of a Catholic middle class. The innovators stopped being identified with the old Catholic families and upper-class Anglo-Scots whose nationalism was over-intellectualised and condescending. They chafed at the hier-archy as well as at the residuum of Scots presbyterian prejudice. The association of Catholicism with left-wing social criticism, which Edwin Muir had made in the 1930s, from outside the Church, was restated in the 1960s by such priests as the Dominican Father Anthony Ross, chaplain to Edinburgh University. Ross, a convert in the 1930s both to Catholicism and to nationalism of the MacDiarmid variety, offered hospitality and encouragement to students of all faiths and none, helping set up the journal *Scottish International* in 1967. Deeply involved in social work, especially in the forgotten Edinburgh of the Grassmarket dosshouses, Ross carried conviction among a gen-eration whose drift from political and religious orthodoxy was evident in declining vocations, with his plea that:

> Before deciding what it is to be Scottish we need to exam-ine our ideas as to what it is to be human, and to be Christian, and make at the start an act of contrition for ourselves and the community in which we live.

Religion had never been the opium of the Scottish masses. The politics of the Kirk had been closer to most people than those of Parliament or town council. But they were run by a male elite, and in the 1960s they were steadily losing their grip.

To young people, who in the 1920s found religion a kind of surrogate politics, politics now became a surrogate religion, a vocation for Christians with a desire to identify with the community, and a distrust of their own conservative establishments: a motivation which created expectations of politics that could scarcely be fulfilled.

THE DOMINIE'S DILEMMA

The most spectacular crisis came in education, traditionally the link between the Scots estates and the opportunities provided by Britain and the Empire. In the late 1950s educational reform appeared imminent, as the trained cadres of a mixed economy would have to be produced. It was also plain that such change would be imposed according to English, not Scottish, ideas. Half a century of neglect and complacency had left a school and university system in need of reform and incapable of generating that reform internally, through its neglect of research and experiment. This challenge was focused by a remarkable book published in 1961 by the Edinburgh philosopher George Davie, *The Democratic Intellect: Scotland and her Universities in the Nineteenth Century*. Davie argued that in the years after 1832 the democratically recruited and unspecialised nature of Scottish liberal education had been cut to fit 'English' demands for specialisation and elitism. The result had been its reduction to an anomalous provincialism:

> The democratic intellectualism which had distinguished Scottish civilisation was being allowed to disappear and the peculiar polymathic values it supported were, increasingly, at a discount among the cultural leaders . . . there has been a marked reaction in twentieth-century Scotland against the historic heritage, but one will misunderstand the situation unless one sees it not as a collapse but as a slow surrender. The ideal of a balanced breadth of mind still remained entrenched in wide educational sectors; what was being swept away was rather the intellectual sharpness required to secure its survival . . .

In some ways Davie's book was an apologia for the old tradition rather than a realistic description of it. He underestimated the practical domination of the universities by the clergy, the lawyers and the medical men; he ignored the superficial nature of the instruction in the huge lecture classes, and the intellectual damage done by sectarianism. He also neglected the impact on the 'democratic' university of a reorganised secondary education, which benefited the middle class, who could sustain their children through two extra school years. But, these apart, Davie's book was a powerful tract, which warned against slow surrender turning into outright capitulation.

In 1964 Labour began its own reform programme, encouraged by Willie Ross. The system was challenged from three sides: by new forms of teaching, by new types of school organisation, and by new ideas about the role of education in society. Despite A. S. Neill, Scottish education was always teacher-centred, but this orthodoxy was challenged by new methods of primary instruction developed mainly in the south, and applied to Scotland after 1965. In the same year comprehensive reorganisation throughout the country was announced. Again, the precedents involved were English, although district secondary schools in the Scottish counties had traditionally catered for all the children in their locality.

Regardless of their scholastic merits, these implied considerable changes in the status of teachers. The reduction of pupil/teacher ratios required more teachers than the ordinary degree courses of the universities and the established training colleges could supply. The latter started to offer a Bachelor of Education degree, and four new colleges were built, with the result that the tradition of a teaching profession in which all the men were university graduates was weakened. Unease was rapidly given political shape. In 1965 a General Teaching Council was set up to govern the profession in Scotland. Initially, teachers saw this as a means of imposing lay control; then when teachers' representatives formed a majority, they accused it of favouring the numerical majority of non-graduates in the profession, and so 'diluting' it. To this end an Aberdeen schoolteacher, J. S. Malloch, backed by the graduates' union, the Scottish Schoolmasters' Association, challenged in the courts the power of the Council to bar unregistered teachers from employment. This lengthy case testified to the continuing influence of the 'surrogate politics' of the old estates, but it seemed to be a defensive response to narrowing horizons. The teachers were no longer the recruiting-sergeants for an army of opportunity.

The university situation was peculiarly sensitive. Relatively, they had been declining in size since 1900, when Scotland provided nearly half the students in Britain. The growth of the English provincial universities cut this to 16 per cent. The Robbins Committee in 1961 promised a numerical expansion, but one which would still lessen this proportion. Fifteen per cent was an advantage to the Scots, but close up their position was much weaker. Sixty per cent of graduates took ordinary degrees; in England, they would have gone to training colleges. Scotland also lacked the polytechnics which were rapidly developing in the south. On top of all this, a larger proportion of staff and students (frequently the abler ones) were coming north from England.

Robbins brought matters to a head. University expansion – a new foundation at Stirling, university status for the Dundee outpost of St Andrews and the technical colleges at Glasgow and Edinburgh – had to be staffed and, in the arts and social sciences, the native tradition was weak. Scotland had always lagged in research; able graduates, if they wanted to persevere, usually went on to Oxford, Cambridge or London. So the deficiency was made up by English or English-trained professors and lecturers. By 1974 there were as many Oxford as Scottish graduates teaching history subjects north of the border, and the the latter was never higher than a third of any department. Although this led to nationalist grievance it had positive effects. Departments were enlivened by digesting new techniques and new research interests; postgraduate studies at last started to develop; and many immigrants seemed keener to launch themselves on the Scottish problem than the natives were.

But by the early 1970s, as the first generation of Scottish postgraduates began to emerge with their PhDs, expansion came to an end. Lecturers in post were mostly English, recruited in an academic sellers' market. An able generation of young Scots, denied academic careers, confronted an establishment which was itself young. This rivalry underlay the mid-1970s conflict about who should control the universities – the proposed Scottish Assembly or the British University Grants Committee – and it powered many of the cultural achievements of the 1980s.

In 1971 Donald Macrae, Professor of Sociology at the London School of Economics, recollected a Scottish education dominated by injunctions to the young to seize a future which was always outside Scotland. That time was now past; academic prizes glittered no more: 'The prestige, the cash value and the cultural importance of what universities do and the qualifications they give, all fall as they are more widely distributed.' But where the university took on a new importance was as a civic educator, something dramatically evident in the success of that 'state-of-the-art' Steam Intellect Society, the Open University, carried into being by and launched before a sceptical academia by two 'bairns o' pairts', Jennie Lee and Walter Perry.

In the late 1960s and early 1970s unease became widespread among teachers, normally Labour stalwarts. In the changed circumstances of post-imperial Britain, nationalism, and the recovery of traditions and values which the schools had on the whole neglected, seemed to offer a plausible alternative. By the mid-1970s a substantial minority – somewhere between a third and a half – had demonstrated this by their votes.

'A LICENCE TO PRINT MONEY'

In the 1960s Scottish society suffered a debilitating series of alterations and reverses. Law, its most conservative if also most national component, was the least affected; religion and education had to accommodate themselves to a changed and rather unfriendly world. Hitherto the problems of the estates had generally been dealt with internally, as part of the effective federalism of post-Union politics. Now their weakness became a national concern. But whose concern? Local government had problems of its own; the Scottish Trades Union Congress, which might have provided a left-wing counterpoise to a declining Scottish capitalism, itself suffered from the southward drift of union authority. As a result, not only did civil society try to compensate for loss of authority by backing devolution, but the discussion of social issues shifted to the 'new' national institutions: the press and the literary intelligentsia.

The Scottish press in 1950 had changed little since Lords Beaverbrook and Rothermere had bought their way in twenty years earlier. In the interval the Mirror Group had purchased the Glasgow *Daily Record* so that the mass-circulation dailies were all in English hands, but the Scottish papers had a lot of autonomy and none of their English stablemates, such as the

Mirror or the *Daily Herald*, was widely on sale in the north. The two quality dailies, the *Scotsman* and the *Glasgow Herald*, remained in Scottish hands; the *Press and Journal* in Aberdeen was independent. The Dundee *Courier and Advertiser*, famous for its ferocious Toryism and one-sentence paragraphs, remained the possession of the reclusive Thomson family, who also owned the *Beano* and the *Dandy* as well as that Kailyard gold-mine, the *Sunday Post*. Most Scottish dailies had companion, and usually much more profitable, evening papers, which supplied an unvarying diet of court reporting, local features and sports coverage to readers indifferent to what was happening in other football leagues, let alone in other countries: something which all the centralising impulses in the British press found it difficult to beat.

In the 1950s the challenge to the old establishment came, once again, from a Scots Canadian. In 1954 Roy Thomson, owner of several Canadian provincial papers and radio stations, wanted to break into the British press. He saw that the junior of the two Scottish quality papers, the *Scotsman*, was for sale and, remarking that the outfit wouldn't have lasted six months in Canada, took it over. The *Scotsman* was plainly only a stepping-stone; within three years Thomson had taken over the *Press and Journal* and, in England, the Kemsley newspapers, including the *Sunday Times*. More critically, he captured the franchise for the first commercial television channel in Scotland.

Thomson was an unabashed philistine. Editorial content was 'the stuff that fills the spaces between the ads'; Scottish Television was 'a licence to print money'. But he was almost alone in backing it; the Reithian tradition died hard. His investment paid off handsomely, as did the Edinburgh papers, though not before the rival and more prosperous *Evening News* had been amalgamated with Thomson's *Evening Dispatch*. Thomson was a Tory but abstained from imposing any line on his papers. Alastair Dunnett, his appointee as editor of the *Scotsman*, had a leftish and nationalist background and, although until 1966 the paper usually swung right just before elections, it provided a platform for left-wing and liberal views. Journalists no longer had to use pseudonyms and anonymous pamphlets to make their voices heard while avoiding the wrath of their proprietor.

Commercial television was a powerful regional motor – the

first Director-General of the Independent Television Authority, Sir Robert Fraser, was a Scots-Australian federalist and socialist – but Scottish Television was a cultural tundra. Its drama output was negligible, its light entertainment banal. It used the services of John Grierson, but it made no attempt to develop documentary, although *Seawards the Great Ships*, made in 1958, showed that Grierson had lost none of his gifts. Only in sport and in news coverage did it compete with the BBC, which had been inert for a couple of decades. Parties and pressure groups saw the value of the increased coverage, and the emergence of newscasters, announcers and reporters with a Scottish reputation provided university debaters with new routes into politics.

Commercial television, and the BBC's reaction to it, reinforced in a much more explicitly political manner the national identity which the decline of the traditional institutions was currently eroding. That identity might only take the form of the small-screen parochialism of the Scottish news bulletins or the neo-Kailyardery of *Dr Finlay's Casebook* and *Sutherland's Law*, but it existed and it was capable of development. It took an English director, Peter Watkins, to dramatise, and de-mythologise, Scottish history, in *Culloden* (1964). The improvement by the end of the 1960s could be seen in the career of James MacTaggart. With Edward Boyd he created a seedy Glasgow gumshoe, Daniel Pike, the first of a sequence of credible and witty *films policiers* which modulated its Chandler and Hammett prototypes in tune with the Clydeside-Atlantic preoccupation with urban tracklessness. With George Mackay Brown in *An Orkney Trilogy*, he transformed a literary vision into memorable images. Bleak and uncomfortable, but with a wild gallows humour, these showed enormous potential for future collaboration. These qualities survived MacTaggart's early death to surface in the work of Tom MacDougall – *Just Your Luck* and *Every Other Saturday* – and the austere films of Bill Douglas – *My Childhood* and *My Ain Folk* – both of whom won major European prizes. Their Scotland fitted no cosy nationalist stereotype, but its predicament was real enough.

'FROM SCENES LIKE THESE'

In 1936, in *Scott and Scotland*, Edwin Muir had written that, despite the efforts of MacDiarmid, the prospect of creating an integrated Scottish literature was remote:

> In an organic literature poetry is always influencing prose and prose poetry; and their interaction energises them both. Scottish poetry exists in a vacuum; it neither acts on the rest of literature nor reacts to it; and consequently it has shrunk to the level of anonymous folk-song.

This stung MacDiarmid to violent rejoinder yet, thirty years later, it still appeared valid. The only major novel-writing talents to appear comparable to the poets had been Neil Gunn, Naomi Mitchison and Lewis Grassic Gibbon. Periodical production and short-story writing limped along from year to year. Muir's own commitment to Scottish culture, his wardenship of the Scottish Adult Education College at Newbattle, gifted to the nation by the imperial administrator and diplomat Philip Kerr, Lord Lothian, ended in disappointment and estrangement. Individual cultural communications developed but without critical standards, intellectual interchange or – all too frequently – social relevance. In a survey of Scottish literature published in 1971 the critic Alexander Scott sounded like a company director announcing record-breaking productivity:

> Even Scotland, where the poets have always outnumbered the novelists – and most of them have been poets too – has never experienced such a pullulation of poetry as in the last decade, and while the cascade of slim volumes pours from the presses, there seems no reason to believe that anything short of a major slump, and a consequent catastrophic cut in Arts Council subsidies, can stem the flood in the foreseeable future.

Poetry, since MacDiarmid the imaginative centre of Scottish culture, seemed, in the 1960s, closer to politics than to literature, not because poets were nationalist, but because they had the same sort of internal discipline and critique as political movements. Scottish poetry didn't travel: apart from MacDiarmid and Norman MacCaig, and perhaps Edwin Morgan, George Mackay

Brown and Iain Crichton Smith, few Scots poets were widely known outside of the country. But it was a participating community. As many seemed to write poetry as to read it. Parties were formed; small magazines assaulted one another; a little Arts Council money went a long way. How good was the output? Who read it? Did it change things utterly? Or at all?

The 'society of the poem' in Scotland has yet to find its historian. What he or she will find will not be of even quality. Much was mediocre or derivative: too many periodicals foundered under the weight of imitations of Ginsberg, Lowell or Brecht. 'Vigour and variety,' as Edwin Morgan pointed out 'don't guarantee a direction or consolidate an achievement'. But at least the Scottish scene was intellectually vibrant, compared with the provincial-lad-made-good ethos of London. Kingsley Amis, Philip Larkin and the Movement ruled out 'philosophers or paintings or novelists or art galleries or mythology or foreign cities or other poems' as fit subjects for poetry. But booze, copulation and death had their limits as inspiration, and ultimately imprisoned both imagination and sympathy. In Scotland this accidie was lacking, as was the coterie spirit. To acquire freedom of any sort the forces of darkness had to be challenged, as in the 1920s, and so the influence of MacDiarmid reasserted itself, not just the vernacular lyricist but the Carlylean sage of the uncompromising dialectic prose and the 'catalogue poetry' who sought to evolve a language complex enough to deal with industrialised materialism.

Paradoxically, the relatively weak pre-war nationalist movement got more literary attention than the 1960s SNP. There were no literary politicians equivalent to Gunn, MacDiarmid or Compton Mackenzie. Did this mean that modern nationalism owed little to intellectual or cultural values? William Wolfe was highly literate, but the SNP had a far more attenuated cultural presence than Gwynfor Evans's Plaid Cymru. Yet the responses of the greater renaissance writers – Muir, Gunn, MacDiarmid and Gibbon – had a complexity that went far beyond politics, being preoccupied with the problem of 'reifying' a Scotland out of a reality riven by the alternative loyalties of local community and cosmopolitan opportunism, and three possible literary languages. Grassic Gibbon – and he was the cosmopolitan opportunist *par excellence* – dramatised it in the address of the Minister at the end of *Sunset Song*:

Nothing, it has been said, is true but change, nothing abides, and here in Kinraddie where we watch the building of these little prides and little fortunes on the ruin of the little farms, we must give heed that these also do not abide, that a new spirit shall come to the land with the greater herd and the great machines.

This was Carlylean threat as much as progressive opportunity. In *Grey Granite*, the last novel of *A Scots Quair*, Gibbon reached the political life of industrial Scotland in the depression, but as his biographer, Ian Munro, has written:

Duncairn has no identity, none of that indefinable yet inescapable atmosphere known to the natives of any Scottish town. Gibbon's city is anonymous and voiceless despite the tumult of traffic and noise of its inhabitants.

Gibbon had at least attempted what Muir and Gunn, and even, for all his communism and materialism, MacDiarmid had seemed to avoid. 'If a city hasn't been written about, not even its inhabitants live there imaginatively,' Alasdair Gray makes one of his characters complain in *Lanark*. This gap could all too easily be plugged by comfortable anecdotage, an urban Kailyard carefully tended by the feature writers of the Scottish local press. Jack House and Cliff Hanley in Glasgow, Wilfred Taylor and Albert Mackie in Edinburgh, Cuthbert Graham in Aberdeen maintained a corporate memory with wit and humanity, but offered only a nostalgic response to the ruthless and mindless destruction of urban life by businessmen, councillors and – most notoriously – the universities.

The problem in the 1950s had still been Calvinism: the near-impossibility of getting out from under the Great Determinist, who lay heavily on the work of Robin Jenkins, George Friel, J. D. Scott and James Kennaway. Liberation could seemingly only come with some act of symbolic destruction wreaked on an imprisoning, semi-metaphysical Scotland. This private torment seemed more salient retrospectively than at the time: so much did Angry Young (and metropolitan) Men dominate the literary publicity machine. It was only in the 1960s that the social inquiry predicated by Gibbon was resumed, into the life of the cities and the 'unknown Scotland' of the central belt, in the novels of Alan Sharp, Archie Hind, Gordon Williams and William

MacIlvanney. Their achievement was uneven, and led Sharp and Williams away from Scotland to the lusher pastures of London and Hollywood. Perhaps they only showed the limitations of the novel in capturing and conveying social reality. But the predicament delineated is important enough, if depressing.

Gordon Williams's *From Scenes like These* accurately delineated a signpostless life in the central belt. Duncan Logan tries to struggle out of an industrial village in Ayrshire – ironically, close to the Reverend Micah Balwhidder's Dalmailing in Galt's *Annals of the Parish*. Life is grim, but meaningless rather than earnest. 'Getting on' no longer leads up and out, only circuitously to the wafflings of Logan's nationalist schoolteacher. Sex, when available, is hurried and insensitive. Love leads to marriage and a council house. Drink and the witlessness of the football terraces offer, at the end of the book, the conditioning which makes life in Kilcaddie tolerable. Logan could be out of Alan Sillitoe and Stan Barstow a decade earlier, but he has deeper, Scots, resonances – the booze-propelled *machismo* (in the 1970s Scotland had five times the alcoholism rate of England), the weak working-class politics, the decay of promotion through education. Throughout, Logan lapses in and out of dialect to suit different situations, an optional Scottishness neither wholly honest nor wholly false. Williams's book was not about nationalism, but he described the classic environment of *anomie* where nationalist politics was to put down its roots.

The problem remained what it had been in Carlyle's day: how to give the Scottish novel artistic and philosophical shape as well as documentary accuracy. Here the new novelists had to struggle; they lacked Walter Scott's and Grassic Gibbon's hard-read grasp of historical process and pattern. William MacIlvanney's experimentation exemplified one side of the problem. His translation of the Hamlet *mise-en-scène* to Kilmarnock in *Remedy is None* (1966) provided a structure, but a rather forced one, his *Docherty* (1975) and *The Big Man* (1985) emblematised the endurance of a sort of 'Iron John' figure from Scottish mining life. He was criticised for an over-allusive literary style, yet somehow this was true to the Scottish working-class predicament, what MacDiarmid had called 'a dream o' beauty dernin' yet/ Ahint its ugsome state'. In the 1980s MacIlvanney seemed to find his true voice as a documentarist of the human tragedies caused by

Smithian market economics divorced from Smithian 'sympathy', and as a political writer and speaker of great moral power.

On the other wing of realism was Alan Massie, briefly involved on the fringes of the home rule movement in the 1970s and subsequently elegant in regretting it. The Lampedusa of Charlotte Square could find little place for Scotland in the modern world, but seemed equally pessimistic about politics in general. Following a melodramatic encounter with nationalism in *A Night in Winter* (1983) he moved away to record the encounters of the old European order with assorted unpleasantnesses of the age of mass society. He remained, however, thornily present in Scottish society, unionism's not altogether consistent defender, the inevitable 'balancing opinion' to raucous home rulers. This was a seller's market, and he did not do badly out of it.

An older novelist, Robin Jenkins, was also moving towards the historical and political, in such novels as *Fergus Lamont* (1979) and *The Temptation of George Darroch* (1985). Themes he had originally rendered as metaphor now assumed the historical density of Walter Scott: the cultural-political career of Lamont, a monster of the Scottish renaissance; the involvement of Darroch in the Disruption of 1843, that fateful point at which Scotland seemed to withdraw from European intercourse and talk to itself.

Was it worth it? Was there a mass public for novels about ordinary people and their Scotland? Or did the ingenious formula still provide the fastest way out? A. J. Cronin had found it so in the past, and George MacDonald Fraser, James Herriot, Mary Stewart, Alastair MacLean, Ian Fleming, Dorothy Dunnett and Nigel Tranter were working flat out in the 1960s. The Scots – and the house of Collins in particular – seemed to have cornered the market for the 'good read'.

Not only social life got the realistic treatment. Sex beckoned delectably, but raised the questions that Victorian puritanism had repressed. The *Scotsman* columnist Wilfred Taylor wrote facetiously that Annie S. Swan handled sex 'more imaginatively and adventurously than D. H. Lawrence'. There was a case against Lawrence, but Annie S. Swan (whose genuine feminism and nationalism were smothered in calculated Kailyard sentiment) wasn't it. MacDiarmid and Grassic Gibbon, thirty years earlier, had treated sex as explicitly, and with much more social realism, than Lawrence. Possibly Lallans acted as a linguistic fig-leaf. What both had to say about sex and consciousness, and sexual roles in society, went beyond conventionalities about freedom and fulfilment, and the Burnsian dualism of sentimentality and bawdry. If their Scottishness allowed them to be read while the old puritanism still applied, their belief that liberty involved sexual equality and social involvement remained after permissiveness had worn off.

At the same time another element of the Scottish intellectual tradition surfaced in R. D. Laing's investigation of schizophrenia, *The Divided Self* (1960), and his notion that madness was a protest against a constricting society. This wasn't simply a reprise of Hogg and Stevenson, but arose from a dialogue on philosophy, personality and society among academics, medical men and the Iona Community which had been particularly lively in post-war Glasgow, where the exiled Jewish psycho-analysts Abenheimer and Schorstein found an unusually receptive ambience. When Laing came north for a visit in 1967 he was lionised, though the Scots distanced themselves from his later mysticism. Despite – or possibly because of – the puritan tradition, they were well placed to exploit the new freedoms, without falling for the bizarre and the outrageous.

UTOPIA NOW!

Leslie Stephen likened the impact of secular ideas on English intellectuals of the 1860s to an ice-cap slowly sapped by warm currents. Suddenly the old environment split and crumbled and altered beyond recognition. Something like this happened over a century later in Scotland. The collapse of religious constraints and prescriptions meant accepted mores – marriage for example – depended more on consent than on convention. The resulting fragility was only partly exposed by a fourfold increase in divorces between 1960 and 1974. Individuals had to work out their relationships for themselves, with results which were as painful as they were liberating. It did not require the frequent production of Ibsen and Strindberg at the local repertories to show that the preoccupations of these great subversives had at last taken root. Brands and Lovborgs were identifiable; all over the place Noras were slamming doors; in every drowsy coastal town there were Bernicks and Manders to be fought and Stockmanns to be supported. Freedom was indivisible. The people who wanted to shut down the Traverse Theatre, ban 'filth' at the Edinburgh Festival, and stop the publisher John Calder from addressing the General Assembly were also likely to think well of South Africa and the atom bomb.

All this was utopian and thus by definition non-nationalist, although some notion of utopia helped when it came to understanding MacDiarmid's achievement. A sense of new possibility challenged all the traditional institutions with aims which were either individualist – like sexual freedom or freedom of expression – or collectivist, like the reorganisation of industry and politics. The connection between the two was direct. Wilde's *The Soul of Man under Socialism* (1891) seemed, more than any of the speeches of the Labour leadership, to embody what was expected from 'the white heat of the technological revolution':

> Unless there are slaves to do the ugly, horrible, uninteresting work, culture and contemplation become almost impossible. Human slavery is wrong, insecure and demoralising. On mechanical slavery, on the slavery of the machine, the future of the world depends . . . the community by means of organisation of machinery will supply the useful things, the beautiful things will be made by the individual.

Laurence Daly, the miners' leader, said in 1965 or 1966 that Wilde had converted him to socialism. It was not only the university-educated youth who regarded the Wilsonian future in this sanguine light. But the new order did not rise on the ruins of the old. However alien the antics of the SNP seemed, by the 1970s utopia had vanished to infinity.

It was, however, during this interregnum that political writing returned, for the first time since the heyday of the *Edinburgh Review*. Hitherto, books and articles on contemporary Scottish society and politics had mainly been propagandist: Professor H. J. Paton's *The Claim of Scotland*, which appeared in 1967, was one of the last of the genre. Now the task was to understand why Scotland was different, and what long-term factors, if any, underlay the current political upheavals. Writing about Scotland became almost an obsession among the red Scots, at home and abroad – and among recent immigrants. There were several symposia: Edinburgh University produced *Scotland: Government and Nationalism* (1969), edited by its American economics professor J. N. Wolfe; Glasgow academics retorted with *The Scottish Debate* (1971), edited by Neil MacCormick; two literary expatriates set to work as well: Karl Miller, then editor of the *Listener*, in *Memoirs of a Modern Scotland* (1970), and Duncan Glen, Hugh MacDiarmid's biographer, in *Whither Scotland* (1971). The contents of these books were variable but they contained enough of value – Nicholas Phillipson's discussion of semi-independence within the Union, Tom Nairn's exploration of the post-Reformation dualism in the Scots intellect, Harry Hanham's studies of the development of Scottish administration – to stimulate a continuing and serious inquiry. Even Ross recognised this and appointed Dr Gavin McCrone, historian of the post-war Scottish economy and regional policy expert, to head the new Economic Planning Unit at St Andrew's House in 1969. With books like James Kellas's *Modern Scotland* (1968), Hanham's *Scottish Nationalism* and Christopher Smout's *A History of the Scottish People* (both 1969), the treatment of Scotland moved away from myth, recollected grievance and the romanticism which had penetrated earlier popular accounts. There was a long way to travel yet, especially in transmitting this new objectivity to the public. The Canadian journalist John Prebble found a ready audience when he recounted the vivid traditions of Highland deprivation. Messrs Berresford Ellis and Seumas Mac a'Ghobhainn invented, in *The Scottish Insurrection of 1820*, some new legends of their own. The Messianic figure of John MacLean was reincarnated by his biographers, rather than understood.

There was at least an apparatus of criticism which would ensure some objectivity. With half a dozen more or less durable periodicals, the later 1960s had come far from the time of the limping *Saltire Review* and the infrequent poetry periodical, *Lines Review*. Political parties and university clubs produced their magazines, and funding by various foundations was now available for several independent publications. The whole thing could be explained by the 'duplicating revolution' and Arts Council subsidies, but it also showed that there were more people to write, and there was more to write about.

As elsewhere in Europe, the universities took the lead. They had traditionally exerted little influence on the views of their students, many of whom were daily commuters, but in the post-Robbins era, more lived in flats and in residences. A student bohemia began to emerge: pretentious, immature and self-indulgent, but validly attempting through little magazines and the student press to articulate and rationalise. The attempts of the international student lefty to settle down in Scotland were hilariously guyed by Gaston le Jobbe, a creation of the future student Rector of Edinburgh University, Jonathan Wills. Gaston, in beard and beret, persistently encountered Embro punters who referred to him in expansive mood as 'Djimmeh' and otherwise as 'wan o' they fung studints'. 'Fung studint' became in 1968 the Scots version of 'Juifs Allemands', and was properly worrying to the students themselves. In the next few years, as some minor disturbances came to a head, with more official panic than student cohesion, the total absence of any student–working-class link became palpable. Much subsequent student literary activity was directed at discovering why this was the case, and what could be done about it. On the whole this produced its dividends. The Edinburgh University Student Publications Board graduated from publishing guides to pubs, and student and charity newspapers, to producing a quarterly, the *New Edinburgh Review*, in 1968, the *Red Paper on Education* in 1969, the first publication in English of essays by Gramsci in 1972, and in 1975 the *Red Paper on Scotland*, a hefty and very valuable symposium on Scottish government and society, edited by the second student Rector, Gordon Brown. Students who had served their apprenticeship on such ventures moved out, not only into television, Fleet Street and the Scottish papers, but into small publishing concerns and a rash of community newspapers, of which the *West Highland Free Press*, founded in 1972, provided a durable and effective radical voice in the Highlands on the eve of the oil boom.

The government, in the shape of the Arts Council, became a major catalyst. Until Labour took office Arts Council funds had been very limited and about half went on opera. The Scottish allocation had actually dropped from 8.4 per cent in 1948–9 to 6.3 per cent in 1963–4. Things improved under the godmotherly influence of Jennie Lee. The Council's grant-in-aid rose by a factor of 3.5 between 1964 and 1970; the Scottish allocation climbed to 11.4 per cent. Hitherto most of this had gone to the Edinburgh Festival and the orchestras, now it was much more widely distributed. The major coup was musical – the rapid expansion of Scottish Opera, founded in 1963 – but funds also reached literature – not simply poetry, but critical and even political magazines. For the first time these had some financial stability, and were even able (occasionally) to pay contributors, while bursaries to writers went some way to stemming the drift south.

The Arts Council helped *Scottish International*, run by three poets, Robert Garioch, Edwin Morgan and Robert Tait, to change from being rather glossy and arty into an impressive platform for dissenting and critical views. Its conference, 'What Kind of Scotland', in April 1973, made clear to many the full implications of the oil boom; and from it John McGrath's 7:84 Theatre Company set out to capture the Highlands for socialism with *The Cheviot, the Stag, and the Black, Black, Oil. Scottish International* succumbed a year later, but the torch was flung on. Mistakes were still being made, but the literary-political momentum continued. The *New Edinburgh Review* survived the left-wing *Galgacus* and the political fortnightly *Question*. The Edinburgh Student Publication Board followed the *Red Paper* with the *Yearbook of Scottish Government*. When, in 1976, the *Scottish Educational Journal* republished MacDiarmid's *Contemporary Scottish Studies*, the veteran could reflect that:

> one of the aims of my *Contemporary Scottish Studies* has now been realised – the recognition that anything that purports to be a contribution to Scottish literature must be judged by the standards applied to literature in all other civilised countries.

PAPERING THE TOWN RED

In 'Parliamo Glasgow' Stanley Baxter translated 'Erra perra toon cooncillors' as 'Here come two intellectuals'. Before the 1950s the Scottish definition of the word was scarcely more comprehensive. In Scotland an intellectual meant a professional man, who lived a life dominated by a few choice institutions: family, Kirk, golf club, former pupils' club. Except when decorously mediated through Scottish Orchestra concerts, the Royal Scottish Academy and touring drama companies, culture, in any creative sense, was alien, part of a Mr Hyde world of Rose Street bohemians. Crossing the divide usually meant assuming another identity. It could almost be the same in politics: one set of views for employer and colleagues, another for propagandising. The pseudonym flourished in the land of Hamish Henderson's Alias MacAlias. But with the post-war decline of the old estates, and a loosening of traditional strictures on behaviour, alternatives grew and something much closer to a classic European intelligentsia began to emerge, with some correspondence between social situation, style of life, and politics.

The Scottish 'state sector' intellectuals – academics, teachers, those in the culture business – realised that if they wanted to stay in Scotland they would be constrained by the geography and society of the place. So they resembled for the first time their counterparts in nineteenth-century Europe. Moreover, they had an ideology to hand which might enable them to rationalise their position. Into a country which had since 1843 avoided political dialectic, 'revisionist' Marxism irrupted in the mid-1950s, challenging (among other things) the traditional anti-nationalism of the red Scots.

Its significance was fourfold: the schism in the Communist Party in 1956 spread a greater ideological awareness among the Scottish left; the New Left's attempt to establish a base among the Scottish working class encouraged a national identification; its Marxism paid unprecedented attention to the effect of the political and cultural superstructure on the economic base. Finally, this complex analysis led to different patterns of intellectual integration with politics, north and south of the border. While the scholarship of left-wing historians like E. P. Thompson and Christopher Hill went some way to creating – for the first time – an English nationalism, the New Left opened to the Scots the prospect of new links with Europe.

The Communist Party's break-up over the invasion of Hungary in November 1956 released a number of articulate and effective writers, thinkers and organisers, who coalesced with non-party socialists. (MacDiarmid, typically, rejoined the Communist Party, although he had protested over Hungary.) By 1962 there were New Left Clubs in all the university towns and one development unique in Britain, the Fife Socialist League, was formed. A successful independent left-wing political party, it was run by Lawrence Daly, the ex-communist organiser of the Mineworkers' Union in Fife. But, this apart, the New Left showed up the weakness of a political intelligentsia in Scotland, the absence of the close identification between working-class power and creative political thought that they admired in Italy and Yugoslavia.

The New Left wasn't nationalist. Indeed it seemed tailor-made for English academic immigrants, analytical and given to the rather moralistic commitment of the likes of CND, apprehensive about the nature of working-class activism, although curious to find out what precisely were the links that bound base to superstructure. Other activists, notably ex-communists, were more positive about politics and more preoccupied with Scotland. Under its Scottish General Secretary, John Gollan, the Communist Party had campaigned on Scottish economic problems and since 1951 had favoured a Scottish Parliament, a solution revived by Lawrence Daly in the *New Left Review* in 1962:

> A Scottish Parliament could certainly contain a majority of Labour and radical members. There is every chance that it could not only revitalise Scotland's economic and cultural life but that it might well set the pace for the progressive social transformation of the rest of Britain.

Even where this was not endorsed, socialists connected with the New Left, such as Norman Buchan and Hamish Henderson in their folk-song and folklore studies, and David Craig with *Scottish Literature and the Scottish People* (1961) explored the connections between culture and political mobilisation, seeking to re-create links that the formal structures of politics had allowed to decay. Politically, most of this activity flowed not into nationalism but into the regional policy which marked Labour's reponse during the late 1950s and early 1960s. By 1966 such New Left activists as Buchan and Neil Carmichael were in Parliament and further committed to the Labour programme. To them, the nationalist upsurge seemed an irrelevant outbreak of lower middle-class false consciousnes. Buchan wrote in 1970:

> If Scotland suffers from the uneven development of capitalism in common with other areas then it is right that the entire UK resources should be used to restore the imbalance . . . if we remove all Scottish political control

and influence over what all accept is a single economic entity . . . then we are left inevitably to be controlled by that total economy. . . . Paradoxically, total separation means less real independence.

There was logic behind this position, given the SNP attempts to prove that English taxation was robbing Scotland blind, but the point remained that regional policy hadn't worked and 'false consciousness' had – not only in Scotland but, more ominously, in Northern Ireland. Scotland's problems might be the same as those of the North-East and Lancashire, but responses were distinctive and didn't validate any 'real' working-class consciousness. Knoxian denunciations by Scottish Labour politicians of those with differing views didn't add to their own democratic credentials. To younger people, who had been outside British politics, this seemed dogmatic and intellectually conservative, even if the Nationalists themselves appealed little. The New Left itself split between those who were now part of Labour's 'patronage state' and defended it, and those who wanted to examine the roots of the revolt against it.

A similar divergence existed by 1968 in English left-wing politics, with the publication of the New Left's *May Day Manifesto*, and the desertion of Labour by many who, like its editor Raymond Williams, had given it tentative endorsement in 1964. The *Manifesto* 'wholeheartedly welcomed' nationalism, rather optimistically conflating it with radicalism – something the left in Scotland was scarcely likely to do. But the revisionism of the Edinburgh historian Victor Kiernan, whose 'Notes on Marxism in 1968' in the *Socialist Register* proved a notable landmark; regarded nationalism as more than 'false consciousness'; especially when, in the following year, Tom Nairn of the *New Left Review* started the first of several bouts with the beast. 'The Three Dreams of Scottish Nationalism' was dismissive, but it did recognise that nationalism in Scotland had a chronology different to that of nationalism in the rest of Europe, and that Scottish civil society – in being both nationalist and assimilationist – was unique. Nairn's conversion to nationalism was in the future, but his work, and the rediscovery of Gramsci, ensured that the question thereafter preoccupied the intellectual left.

At that stage, the right was silent. It was difficult to see what it could say, as Enoch Powell, the prophet of the market economy,

166

saw emigration as the solution to the problems of the Scottish economy. 'Scientific' middle opinion surfaced in January 1972 in the *Ecologist*'s 'Blueprint for Survival', roughly a third of whose signatories were Scots. The 'Blueprint' scouted nationalism as 'a dangerous and sterile compromise' but in its invocation of small-scale industry and agricultural self-sufficiency it met the views of some nationalists as well as those of the environmentally aware young, Marxist or not.

In the 1970s it seemed that new thought had to come from the left. In a country so dependent on government, the prescriptions of the market economists had little relevance. The problems at issue were those of authority and control. As Neal Ascherson, who returned in 1975 from being European correspondent of the *Observer*, put it:

Scotland is not really within the category of 'capitalist economies' as they are usually classified. Neither is it socialist. It hangs somewhere between Eastern and Western Europe, a stateist economy without a state.

The links between the intellectuals and publicity and administration were strong; always useful in an 'administrative state'. But in another direction, where their formal loyalties lay, there was a serious weakness. The Scottish working class might indeed be, in John McGrath's words, 'one of the strongest in Europe, with a considerable experience of struggle and great maturity as a result', but the intellectuals had little real contact with it or knowledge of its political behaviour. Reviewing the *Red Paper*, Kiernan commented pessimistically that Gordon Brown,

laments, as he well may, that after all these years Scotland has 'no socialist book club, no socialist labour college . . . only a handful of socialist magazines and pamphlets'. If any large part of the working class wanted such things, Scotland would have them.

The university *men* – there was hardly a woman among them – who wrote the *Red Paper* had become politically involved. But their prospective allies were far from being Gramsci's conscious proletarian intelligentsia. Battered by economic decline and the ineptitude of their own representatives, the people of the tower

167

blocks and the bleak estates – the Scotland that no one ever visited – responded to the old loyalties and the old songs. Fletcher's prophecy – that ballads and not laws made a nation – seemed to be coming true.

6

A DANCE TO THE MUSIC OF NATIONALISM, 1945–1979

At any rate, I think we should pay more attention to the small but violent separatist movements which exist within our own island. They may look very unimportant now, but, after all, the Communist Manifesto was once a very obscure document, and the Nazi Party only had six members when Hitler joined it.

George Orwell, *Tribune*, 14 February 1947

MACCORMICK'S MOMENT

In the spring of 1962 Max Aitken, Lord Beaverbrook, returned briefly to Scotland. Thirty years before, he had been a goblin godfather to Scottish nationalism; now, old and ill, he travelled to the village of Torphichen in West Lothian, a rural island in the wastes of the industrial belt, from which the Aitkens had emigrated to Canada over a century earlier. Bizarre coincidences are the bonuses of history. The dying prophet of a dying Empire – the most restless of the red Scots – visited the place where, within a few weeks, the revival of nationalist politics was to begin. The Scottish National Party had one of its few branches in the village, but it was from this branch that the initiatives which were to transform it, and Scottish politics, were to come.

The party that William Wolfe, a local chartered accountant, had joined in 1959, had changed little since its victory at Motherwell fourteen years before. Its membership was around the 2,000 mark, its leadership had changed only by resignation and expulsions – a resilient little sect, rather than a political movement. In 1946 it had adopted a new constitution, the work of a group of members around Dr Robert McIntyre, which was

169

less a programme than a set of values. Influenced by social credit, populism, Catholic distributism, it repudiated size, centralism and the concentration of economic power in private or state hands. Beyond this, it was eclectic. As Hanham wrote, it found a place for just about everything 'except a frank acceptance of the modern state and of modern bureaucratised industrial, political, trade union, and commercial empires'. McIntyre justified this by arguing that contemporary ideologies made for clumsy, preconceived 'solutions', but his dominance in the party imposed its own constraints. The SNP lacked the European profile of the post-Saunders Lewis Plaid Cymru: the interest in Danish co-operatives and people's colleges, the small-scale socialism that attracted 'green' thinkers such as Leopold Kohr. Its 'Sinn Fein' line of putting independence first – once a majority of SNP members was returned to Westminster, they would withdraw and set up their own Dáil – coexisted with a much more exclusive party spirit. The 'open party' which, despite their mutual hostility, Douglas Young and John MacCormick both favoured was abolished in 1948. Young, and MacDiarmid, joined MacCormick in apostasy.

Roland Muirhead remained a member, but wrote in 1957 (he was then 89) that 'the present policy of the party has proved a complete failure'. Its impact was limited to winning a few seats on the councils of small burghs, but it fared no worse than his own movement, the Scottish National Congress, founded in 1950, which remained in communion of a sort with the ILP, and shared in the decline of the old libertarian left. Between 1945 and 1960, to Muirhead's and the SNP's chagrin, the man at centre stage was 'King John' MacCormick himself.

When MacCormick set up his 'Scottish Convention' after leaving the SNP, little love was lost between the two groups. A squib 'On a North British Devolutionist' appeared in the *Scots Independent* in 1944:

> They libbit William Wallace.
> He gar'd them bleed.
> They dinna libb MacFoozle.
> They dinna need.

But after 1945 MacCormick took the initiative. In March 1947 Scottish Convention held a National Assembly in Glasgow, on the lines of the one planned for September 1939. Representatives of political parties, local authorities, the churches, trade unions and so on were invited. A resolution demanding home rule was passed almost unanimously, and a committee drafted a constitutional scheme to be presented to a second assembly in 1948. Once endorsed, this was made the burden of a Scottish Covenant, the signing of which started at the third assembly, in October 1949. Nearly two million put their names to it.

MacCormick was a gifted orator and organiser, but an unsubtle strategist. Scottish Convention was campaigning for a consensus on home rule, which meant holding Labour MPs to their election pledges of 1945, when, with Motherwell in mind, they had promised it high priority. But it was too easy to swim with the anti-centralist, anti-socialist tide. In late 1947, believing he had united the Unionist and Liberal Parties on devolution, MacCormick stood against Labour at Paisley. The Liberals repudiated the 'pact' and he found himself supported by some rather implausible converts like Walter Elliot and Peter Thorneycroft: not the best opening to an all-party campaign.

MacCormick won – not Paisley but the enmity of the government. Arthur Woodburn, the Secretary of State, a supporter of devolution during the war, became bitterly hostile. However many signatures the Covenant gained, even when it was endorsed by the likes of Tom Johnston, the Kirk and the Communist Party – this factor was critical. Woodburn made some slight alterations to Scottish business in the House – an initiative which was recalled in Ian Lang's 'taking stock' exercise in 1993 – but otherwise his panicked responses made Attlee fire him in 1950. His successor, Hector McNeil, a former Beaverbrook journalist and high-flyer in the Foreign Office who had got rather too close to the flare of Guy Burgess, took an even harder line. The Unionists made sympathetic noises, but no more. Revivalism could not guarantee sustained pressure, and MacCormick failed to take the chance presented by the two elections of 1950 and 1951. Instead, he recaptured his undergraduate past by helping steal the ancient Scottish Coronation Stone from Westminster Abbey on Christmas Day 1950 and smuggling it north to Arbroath, where it was recovered on 11 April 1951. The escapade was popular but inappropriate, enhancing emotional nationalism rather than MacCormick's usual canny moderatism.

After this, the Convention ended in circumstances at once

anticlimactic and, on the government's part, slightly sinister. Churchill conceded greater administrative devolution, but instructed the Balfour Commission on Scottish Affairs (1952) to avoid the home rule issue. The result conformed to what James Bulpitt has called the 'central autonomy' pursued by the Conservatives, with 'high politics' reserved to Westminster and Scotland left to the local establishment, governing through consultation. The Convention involved itself in a lawsuit in which MacCormick challenged the title of the new Queen to be called Elizabeth II in Scotland. This produced a famous judgment by Lord Cooper, a Unionist politician but legal nationalist, denying that the concept of parliamentary sovereignty had any place in Scottish constitutional theory, but the government won anyway. Some youngsters took matters a stage further and blew up pillar-boxes with the new royal insignia – the Special Branch egging them on. This conveniently coincided with an IRA offensive, and helped discredit the Convention, which faded out. MacCormick had lost his health, and his lawyer's business, through his devotion to it. His old opponent, Muirhead, helped keep him going and he contested Roxburghshire in the 1959 election, as a Liberal. He died in 1961.

Scottish Convention demonstrated the benefits and the penalties of seeking consensus support from the Scots estates. When they thought themselves under threat – in this case from Labour – their role in a 'popular front' could be impressive. But MacCormick's front never included the ordinary people who were, in the late 1940s, creating the mass Labour Party. Only they could have given his schemes political continuity, as the Irish had a century earlier supported O'Connell. Scottish Convention sustained the nationalism developed during the war – a reservoir of support awaiting the next concurrence of institutional and political unease. But the equilibrium of the estates had been restored, and they deserted.

Two events in 1953 were emblematic of a deceptive tranquillity. After the Coronation – Churchill's last pageant – the young Queen visited Edinburgh and had the 'Honours of Scotland' presented to her in St Giles. The historian Dr Gordon Donaldson, an undemonstrative man, observed in Lady Bracknell-like tones that, confronted with the panoply of the Scots crown jewels, the monarch was dressed in a short blue costume, and carried . . . 'a *handbag*'. Later that year Hamish

Henderson, folk-song collector and communist, knocked at a door in an Aberdeen housing scheme, and started stumbling through a traditional ballad. 'You're terrible,' said the housewife who had opened it. 'You'd better come in and I'll sing it to you right.' Jeannie Robertson, a traveller, had all the classic ballads in her head. The assertion of Maurice Lindsay that 'the tradition in which Burns wrought . . . is gone for ever' had been disproved by a phenomenon as dramatic as – and much more genuine than – Ossian.

THE SNP REVIVES

The leadership of the SNP might appear ineffective, but it survived like a modest family business. It was not sectarian in the left-wing sense, with an elaborate liturgy and frequent backslidings. It had the simplicity of eighteenth-century Scottish religious dissent: a single political tenet which was the 'one thing needful'. Relevant enough, as McIntyre pointed out, when the policies of the major parties produced a continuing drift towards centralisation: anything more complicated would trap itself in its own logic. This philosophy served the party well in its rise in the 1960s; by the time its drawbacks were apparent it was a far different organisation from the one which Wolfe, who had been a Convention and Saltire activist, had joined.

Scotland went its own way in the election of 1959 but the Labour Party was the beneficiary. The five SNP candidates had the curiosity value of the ILP, or other revenants from the red Clyde, but saved only one deposit: Dr McIntyre's. Within two years, however, the party was doing well at by-elections, which brought into the leadership two men, Wolfe and Ian Macdonald, who modernised it and created a remarkable publicity machine. Out of the 'unknown Scotland', both took advantage of the Labour Party's uncertain grasp. Macdonald, born in India, was a farmer and had been a pilot in the RAF. He had become a Nationalist at Glasgow University, McCormick's former stronghold, now a nursery of ambitious young Labour politicians. In November 1961 he stood at Glasgow Bridgeton, James Maxton's old seat, where Labour's choice of a pedestrian Glasgow councillor presented the SNP with a claim to the ILP home rule tradition. Macdonald was no left-winger, but he benefited from this disillusionment and took 18 per cent, nearly beating the Conservative into second place. He gave up his farm and, at £5 a week, joined the SNP as full-time national organiser, without guarantee of salary or tenure: the sort of gamble an earlier Scotsman might have made in business or colonial enterprise. Within a year he had the West Lothian election on his hands.

In West Lothian in February 1962 Labour's selection went to the other extreme. Tam Dalyell of the Binns, descendant of 'Black Tam', the scourge of the Covenanters, educated at Eton and Cambridge, was straight out of George Meredith or Henry James, an engaging and (as it proved) tenacious radical but, on the face of it, an odd choice for the most depressed constituency in Scotland. The Tory was downed by his own government which, in the 1962 budget, removed the tax concessions which kept the West Lothian shale oil industry alive. Only weeks after the Liberal triumph at Orpington, a third party now had a chance.

It was at this point that Wolfe, recuperating from a bout of flu, was approached by a scratch SNP Constituency Committee. Reading *A Scots Quair* had put him in receptive mood:

> I was moved to indignation and frustration not because of the loss of old and hard ways of life, but because I realised anew that the essence of Scotland was being so diluted and near destroyed without the people, the real folk of Scotland, being able to do anything about it. It was a kindly English imperialism that was destroying them, and their own vulnerability was making it so easy.

One chicken of the literary revival had come home to roost, if hardly in the way Gibbon had intended. He had taken his Kincardineshire folk into the new world of industrialisation and class politics. Wolfe was going to stop short and fight for the older ideal of community: his roll-call of his party workers – Kerr, Hamilton, MacDonald, McGillveray, Rankin, Kellock, Ross, Sim – and their jobs – papermill worker, watchmaker, seaman, painter, draughtsman, steelmill worker – is almost Gibbon's salute to the crofters of the Mearns at the end of *Sunset Song*. In the circumstances, and combined with Wolfe's personality, it proved a remarkably potent symbol.

Wolfe's role – as Vice-Chairman and after 1969 Chairman of the party – reflected distinctive qualities in the SNP's organisation, paralleled only by Gwynfor Evans in Plaid Cymru. Never a successful candidate, he was no tactician, no theorist, not even an organiser. He did not dominate his party but between 1960 and 1982 he symbolised it through an Orwellian 'decency'. Even left-wing critics, like Neal Ascherson or the playwright John McGrath, qualified political criticism with personal regard. His role symbolised the SNP's sense of being a community as well as a movement, with Wolfe its conscience rather than its leader, conciliating and inspiring, like Keir Hardie in the ILP, and by instinct rather than skill negotiating an openness to democracy in the agreeable chaos of the SNP annual conference. This was the old Scotland at its most responsible, transferring its essentially religious values to secular life.

West Lothian created, in embryo, the alliance that underwrote later SNP success. Activists included veterans of 1950 (when scarcely a thousand votes were polled) and left-wingers who had left the Labour Party because of its renunciation of unilateral nuclear disarmament, a cause with which Wolfe sympathised. Macdonald's team battened on the shale oil issue – not the last time when oil and the fortunes of the SNP were to be linked. Wolfe stumped energetically round a landscape which anthologised the condition of Scotland: old royal burghs, anonymous colliery villages, run-down factories and docks, looming over them the surreal dereliction of vast red tips of burnt shale. Even a mediocre Labour candidate would have won, and Dalyell proved a tough opponent. But Wolfe came second, the Tory and Liberal far behind. Since the Tories had been the majority Scottish party in 1955, and the Liberals under Jo Grimond were bidding to become the 'third force', both had real cause for concern.

THE LIBERAL CHALLENGE

The SNP fought four by-elections before the 1964 general election, without much impact, but Wolfe and his West Lothian activists rapidly changed the party. At the 1963 conference they made up about a quarter of the delegates and helped elect Wolfe Vice-Chairman, the first recruit to the national executive for years. The party went left on issues like disarmament and land nationalisation and, largely through Wolfe's shrewd patronage of younger members, especially students, managed to create a strong (by Scottish standards) project-based structure which solved the perennial problem of combining activism with cohesion. The recession made radical ideology acceptable, and the SNP could draw on individuals and single-issue causes – nuclear disarmament, opposition to railway closures, or the co-operative control of industry – of great value in directing its subsequent campaigns.

After 1963–4 Wolfe directed publicity and development, his colleague Douglas Drysdale, a foundry-master from Falkirk, organisation and finance. In 1965 they were joined by Rosemary Hall as Publicity Secretary. Like Wolfe, she had been involved with the Saltire Society, and transferred its preoccupation with design to the SNP's publicity, which soon became the best of any British party. Central to this was the party symbol, a combined thistle and saltire, like an alpha sign stood on end. White and red on a blue ground, this stood out on documents and badges, but (in a country addicted to graffiti) it could also easily be scrawled on bus shelters and lamp-posts. There had been nothing like it, opponents said, since the swastika: but this was sour grapes.

Good organisation and a nose for issues were not enough. The SNP faced Liberal rivals. The latter had revived in Scotland, particularly in the universities. They promised home rule and, in any head-on clash, would probably have seen off the SNP. In February 1964 Wolfe persuaded the National Council to offer them a pact. He argued, against the older members, that this would force the Liberals to come clean on Scotland: would they put home rule before their other commitments? Although a precedent existed in the pact of 1938, this placed the Liberal leadership in a quandary. It replied that home rule was integral to Liberal policy and could not be advanced as a joint demand. Yet enthusiasm for a pact endured; during the 1964 election both parties were on the whole careful not to contest the same seats.

In hindsight, this partial truce cost the Liberals dear: for the price of a few deposits they could have shattered the confidence of the SNP. Only where they were absent did the SNP poll well, and its performance was, overall, inferior to its last major campaign, in 1935. But it did creditably in seven seats, mainly in central Scotland, and membership more than doubled annually. In 1962 it had been 2,000; by 1966 it was 42,000. In that year the Liberals faltered, with a drop of about 15 per cent in the party's

Scottish vote, while the SNP doubled its poll. Although Scotland supplied half their MPs, the Liberals did not recover. Jo Grimond resigned in 1967, having led them to the federal gunfire. Although in 1968 federalism was endorsed by the Scottish Party, the Liberal Assembly, who favoured equating the position of Scotland and Wales with that of the English regions, repudiated it. Grimond could have mediated between the centre and the Scots; the new leader, Jeremy Thorpe, looked to the English suburbs. The ambitions of the ablest of the Scottish Liberal MPs, David Steel and Russell Johnston, were firmly oriented to Westminster and Europe, so their reaction was predictable; but other prominent activists, the party treasurer Michael Starforth and the broadcaster Ludovic Kennedy, moved to the SNP. By 1970, when the party lost a further two seats, the Liberal hour had passed.

THE FIRST WAVE

In 1970 the Nationalist hour seemed to have passed as well. Between 1967 and 1969 the SNP boomed and then, as spectacularly, slumped. In 1968 it had the largest party membership in Scotland, gained the highest proportion of the vote in the local elections, and expected major parliamentary gains. A year later it seemed unlikely to retain anything. Was this oscillation the natural fate of a mid-term protest, or of a genuine will to independence, vitiated by the immaturity of the party? In 1973 the first line would have won, but the resilience of the SNP and growing support for devolution showed that, even before North Sea oil changed the agenda, it was exploiting inadequacies in Scottish society which the other parties could not deal with.

Mid-term unrest set in only weeks after the election of March 1966. Right-wing and Liberal candidates gained 26 seats from Labour in the May local elections, but while the right was split between local 'Progressive' and national Conservative parties, the SNP was boosted by Plaid Cymru's victory in the Carmarthen by-election of 14 July, and started to win local council by-elections. Then, in early 1967, the MP for Labour's most marginal seat, Glasgow Pollok, died. The Conservatives produced Professor Esmond Wright, a political commentator for the BBC. Labour approached Alastair Hetherington, then editor of the *Guardian*, but ran Dick Douglas, a technical college lecturer renowned as a pillar of party orthodoxy. The SNP's choice, George Leslie, a Glasgow vet, turned out an impressive orator rather in the style of Maxton. Wright won – the last Tory to gain a Scottish seat at a by-election – the SNP polled 28 per cent and the Liberals came nowhere. This highlighted a swing to the SNP and the instability of 'mainstream' Labour when thus confronted. Dick Douglas would finish his parliamentary career as an SNP MP.

The SNP had now become news. Two months later it broke through in the councils, gaining 27 seats in the burgh elections and 42 in the counties, and increasing its poll from 4.4 per cent in 1966 to 18.4 per cent. The right-wing revival was stopped in its tracks and Labour, still hanging on in the major cities and towns, was badly rattled. Hitherto polls had been around 30 per cent and results reflected the popularity of the major parties. Issues were to do with rents and rates, but 'we're a' Labour here, son' council tenants usually didn't vote, even when a right-wing council was raising their rents – until they responded to the SNP's call to 'put Scotland first'. There was no SNP municipal policy, and few experienced candidates. New councillors appeared out of the blue. Mainly small businessmen, housewives and the self-employed, only about 40 per cent of one sample had more than three years' membership of the SNP and only 13.5 per cent had been members of other parties. If they offered an alternative to Labour's trade unionists and the Progressives' shopkeepers, it was only because they had little idea what council business entailed. With the exception of several middle-sized burghs in central Scotland, the SNP councillors made little impact. Defections and resignations, and a Labour recovery in 1969, made the aftermath of this coup an extended embarrassment. But in the summer of 1967 this was still the future. Greater victory was at hand.

Tom Fraser, the Minister of Transport, had not been a success and after leaving the government in December 1965 became chairman of the North of Scotland Hydro-Electric Board in May 1967. This meant a contest in the solid Labour constituency of Hamilton. The National Union of Mineworkers got their own man selected, although Hamilton had no working collieries. Alex Wilson, an elderly councillor, was in direct contrast to the SNP's Winifred Ewing, a prominent Glasgow solicitor with an ILP background: attractive, articulate and usefully emotional,

178

her selection reflected on the neglect of women candidates by the other parties. Although well projected by the SNP machine, she also had the good luck that the by-election, on 2 November, came at the nadir of Labour's fortunes, with a disastrous trade deficit making devaluation inevitable: too much even for a 16,000 majority. Mrs Ewing left Glasgow for Westminster on a special train, like Maxton and his Clydesiders forty-five years before. The point was not lost.

Hamilton registered in Downing Street, but the Conservatives were first to take action, setting up a study group on devolution. Edward Heath endorsed its report in May 1968, and formed a more authoritative 'Constitutional Committee' under Sir Alec Douglas-Home. Was this similar to Churchill's pseudo-endorsement of the Covenant in 1950? As then, the Scottish Labour hierarchy and Secretary of State were against any concession, and this – plus the economic situation – seems to have held Wilson's hand. A pro-devolutionist manifesto by the Berwickshire MP Professor John Mackintosh, the ablest constitutionalist in the House, didn't help; his relations with Ross and Wilson were icy. For a year Labour led with its chin, until Wilson announced the Crowther Commission in December 1968. This hiatus helped reassemble a home rule consensus. Churchmen, lawyers and academics – from the institutions which had, two decades before, backed the Covenant – rediscovered devolution, organised symposia and conferences. But, with Labour hostile and the Liberals weak, such publicity worked in favour of the SNP.

The media now became almost indulgent. Mrs Ewing was quickly signed up for a weekly column in the *Daily Record*, the only Scottish daily that supported Labour, while the *Scottish Daily Express* reanimated Beaverbrook's nationalism and covered her Westminster activities with a weekly report. Roy Thomson's northern outposts went devolutionist, the *Scotsman* producing in February 1968 a plan for the federal reconstruction of the United Kingdom; even the Dundee diehards, the *Courier and Advertiser* and the *Sunday Post*, made sympathetic noises. Alone of the major papers the *Glasgow Herald* remained hostile, providing a vehicle for high Tory and (oddly enough) far left attacks on the SNP.

This combination of respectable fellow-travelling and the SNP's impracticalities in local government provoked Labour.

Some MPs and activists supported devolution – the Scottish correspondent of the *Financial Times*, Andrew Hargrave's 'Devolution: the Third Choice', a Fabian tract of 1969, anticipated what was eventually offered in 1976, and the line of the rank and file was voiced by a strident pamphlet, 'Don't Butcher Scotland's Future', produced by two MPs, Alex Eadie and Jim Sillars, in the same year. This damned a Parliament of any sort as a concession to irrationalism and reaction. Despite the endorsement of some leftish literati like Sir Compton Mackenzie, Claud Cockburn and Cliff Hanley, who a couple of decades earlier had written 'Scotland the Brave', there were signs within the SNP that such suspicions had foundation.

Shortly after Hamilton the government announced the disbandment of the Argyll and Sutherland Highlanders, who had just sorted out the Arabs in Aden; their tough commander officer, Colonel Colin Mitchell, conformed to the traditional Scottish image of the popular fighting-man. They returned to a hero's welcome, especially in their depot town, Stirling, now controlled by the SNP. A 'Save the Argylls' campaign was mounted by the *Express*, and rumour had it that 'Mad Mitch' would stand as an SNP candidate. Mitchell turned out to be a Tory, and won West Aberdeenshire from the Liberals in 1970. (Subsequently he showed little taste for politics and so he didn't help them much.) But the imperial nostalgia of the episode jarred against the SNP's radical pretensions.

The SNP was further embarrassed by the 1320 Club. Founded in 1967 to commemorate the Declaration of Arbroath, it sought to supplement the SNP with a broader-based consensus, along the lines of the pre-1948 'open party'. Douglas Young was a founder member, along with such veterans as Wendy Wood, Oliver Brown and Hugh MacDiarmid. The SNP rapidly banned it, remembering its own past history. With good reason: conspiratorial and authoritarian tendencies within the Club came to the surface and in 1975 landed its secretary, Major F. A. C. Boothby, in prison for terrorist conspiracy. This sort of thing doubtless inspired the former editor of *Private Eye*, Andrew Osmond, and Heath's private secretary, Douglas Hurd, to fantasise about a takeover of part of the Highlands by Nats with Russians behind them. *Scotch on the Rocks*, thanks to Dr Iain MacLean of Oxford, contained not altogether fictional nationalists, annoying those parodied and infuriating those left out. Six years later the eccentric dictator of Uganda, Idi Amin, claimed to have had consultations with the provisional Scottish government, and telegraphed an embarrassed Wolfe to support 'the Scottish [who] are among the most brave people I have known in the world'. His message coincided with the trial of some very real terrorists.

Apart from backing Radio Free Scotland, which broadcast after hours on the BBC TV wavelength, the SNP kept to the letter and spirit of the law. Yet six trials, between 1971 and 1976, uncovered 'physical force' fringes to nationalism. Trifling compared with Northern Ireland, or the militant Welsh, could these still have ominous implications in the event of a constitutional breakdown? In 1972 three activists in a crazy little left-wing organisation, the Scottish Workers' Party, were sent down for over twenty years for bank robberies in Glasgow. In April and May 1975 two 'Army of the Provisional Government' trials – resulting from an inept bank raid – exposed a bizarre milieu of death oaths, assassination squads, and plans for military subversion. In 1976 a further batch of activists, some of whom had been SNP local officials, came before the courts on explosives charges. Although some convictions were secured, the existence of a 'Tartan Army' remained as shadowy – and as alien to the SNP's legalism – as before.

The SNP's problems were not due to militancy but to its own policy and its shaky support. Independence wasn't enough; it had to deal with local government and any steps towards home rule that the other parties might suggest. So, under pressure from Wolfe and the younger people in the party, policy formation groups were set up in 1968, which reported at the Oban conference in 1969. The SNP moved left of centre, subject to a degree of populism over crime and punishment. But the party constitution, which gave equal weight at conference to every local association, still divided the 'freedom first' school from the 'social democrats', although the latter secured the election of Wolfe as Chairman over the veteran Arthur Donaldson. This did not save the party from serious electoral trouble. In the May local elections its vote slumped from 30 per cent to 22 per cent; although 20 seats were gained, this was a fall of 80 on the 1968 performance. Labour was beginning to climb out of the trough. At an October by-election in Glasgow Gorbals, the centre of Catholic-Labour Clydeside (where the Labour posters were printed in green), the SNP vote fell to 25 per cent, and in the by-election in South Ayrshire in March 1970 – caused by the death of Emrys Hughes, Keir Hardie's son-in-law and former *Forward* editor, who had sponsored Mrs Ewing at Westminster – their poll fell to 20 per cent. The strongly unionist Labour candidate was the young Jim Sillars. In May, Labour revenged its 1967 losses by recovering its position almost completely. The SNP, its membership shrunk to half its 1968 level, did not look forward to the general election.

Political adversity had, however, produced a greater realism. Attitudes to independence became less absolute: there was talk of an Association of British States, or at least a customs union. This moderation stemmed partly from one of the SNP's pet propaganda points: the calculation that Scotland was, through taxation, subsidising England at sums variously computed at between £30 and £120 million per annum. This was questioned by the regional economist Dr Gavin McCrone, in *Scotland's Future: The Economics of Nationalism*, published in 1969. McCrone calculated that Scotland remained indebted to England to the tune of £56–£93 million per annum and, as a strong critic of government economic policies for Scotland in his earlier book *Scotland's Economic Progress, 1951–1960* (1965), this analysis seemed authoritative. But it was also a two-edged weapon, as in the early 1970s it provided an accurate basis for calculations about the surplus that would accrue to Scotland through the extraction of North Sea oil.

HANGING ON

If Harold Wilson was unexpectedly defeated in June 1970, the SNP surprised by surviving. Although it doubled its vote to 11.4 per cent it had upped its candidates to 65 from 23. Forty-two lost their deposits. In the cities its performance was poor, in Glasgow Gorbals falling to 7.4 per cent. At Hamilton Mrs Ewing was out by over 8,500 votes. The only consolation came in the Western Isles where Donald Stewart, the Provost of Stornoway, overcame a 40 per cent majority to oust Malcolm Macmillan, the non-resident Labour MP. The politics of Lewis and Harris ensured in their idiosyncratic way that a parliamentary presence continued. The Liberals lost two of their five Scottish seats, and took just 5.5 per cent of the vote. The SNP did well in central

Scottish counties, and in seven seats – Aberdeenshire East, South Angus, Argyll, Banff, Galloway, Hamilton and West Lothian – it lay second, a solid presence in the north-east, which oil developments, as yet only shadowy, were to make significant. And they were still able to hit Labour, by delivering a protest vote in the cities.

The rise of the SNP was not a one-off. In early 1967 the future *Sun* commentator Professor John Vincent, criticising the 'radicalism' of the Liberals, wrote in *New Society*:

> There is definitely room in British politics for a party based on middle-aged opposition to the secular humanism (to use no more actionable term) of the Oxford Union, on the opposition of the less demoralised and modern areas to the solipsism of the M1 country. There is room for a party which puts locality before party conflict.

The SNP could be fitted into a pattern which included the English as well as the *Blaid*, involving some populist Liberals and Enoch Powell, whose popularity was transmitted at by-elections to other Tories. Although there was no immigration issue in Scotland, there were similarities – the idea of a community under threat; the suspicion of bureaucratic machination. Powell reflected a defensive ethnicity uncharacteristic of Scotland, although he wasn't slow to prescribe for its ills:

> I don't think that because Scotland has five million people it has a right to that size of population . . . if you don't like your geographical position – being away from the dense population markets – get out of it . . . but don't ask people to give you handouts. That's the begging-bowl mentality.

He was blunt about independence. If the Scots wanted it, they should take it. Anything would be preferable to continued subsidy or devolution. English nationalism did not figure in the 1970 election, but it would recur in 1975, in the shape of Mrs Thatcher.

THE BLACK, BLACK OIL

From 1967 the ports of eastern Scotland started to fill up with odd-looking vessels, high-prowed and low in the stern, like floating lorries: tenders for oil-drilling rigs. Old shipyards and warehouses sprouted the insignia of international oil and engineering companies; local grocers stocked exotic American tinned foods; house prices rose. The hunt was on for North Sea oil. It had started over a decade earlier, when the discovery of a natural gas field in Holland suggested the likelihood of undersea oil-bearing strata. By 1965 gas was being piped from the sea off East Anglia, and in 1969, following the partition of the sea between the neighbouring states, a commercially viable field – the Ekofisk – was located in the Norwegian sector. As pressure on world supplies increased, the rigs were towed north to the treacherous waters off the north-east coast.

The finds would have to be rich indeed to justify £1 million for a test borehole and up to £500 million for a production platform the height of the Post Office Tower and as wide, at its base, as Edinburgh's New Town, from Princes Street to Queen Street. By late 1970, however, the investment seemed to be paying off. BP discovered a large field – the Forties – 120 miles north-east of Aberdeen. They talked in terms of a total output of 12 million tons a year in 1980. Then a sequence of events occurred which resulted in output forecasts rising by a factor of 13, to 158 million tons a year in 1980.

'It's Scotland's Oil!' Whatever the ethics of the proposition, the SNP chose an opportune moment, in September 1972, to launch a sophisticated and well organised campaign. The United States government was rumoured to be about to suspend quotas on oil imports, admitting an oil shortage, and the Middle East states were already beginning to show their bargaining strength against the cartel of the 'Seven Sisters'. A year later, after the Yom Kippur War, prices per barrel had risen by a factor of between six and eight on their 1972 levels. The North Sea oilfield was no longer a marginal economic proposition, and the SNP, with a lot of informed advice from the universities, a research officer, Donald Bain, who had studied the Alberta oil boom, and a press department run by a former Fellow at Chatham House, Stephen Maxwell, was well placed to exploit Scots disquiet about the descent of the multinationals on their coastline. The other parties might denounce the demand for Scottish control of oil revenues as selfish but, in a Scottish context, the oil issue was more complex than crude. To an extent not appreciated by politicians in the south, it presented the Scottish economy with as many problems as opportunities, problems which ultimately brought, as no other issue did, the whole concept of the Union into question.

The central issue was the result of geography aggravated by government policy. The economy of north-eastern Scotland was still largely agricultural, industry was limited, and, following decades of rural depopulation, the labour surplus was small. The local economy could not respond to the oil stimulus, while competition for labour, houses and services brought great economic disadvantages. Oil equipment could be supplied from the Clyde, with heavy engineering capacity – and unemployment – in abundance. But as time and investment for re-equipment were required, extraction would have to be slowed down. But the government, obsessed with disastrous balance of payments deficits, and reluctant to increase public expenditure, inevitably backed rapid extraction and the dispersal of 'onshore' activities around the northern coast, a policy which seemed deliberately to exacerbate the situation.

This threat was dramatised when an oil platform construction company, Taylor Woodrow, proposed to acquire land at Drumbuie, on Loch Carron in Wester Ross. The land had been covenanted by a previous owner to the National Trust for Scotland, yet the Heath government in early 1974 intended to help the company with an Act giving it general powers to acquire coastal land for oil-related use. Drumbuie was not the first – or the last – area of great beauty to be thus threatened, but the government's insensitivity promised the rape of the Scottish environment, while the credibility of conservation groups was endangered by the wholehearted participation of the Scottish upper classes in the oil business.

Although Scottish industry was increasingly dominated by the state, native capitalism had revived in the late 1960s. The five banks were now reduced to three, but the two largest were controlled from Scotland. Five merchant banks had also been set up, and the Bank of Scotland had established the International Energy Bank, with assets of £50 billion, to finance oil exploitation. In 1973, with the City of London winded by the collapse of fringe banks, 'Charlotte Square' surged forward, although its integration with the Scottish elite seemed almost incestuous. The left made much of the involvement of George Pottinger, jailed for corruption in February 1974, with the business empire of the first Sir Hugh Fraser; there were other examples in local authorities and in the Highland Board. When Heath brought Lord Polwarth, Chairman of the Bank of Scotland and of the Scottish Council, into the government in March 1973 as 'oil supremo', he seemed to sanction a lash-up of big business, government, Scottish institutions and multinationals. That summer John McGrath's 7:84 Theatre Company punched the message home throughout the Highlands with *The Cheviot, the Stag and the Black, Black Oil*:

> Now all you Scotties need have no fear,
> Your oil's quite safe now the trouble-shooter's here,
> So I'll trust you if you'll trust me,
> 'Cos I'm the ex-director of a trust company.

The Cheviot was the highlight of the SNP's conference at Oban in August. 'How can they put on a play like that and then say they are not Nationalists?' a *Scots Independent* reporter asked Wolfe. 'If we knew the answer to that, we would sweep Scotland tomorrow', was the answer he got. But for every one of McGrath's audience who was converted to his own Marxist position, ten saw the confrontation in national rather than class terms. Tactically, the SNP was well placed. It could mobilise Scottish resentment against the multinationals and the British state without committing itself to a positive policy, left or right. Oil had brought about Muirhead's hope of the 1930s: the equation of nationalism with anti-imperialism. But, when Labour took power in February 1974, the SNP was also courted by businesses fearing government interference, symbolised by the adherence of the second Sir Hugh Fraser in April 1974.

Inevitably, oil enhanced the prospects of the Scottish economy. The choice 'rich Scots or poor British' appealed to some of the remaining industrialists and some fringe finance operators. But doubts remained. Wouldn't the huge balance of payments surplus prove a curse in disguise, pushing up the value of the Scots pound and strangling Scots exports? Had Scotland, anyway, enough industry to absorb the wealth? The SNP answer – a slower rate of extraction – might bring redundancy to those involved in oil-based industry. After the initial impetus of 1974, in fact, the equation of independence with oil looked much less straightforward.

But the problem of industrial structure remained, and while it did the SNP's case remained plausible. Oceanspan, with its prospect of the Clyde as a major European entrepôt for imported oil, was struck a fatal blow by the North Sea discoveries and by the slackening of European demand. The axis of Scottish economic development was no longer the Forth–Clyde isthmus but the south-west/north-east corridor. Investment was also likely to be monopolised by oil-related developments. While encomia of the Scottish revival such as the Hudson Institute's notorious *The United Kingdom in 1980* (1974) looked flattering, on closer inspection this seemed perilously restricted to oil and plentiful government investment. No party had any post-oil ideas, but at least the SNP promised to retain the revenue for industrial reconstruction. From late 1973 it could also make use of the political impetus towards devolution released by the Kilbrandon Report.

KILBRANDON AND THE SECOND WAVE

The Royal Commission on the Constitution reported on 31 October 1973, about two years late. The evidence it took from individuals and institutions in Scotland in 1969–70 seemed to show that opinions on devolution bore no relation to traditional polarities. The Communists, the Scottish Trades Union Congress, the Liberals, the Tories and the Kirk were in favour. Labour and the Confederation of British Industry were against. Practically every group had its dissenters. Only the SNP was straightforward about what it wanted, and it was on the slide. The Commission's reports came to 850 pages and the whole exercise had cost just under £500,000. Had this been paid to further devolution or to frustrate it?

Kilbrandon's conclusions were neither distinct nor unanimous Although all its members favoured devolution, their definitions of it were endlessly varied. Moreover, several of the original heavyweights had dropped out, including the representatives of the – English – Labour centre, Douglas Houghton MP and David Basnett of the General and Municipal Workers' Union. After Crowther died in 1972, Kilbrandon and a clutch of 'Celtic fringe Liberals' moved the reduced Commission to 'home rule all round', devolving power to the 'historic nationalities'. There was some individual dissent from this position, and a coherent revolt by two academics, Dr Norman Hunt of Exeter College, Oxford and Professor Alan Peacock, of the University

187

of York, who backed a uniform system of regional councils throughout Britain. The two were far apart in their politics – Hunt later joined the 1974 Labour government and Peacock, then a Liberal, was a member of the free-market Institute of Economic Affairs – but they at least attempted to square devolution with regionalism, although too late to influence local government reform. Otherwise the assumption was obvious: no unanimity was required because no action would be taken.

This was evident in the reaction to the report. The Liberals and the Nationalists, Scottish and Welsh, were naturally in favour; the government evasive, the Scottish Tories sceptical (they had thrown out their Assembly commitment at their conference in May). Labour's Scottish Council found the report 'at first glance totally unacceptable'. But Kilbrandon's time of peril was short. A week later Margo MacDonald won Glasgow Govan for the SNP.

The miners' work-to-rule, the fuel crisis, and another Liberal revival (they captured Berwick on the day Govan fell) deflected English attention, so that the SNP's breakthrough in the February 1974 general election was unexpected. Although it lost Govan, it captured Dundee West and Stirling East from Labour, and Argyllshire, Aberdeenshire East, Moray and Nairn and Banff from the Tories, and polled 21 per cent of the Scots electorate. The result was no freak: five of the six seats the SNP took from second place were in north-east Scotland, where its oil campaign was particularly relevant. This concentrated wonderfully the minds of the other parties, and the new Labour government.

Labour's February manifesto was intransigent – going no further than suggesting meetings of the Scottish Grand Committee in Edinburgh. But after February action had to be taken. On 6 March four Labour MPs – John Robertson (Paisley), Alex Eadie (Midlothian), Jim Sillars (South Ayrshire) and Harry Ewing (Stirling), two of whom, Sillars and Eadie, had previously been anti-devolution – demanded an assembly on Kilbrandon lines and moved a resolution at Labour's Scottish conference. It was rejected, although Willie Ross, back as Secretary of State, reserved his position.

It was then that the going got interesting. On 8 May elections were held for the new regional and district council seats. Of 432 seats in the regions Labour won 171, the Nationalists only 18.

On 18 May, addressing an apprehensive Scottish Conservative conference, Edward Heath promised a Scottish Assembly – indirectly elected from members of Scottish local authorities – and a Scottish Development Fund, doubtless calculating that a coalition of Conservatives and Independents could stand a chance against Labour. On 3 June the government published its own Green Paper, offering several options though in practice hinting at a Hunt–Peacock type of settlement – executive but not legislative devolution.

These changes strengthened the anti-devolutionists within Labour's Scottish executive. On 28 June, with only a third of its members present, it rejected all the schemes with the verdict: 'Constitutional tinkering does not make a meaningful contribution towards achieving socialist objectives.' This insubordination was not allowed for long. On 25 July the national executive, meeting at Transport House, brusquely and unanimously commanded the Scots to reconvene their annual conference on 11 August. The big unions, which had rejected devolution in March, ensured that after only two hours of debate an elected legislative assembly became policy – three weeks before the second general election campaign began.

At the election of 10 October the SNP vote rose by 10 per cent to 30 per cent, but Labour held on to its seats. The SNP gained Galloway, Dumbartonshire East, South Angus and Perthshire East from the Tories, reducing them to 16 seats and a total poll of only 24.9 per cent. The margin between the total votes of SNP and Labour was narrow – only 6.4 per cent – and in 35 seats the contest was now between the two. The state of parties in the new House, moreover, left the Nationalist MPs in a strong position.

THE MAGIC PARTY

Devolution was to preoccupy Labour in Scotland throughout 1975. The right wing of the government – Anthony Crosland, Roy Jenkins, Shirley Williams, Reg Prentice – said nothing and was thought to be hostile. Social democracy, to which pluralism was supposed to be second nature, seemed catatonic. The orthodox left, personified by Tony Benn, the Industry Secretary, had some enthusiasm for the principle, but worried that it would detract from parliamentary sovereignty. Its 'democratic' alternative was the vertical devolution of authority to the workplace. But in 1975 this mirage dissolved as well. The 'work-in' at Upper Clyde Shipbuilders in 1971 had suggested a revolutionary *démarche*, and attracted Labour notables, although it was good propaganda rather than a success for workers' control. Its much-advertised sequel – the takeover by a workers' co-operative of the Beaverbrook printing plant in Glasgow after the move south to Manchester of the *Scottish Daily Express* in February 1974 – ended in farce. The *Scottish Daily News*, launched in May 1975 with government backing and the goodwill of the SNP (Wolfe was an auditor to the co-operative) as a 'left-of-centre' daily, succumbed to editorial mediocrity and the loutish intervention of the 'socialist millionaire' Robert Maxwell, whom Benn had allowed to take a minority shareholding. The damage to the Scottish press was nothing compared to the damage to 'socialist democracy'.

The same thing happened with the referendum on entry into the European Community. The SNP achieved near-unanimity for its proposition: 'NO – ON ANYONE ELSE'S TERMS', as the posters put it, although many of its leaders were privately pro-EEC. Labour conducted its disputes publicly, with full comradely venom and many MPs at odds with their constituency parties. Sixty per cent of Scots voted for entry. This was 6 per cent less than in England on a low poll of about 62 per cent – only a minority of the electorate. But so sweeping had been the claims of the SNP and Labour that they received the result in silence. The SNP, who could at least claim an overwhelming 'anti' vote in the Western Isles, unobtrusively reversed their policy, and Mrs Ewing went to Strasbourg as a Euro MP. Labour was left to self-recrimination. For a time the right in the Cabinet may have seen the vote as an excuse for ditching devolution, but the SNP held its position in the polls, even knocking Labour into third place in one of its safest regional seats. The referendum had shown, however, a context in which the 'popularity' of the left might prove illusory.

Wilson had promised a White Paper on devolution early in 1975, but the Scottish party conference passed and nothing happened. There was little unanimity. Tam Dalyell endorsed devolution in November – 'There is really no backsliding of feeling on the Assembly' – and forecast the Assembly meeting by autumn 1976, but opposed it in April 1975, and the Scottish

Council tried in June to have its powers reduced to the minimum. Two of the Assembly's protagonists – Eadie and Ewing – were now in the government, leaving Jim Sillars and John Robertson isolated and vociferous. The Scottish Labour MPs, more impressive and ambitious than they had been for a long time, had a case for apostasy. Not only did they fear reduced representation at Westminster, but the more powers that were devolved, the less chance there was of gaining office, the convention being that no Scottish MP could take Education, Health or Environment, which had no authority in Scotland. What Dalyell shrewdly advertised as the West Lothian Question – the disqualification of Scottish Westminster MPs from speaking or voting at Westminster on issues reserved to the Assembly – made them look potentially as marginal as the Ulster Unionists.

Our Changing Democracy finally appeared on 27 November, offering a legislative Assembly to Scotland and an executive Assembly to Wales. It was more the product of an inter-departmental power struggle in Whitehall than of any desire to settle the issue permanently. Edward Short, the minister responsible, took away with one hand what he gave with the other. The Assembly would have 142 members elected in two-member constituencies by the first-past-the-post system. It would be housed in the Grecian Hall of the Royal High School, a late flowering of classical Edinburgh perched above the city on Calton Hill. Its powers would cover local government, health, education (except universities), social work, transport (except railways), economic development agencies (except the Scottish Development Agency), natural resources (except most of agriculture), private and criminal law (except the courts) and tourism (except tourist promotion abroad). The authority of the Secretary of State was increased to counterbalance such concessions. His control was strengthened over economic policy, electricity, police, agriculture and fisheries and the judiciary. He was to organise the Assembly, appoint its executive, adjudicate on the legality of its enactments, to have, in fact 'the powers over the Kingdom of Scotland of the Secretary of State for India and the Viceroy combined'. The Assembly could raise no revenue other than that allocated by Westminster in a block grant, although the White Paper rather unenthusiastically suggested the possibility of a rates surcharge. So much for the 'real measure of economic power' Labour had promised in August.

Reaction was lukewarm, not only in the SNP. In mid-December, Jim Sillars announced his intention to found a 'parallel' party – the Scottish Labour Party. Although hostility to Sillars was immense this challenge at last stung Labour MPs into positive, if momentary, action. By March 1976 all but two of them were demanding a much greater range of powers, embracing the economy, the universities and the Scottish Development Agency. A month later Willie Ross, having led his party to devolution, followed Harold Wilson into the shadows.

This conversion did Labour little good. The SNP continued to win local elections, even when Labour tried to convert them into plebiscites on separation. But only one other MP, John Robertson, an unexciting middle-of-the-roader from Paisley, joined Sillars. The SLP claimed 2,000 members in some forty branches, and attracted some support from dissident Labour office-bearers, journalists and the New Left – Tom Nairn and Neal Ascherson were early members – and Alex Neil, Labour's Scottish research officer, became its first General Secretary. But although polls showed it might take as much as 28 per cent of the Labour vote, the 'magic party' was an army of officers looking for a rank-and-file. Attempts by militant left-wingers from the International Marxist Group to infiltrate in October 1976 led to a brutal purge of the left at its inaugural conference. Sillars and his 'moderate' allies then clashed repeatedly, until even the most enthusiastic lost interest. The SLP's first conference turned out to be its last.

DEVOLUTION AND WESTMINSTER

By the time the Devolution Bill was tabled on 13 December, the Conservatives were in comparable disarray. Mrs Thatcher regarded devolution as a Heath ploy (although he had shown little enough enthusiasm for it between 1970 and 1974). Her declaration that Tory MPs would be put under a three-line whip to defeat the bill provoked dissent from Heath and the resignation of the Tory spokesmen on Scottish affairs, Alick Buchanan-Smith and Malcolm Rifkind, to be replaced by the apostle of populist unionism, Teddy Taylor. The threat of Labour dissidence seemed mitigated, when on 17 December the bill passed its second reading by a majority of 45. Out of the 71 Scottish MPs, 55 voted for it and only 7 against, 6 of them Tories.

However, in order to win over the dissidents in his own ranks, the Leader of the House, Michael Foot, conceded their demand for referendums in Scotland and Wales after the bill had become law, probably in November 1977. It seemed, at that time, difficult to explain this decision. Some unionist Welsh MPs led by Neil Kinnock believed that their line would be confirmed by a popular vote. The case appeared quite different in Scotland. Had a write-in poll held by the *Daily Record* not shown 45 per cent of respondents supporting *independence*?

'History repeats itself,' wrote Marx, 'first as tragedy, then as farce'. Despite the warnings of Foot about the consequences of the rejection of Irish home rule in 1886, there was little Gladstonian dignity around when, in January and February 1977, the first Devolution Bill was destroyed. There was no clash of principles; the bill was killed in committee, the victim of mediocre leadership by government, Conservative frondeurs, and sectional pressure groups. Foot, effective enough as Minister of Labour, was a weak Leader of the House; the new Scottish Secretary, Bruce Millan, was competent but grey; the Scottish Labour MPs were largely silent.

The initiative passed to English and Welsh MPs who eluded Foot's control. North-eastern MPs combined with Tam Dalyell to immolate themselves on a pyre of amendments. Conservatives were encouraged by Mrs Thatcher to launch gadfly attacks. Liberal support depended on the bill moving towards federalism and proportional representation – which would benefit them nationally. When such concessions were not forthcoming, they became hostile. The 350 amendments tabled when the bill went into committee on 13 January immobilised it. Only a timetable or 'guillotine' could get it through. Foot attempted to buy support for this by sanctioning the referendum but ruled out the independence option (the only reason Scots Labour MPs had for wanting it), and made it consultative rather than decisive. To no avail. On Tuesday, 22 February, the guillotine motion was lost by 29 votes. This was not a regional revolt or a rejection of the principle of devolution. Labour dissidents were in fact strongest in London constituencies. Some objections from Liberals and Tories were fairly directed at its inadequacies as a settlement. Could, they asked, devolution stop short of federalism? Michael Foot, as besotted with parliamentary sovereignty as A. V. Dicey, wasn't the man to answer this.

THE SNP IN TROUBLE

The collapse of the bill saw a momentary rise of the SNP in the polls to 36 per cent, which might have given it a majority of Scottish MPs. But there was no convenient by-election. Not until April 1978, when in rapid succession there were contests at Garscadden, Hamilton and East Lothian, the last tragically occasioned by the death of John Mackintosh. By this time the economy had recovered somewhat under the rigours of IMF supervision, inflation had fallen, Tony Benn's direction of oil-based economic activity to Scotland was having some effect, and the Lib–Lab pact reassured those who feared socialist 'extremism'. All three contests were setbacks for the SNP: in the circumstances, disastrous ones. Matters were made worse by the ebbing in its local government vote. A factor was salient which would hit Labour throughout the 1980s, but at this point worked in Labour's favour. Unemployment was not the vote-loser it was usually made out to be. Although it doubled from 3.6 per cent in 1974 to 7.6 per cent in 1978, the Labour vote didn't shift from around 40 per cent in the regional elections, while that of the SNP fell to 21 per cent. It took the industrial anarchy of the winter of 1978–79 to destroy the command that Callaghan had established.

The SNP was in internal trouble over policy. A team under Douglas Crawford, MP for Perthshire East, declared that 'a self-governing Scotland will not need to over-emphasise production for export'; this was a prudent way of saying that exports of everything except oil were going to be priced out of world markets by the appreciation of the Scots currency. Crawford visualised an economy producing high-technology and luxury goods, largely catering for the home market, 'a future economic structure . . . more like Switzerland's than Detroit's . . . very little dependent on large-scale assembly industry', yet the collapse in 1976 of the British television tube industry was an unfavourable augury for this. Would a post-industrial world have much need of Switzerlands? And what if, before Scotland's Detroit were tidied away, the price of oil were to fall? The notion of a cosy little autarky living by international trade in a single commodity was less than beguiling.

The policy-making dynamic within the SNP was corporate rather than radical, directed by middle-class activists in the interests of their professions. Doctors prescribed for medicine, teachers for education, economic consultants for industry. They represented an enfeebled projection of the old civil society, purged of the wide social and governmental claims of the estates. There was no 'radical' questioning of the role of doctors or teachers. The parliamentary party leader, Donald Stewart, could commend the views of the party's token environmentalist, Dr Malcolm Slesser, to the annual conference, and get applause for the proposition:

> A new economic order is on the way when the countries with a reasonable balance between population, land and resources (i.e. like Scotland) will have the capacity to flourish, and states with a preponderance of manufacturing, a lack of land and high population density are simply in trouble.

But Slesser's 'greenish' attack on the party's industrial policy as resource-consuming, and tending to create a 'mini-England', got hardly any support. The loyalty of pacifists was difficult to square with a defence policy group, under the economist Dr Gavin Kennedy, suggesting a budget of £450 million a year, roughly six times that of Eire. The SNP tried to appeal to business interests who wanted to be free of London collectivism, but found itself overtaken by the Conservatives' conversion to free-market economics; it tried to appeal to traditional Labour supporters but found that once the party had made its peace with home rule, these weren't tempted to stray.

The tactical advantages the SNP had enjoyed in 1974 no longer held good, something which seemed more obvious to local activists than to the MPs at Westminster.

THE *DÉBÂCLE*

In Parliament, the Scotland Act got its third reading on 22 February 1978, subject to a referendum to which a hostile expatriate MP, George Cunningham, had attached the condition that the 'Yes' vote should reach 40 per cent of the entire Scots electorate. The Act had served the government well, as Lord Croham, head of the Civil Service, later recalled: it had taken the issue off the boil. In this situation, however, the Labour anti-devolutionists took the initiative. Out of 41 Labour MPs the vast majority were devolutionists without expertise or enthusiasm. Not one showed enough commitment to counter the hostility of Robin Cook or Tam Dalyell. They echoed a widespread view at constituency party level, which roughly ran thus: while the principle might be OK, devolution wasn't much of a priority, and was not worth allocating funds to while a general election was pending. In the short term the Conservatives manoeuvred with lack of scruple and great skill, exploiting these divisions and, through 'anti' organisations, giving the Labour dissidents a platform. The voters were assured by Mrs Janey Buchan, the Chair of Labour's Scottish Council, and the *West Highland Free Press's* Brian Wilson (living down a teenage flirtation with the SNP) that devolution had nothing to do with socialist principle. Lord Home stated that while he (of course) stood by the principle of devolution, a 'No' vote would bring forward a Conservative proposal of 'something better'. As referendum day, 1 March 1979, approached, nationalist misgivings, trade union misbehaviour, government unpopularity, inept organisation on the 'Yes' side, and truly hellish weather which had endured for months (it was still snowing at the general election in May) promised at best a very close result.

The vote went 32.85 per cent in favour, 30.78 per cent against, a lot better than the humiliation sustained by home rulers in Wales (where the vote was almost 5:1 against) but still well short of the 40 per cent which the Cunningham amendment required. Highland and Strathclyde regions voted yes, Lothian only just yes and Tayside only just no. Labour voters, therefore, were favourable but only sluggishly so. The Borders and Northern Isles, the redoubts of the devolutionist Liberals, were overwhelmingly hostile. In the nature of the British constitution the referendum could only be advisory, but Callaghan could not be counted on to carry the Act through against his dissidents. Plaid Cymru and the SLP were still prepared to back Labour in a vote of confidence. The SNP, in a miscalculation that turned out disastrous, were not. The government fell by one vote.

In the May general election the Labour voters it had earlier attracted paid the SNP back for voting Callaghan out, and the SNP vote fell by nearly 13 percentage points, from 30.7 to 18. They lost nine seats, retaining only Dundee West and the Western Isles. The Conservative recovery wasn't dramatic, from 24.7 to 30 per cent – and they lost Teddy Taylor at Glasgow

Cathcart – but they enjoyed a further boomlet of support, and even took five of the eight Scottish seats in the first elections to the European Parliament. Lord Home was wheeled on stage yet again, this time to say that far from devolution discouraging the SNP, it would only encourage a move to independence. 'Something better' meant 'No change'. A career which had begun with the betrayal of Czechoslovakia ended with the betrayal of Scotland.

Everyone, as Andy Warhol said, should be famous for fifteen minutes. One such was Ally MacLeod, the manager of Scotland's World Cup football team at the end of 1978. MacLeod's publicity machine managed to convince the Argentina-bound Scots that they were going to thump everyone and win. But it was Darien all over again. Scotland went down to Peru, and although perversely they beat Holland, they went out in the first round. Matters political might have been a lot different had they won, and the 'we were rubbish' hangover certainly contributed to the 1 March outcome. Was the national movement to share the same fate as Ally's Tartan Army? Patience, reader . . .

7

ON THE EVE

In practice the left, not the right, had held on to the levers of power. It had its arguments voiced by both Catholic and Protestant churches and parroted in the media – hardly any Scottish newspapers supported us and the electronic media were largely hostile.

Margaret Thatcher, *The Downing Street Years* (1996)

Work as if you were living in the early days of a better nation.

Denis Lee, cited by Alasdair Gray, *1982 Janine* (1985)

IN AN OLD BUILDING

In 1917 the Glasgow Marxist John MacLean proclaimed Scotland 'in the rapids of revolution'. Over seventy years later, with the breakdown of the 'scientific socialist' order which MacLean had striven for, the metaphor again seemed valid. 'Wunds wi' warlds tae swing' gave Scotland a particular battering. In July 1988 the Piper Alpha production platform blew up with huge loss of life, after a long period of lax maintenance and superficial inspection. In December an American airliner was destroyed by a bomb – planted by whom? – over Lockerbie, killing nearly three hundred people. In 1993 the tanker *Braer* crashed into the Shetland Isles, polluting sea and land. A year later the attempt of Shell to scuttle the Brent Spar platform led to world-wide protest. Most tragic of all, in Dunblane in March 1996, a misfit obsessed with guns and young boys murdered half a classful of innocents and their teacher before killing himself.

For the rest of the world these headlines *were* Scotland, backed up by inside-page stories about *Trainspotting* or *Braveheart*, or the continuing tourist pabulum of whisky, tweeds, the Loch Ness Monster and the Edinburgh Festival. Pretty far down the line came the political changes which were obsessing the Scots elite. Yet the country's unsettlement could not be detached from those catastrophes.

The first edition of this book concluded on a reassuring note. Scottish political identity had become real, and a devolutionist elite – left and right – had developed to cope with it: a new governing generation. The descent into the rapids modified this optimism, not altogether negatively. 'World is various, and more of it than we think': somehow the movement towards Scottish consciousness had interacted symbiotically with the forces which, in their dynamic, disoriented way, had flayed most countries and wrenched old habits and practices from their moorings.

Not the least affected was the British state. When devolution was torpedoed the Scots elite moved into British politics. In 1993 there were five Scots in John Major's cabinet – Norman Lamont, Malcolm Rifkind, John MacGregor, Iain Lang and Lord MacKay – and rather more Scots Tories sat for English seats than survived in the north. In that year more than half of the Liberal Democrats' MPs represented Scottish constituencies. Even the voice – of right-wing British populism or global media capitalism? – which bellowed from the Murdoch press came from Norman Stone, Andrew Neil, Norman MacRae and Kelvin MacKenzie, not to speak of Murdoch himself, reared in the Free Kirk of Australia.

On 1 May 1997 a new Labour government came in on a landslide. A third of the Cabinet was Scots. However, this raised problems of definition. Did Tony Blair, born in Edinburgh of a family with left-wing Glasgow connections, fit in? He had attended Fettes College, in Edinburgh but not of it. He was unaware of the SNP revival which had constituted Scottish politics in his schooldays. Yet he claimed to be a disciple of the Scots philosopher John Macmurray, also an influence on John MacCormick, and his legal patron who became his Lord Chancellor, was Lord Irvine of Lairg, the second successive highlander to perch on the English Woolsack.

Blair's Chancellor was Gordon Brown, his Foreign Secretary Robin Cook, his Defence Secretary George Robertson. Not since Asquith's day had so many Scots MPs sat in the Cabinet – and these *were* Scots, not carpet-bagging London barristers. But was this *real*? Paul Routledge's biography of Gordon Brown suggested tensions – hitherto expertly masked – between the Premier and his Chancellor which contrasted metropolitan manoeuvre with a Scottish social democracy which the 'Islington fusiliers ... despised, hated and feared'. If a Westminster vacuum coincided with a generation which fancied its chances, was this a plus? In 1992, when Labour's elite had been responsible but inexpert in its economics, a young City dealer could make more in his annual bonus than a minister in his entire career. For Douglas Hurd to persist in politics for £65,000 when he could draw £250,000 as a part-time banker would have seemed as quixotic as his uncle Robert's espousal of Scottish nationalism in the 1930s. Were the Scots around Downing Street like Sicilians in an Italian cabinet – politics being the only game (apart from crime) in Palermo? In the fractured world of post-modernity could one any longer talk of an elite?

The 1980s in Scotland were intellectually and culturally comparable not only with the 1920s but with the high years of the Scottish Enlightenment. This 'success' seemed to coincide with the British state – economy, parliament, City, monarchy – crumbling under the assault of what Edward Luttwak called 'turbo-charged capitalism'. The 'British' solidarity of war and welfare state atrophied, as the generation which had experienced it passed from the scene. Economic authority was migrating to Europe or to global financial markets, firms were being taken over, like Rover, or taken to bits, like ICI. The fate of the Scots economy earlier in the twentieth century was being repeated on a grander scale; and the disciplines which should have been interpreting this seemed bereft of ways of doing so.

In the 1960s the South Korean economy was thrust into its remarkable rise by Scots entrepreneurs, notably Sir William Lithgow. In early 1998, now a major investor *in* Scotland, it crashed. A credit was arranged with the International Monetary Fund for $60 billion. This scarcely retarded the collapse of the 'little tiger' economies, but made those with long memories reflect on the Callaghan government's humiliation at the hands of the same IMF in 1976 when the UK debt involved – firmly guaranteed by the collateral of North Sea oil – was about $5 billion. The tribulations of the British state had to be set against a globalism which was more anarchic than logical.

The period 1992–7 proved crucial in this process. The election of April 1992 was supposed to see some sort of home rule settlement. It did not happen. Instead, the Conservatives made the Union into an icon while as a party they imploded. Autonomy was not top of the Scottish voter's list of priorities, but it was a constant theme. The behavioural framework of Britishness, which the first edition of this book implicitly took for granted, had been shifted to the margin.

NATIONALISMS IN CONFLICT

The 1980s did not begin well for the Scottish National Party. Its May 1979 result was only three points down on February 1974, but its solidarity collapsed. Its MPs had been above the modest Scottish average, but they conflicted with their rank-and-file, coincided with an impressive Labour intake, and miscalculated badly in voting Labour out. 'Turkeys voting for an early Christmas' was Callaghan's quite appropriate parting shot. The SNP's problem was that its efforts were awkwardly split between holding north-eastern rural seats, where it continued a tradition of non-socialist radicalism, and trying to storm the Labour fortresses of the central belt. In 1979, by supporting Labour, it might have held on to most of its MPs, but only by opposing Labour could it gain the critical mass necessary for an independence bid. A growing number believed this could only be achieved on a socialist programme. Organised in the "79 Group', reinforced by the dynamic and disruptive Sillars (who rapidly abandoned the Scottish Labour party), they clashed with the purist nationalism of Donald Stewart and Gordon Wilson. In 1980 the '79ers were suspended from the party. They remained in the wilderness until 1985.

There was little need for the other parties to exert themselves, given this enthusiastic self-mutilation. The SNP underwent the sort of split which bedevilled Labour *in England*, while Labour in Scotland seemed gratifyingly immune. A social democratic ethos persisted. Yet one of the more critical nationalists, Stephen Maxwell regarded this 'public relations gloss of moderation and even of Conservatism' as something which inhibited a more flexible, greener radicalism, a *Plaid Cymru*-like dispersal of power to local authorities and co-operatively-owned industries. But the electoral system always placed Greens and left-wing Socialists at a disadvantage, and favoured the centre-right, though this would change. When the Bennite left prompted Labour's disruption of 1981, Scotland remained faithful. Despite the appeal the dissentient Social Democrats made to Conservative, often Catholic, machine politicians, only two right-wing MPs – Robert Maclennan and Dickson Mabon – seceded to them. In 1983, Labour's *annus horribilis*, the Alliance made its Scottish inroads against the Tories.

Labour could not temper the cold monetarist wind, which decimated the industries expensively induced to settle in the north since the 1960s, and harried the autonomy of the local authorities which the reform of 1974 was supposed to secure. But Scottish Labour's subordination to the English unions diminished as the latter were sapped by unemployment and Conservative legislation, and its power grew when the Oxbridge elite was weakened by the secession of the SDP. The civic and Scottish universities became the nurseries of the Kinnockite soft left. By contrast, the Scottish Conservatives were overshadowed by the City of London, along with what remained of an independent Scottish industrial capitalism. Protestant Unionism, touchily Scottish *and* southward-looking, was no longer an option. An ITV reporter in 1987 likened the Scottish Tories at their annual conferences – extraordinary affairs dominated by the descent from the sky of the leader, ringed by men with guns – to unsuccessful McDonald's franchisers: the brand name was doing well; they were not. They had dwindled by 1987 to scarcely 2.6 per cent of the parliamentary party. Walter Elliot's 'endless adventure' of Tory careerism had been experimental and innovative; now an English seat was the only sure way forward, a shift from elitism back to money and class. In the 1970s the Assembly had offered the chance of consensual commitment to it. Now every man on the right, with a few incorrigible exceptions – Brian Meek, Michael Fry, Sir Russell Fairgrieve – had his price.

Forget Thatcher's revolutionary pretensions. The decade 1979–90 was in fact a crisis of British social democratic nationalism, with Thatcher's state closer to that of Attlee than that of Tony Blair. Her moment of originality, the excursion into monetarism, 1979–81, was disastrous; thereafter she lived on past public investment, if only by selling it off, and on the welfare state, which stopped discontent becoming violent. Under a rhetoric of liberationist economics, she played the Gaullist *dirigiste*. She had fingered the mandarinate of metropolitan liberals, the cast of Noel Annan's *Our Age* (1993), but centralisation still prevailed over civil society. Some old elitists joined the Downing Street court and savaged the mixed economy; some – perhaps most – of the *Marxisants* of the 1960s found their destiny in going with the flow of market liberalism. Thatcher herself was cannier, luckier, and less consistent.

The cultural revolution that was supposed to accompany the advance of the market was eccentric rather than Anglocentric. 'Understand less and condemn more': a *bétise* of John Major seemed to describe the confused Conservative intellect, with Murdoch and a few oilmen and fringe bankers financing a grab-bag of mutually-incompatible libertarians and fogeys. What *had* Roger Scruton and Madsen Pirie in common, or Maurice Cowling and Patrick Minford? The *Salisbury Review* represented an Englishness which had died with the old boy in 1902. Essex Man *was* English – the first regional stereotype to impose himself since Manchester Man in the 1830s – but he wasn't a deferential Tory, and hadn't a clue about authoritarian individualism. In 1950 John Macmurray had worried about what would happen to the Union if its basis of 'freedom in fellowship' was disrupted by English nationalism. Thatcher and Major were clueless rather than nationalist, but the damage was being done.

SOUNDING CIVIL SOCIETY

'Bizarre coincidences are the bonuses of history' your man remarked when Beaverbrook turned up in Scotland exactly where the SNP revival was launched and just a few days before it. He wasn't the last. On a visit to Edinburgh in 1985 Mikhail Gorbachev learned of the death of Alexander Chernenko (how could they tell?) and became Russian leader, to begin the process which in six years would end the Soviet empire. Nationalism – earlier regarded as only one of several explanations of the Scottish situation – would by 1992 have evicted most of the others. Yet in *Janus Revisited* (1998) Tom Nairn noted the peculiarity that as Scotland became more European in admitting this, European nationalism (of the acceptable 'nation as a frame for civil society' sort) became in content more Scottish.

Scottish institutions and assumptions contradicted each other less, became more aligned and – given a positive and original sense of identity – more confrontational. Three elements figured: the consciousness of the Scots; the direction of economic change; and the condition of the political framework. Ideas were central to reformulations of European nationalism, like that of the Czech revisionist Marxist Miroslav Hroch, with his three-stage pattern of intellectual, institutional and finally popular mobilisation. They had never mattered much at Westminster, because Conservatives regarded Diceyite parliamentary sovereignty *as* nationalism, with the Union 'a partnership for good', *their* final stage. Yet with the possible exception of Allan Massie, the 'cultural nationalist/political unionist' position of Elliot or Buchan had vanished. The social and intellectual developments of the 1980s and 1990s went unnoticed by every Conservative Secretary of State, Ian Lang telling a Scottish Liberal in 1992, 'You chaps gave Ireland home rule in 1886, and look what happened!' This cocktail of dogma and dimness stood in ominous contrast to the subtlety of the Balfour brothers and George Wyndham in *fin-de-siècle* Ireland, or for that matter with the nifty footwork of 1979.

Further, Labour unionism, powerful in 1979, weakened in the 1980s and died out after the Communist collapse. To Nairn, Scottish nationalism as modernisation instrument implied a new *démarche*, brought into play by changes in the structure of capitalism and overarching patterns of development. This was comprehensible through the international system paradigms of Immanuel Wallerstein and André Gunder Frank and the theory of international capitalism, while the sociology of Ernest Gellner – influenced by teaching in Edinburgh in the 1940s – explored the role of state and nation in attempting to make space for civil society. Post-1989 Europe provided plenty of parallels to explore, and the macro-patterns it generated framed one important *tour d'horizon*, David McCrone's *Understanding Scotland*, in 1992.

McCrone argued that Scotland was nationalist because of its political life. International systems squeezed the space for ethnic nationality, Versailles-style. There was no longer any major economic or social divergence from the south; the traditional estates had been marginalised; Scots culture – the Kailyard, macho Clydesideism, the Gaelic inheritance – was usually an embarrassment to the Scottish elite. But in place of these an accumulation of *ressentiments* had taken on their own dynamic: compromise and negotiation had now attached themselves to the cause of self-government, and were validated by its progress. The distinctive thing about the stateless nation was its expectation that some day its state would come.

Yes, but. McCrone's problem (and that of most commentators on the theme) was that his nation was painted with a very broad brush. Actual nations differed from one another in size, calibrated from great imperial powers through ethnic nation-states to cities. The first – France, Germany, etc. – evolving through large-scale conflicts, had supplied most of the national vocabulary but still ran into the opposition of minority groups. Did the latter want to be miniature versions of France or Germany? Or had they distinctive notions of community? Or were they out for civil rights and equality *inside* some national market? This intrinsic variety raised a fresh range of social issues, or uncovered old ones, as the cold war framework disintegrated. Did an achieving people like the Scots generate anti-community tensions, as Paul Halmos oberved? Were ethnic differences – between Celt and Saxon – back on the table, rooted in the deep structures of the family – political in the former, affective in the latter – as Emanuel Todd argued? The peculiar thing was that the Scots contrived to be on both sides of the argument: simultaneously imperialists and the tribunes of put-upon communities.

McCrone's model had nailed a lot of the myths and self-deceptions of the Scots elite, *en route* to self-government. But was Scotland the sum of this? Had he paid enough attention to the way rural and urban communities functioned – or didn't function – as in the studies of James Littlejohn and Ronald Frankenberg? What was the role of such socialising factors as regional culture, psychology and education – in the country of Patrick Geddes, R. D. Laing, Ronald Fairbairn and A. S. Neill? Above all, had he given sufficient credit to the country's culture? Creative Scots, whether Alasdair Gray or Robin Jenkins, Liz Lochhead or William McIlvanney – or fifty others – had been thinking, writing and organising furiously for a couple of decades, and they had produced something quite different from any of his stereotypes, which helped define a national community in the flux of unrelenting change.

A NEW ECONOMY?

In the summer of 1996, Big Blue, the huge gasometer of British Steel, Ravenscraig, was ringed with explosives and blown up. Within a few months one of Europe's most modern steelworks, opened in 1961, was a hole in the ground. This wasn't the suspended animation of the 1930s: there could be no return to the world of the heavy industries, the ships surging down the Linthouse slipways, the great locomotives swaying above the Clyde at Finnieston. The Conservatives could console themselves that the socialist element in the economy had dwindled with the privatisation or closure of the Scottish element of British nationalised industries – the shipyards, steelworks, coal-mines, British Petroleum, Ferrantis, Rolls Royce and British Leyland – and the reduction of public sector housing from 52 to 39 per cent of households. Not to speak of the disappearance of the COMECON planned economies, with which Neal Ascherson had compared Scotland. But what remained of *their* world? Of Orange foremen, Rotarian ironfounders, imperial pensioners?

If it was supposed to revitalise the British *mittelstand* – and the above weren't far from her Grantham paradigm – then the Thatcherite project failed early on. Between 1979 and 1990 the petro-pound rose to five then fell to three Deutschmarks, and knocked the manufacturing proportion of GNP down by a quarter. The bounty of oil, over 5 per cent of GNP in 1980, went to pay the dole, not to secure industrial reconstruction. Hit by a price-fall from \$30 to \$10 a barrel in 1985, the year of peak production, it could not resolve a balance of payments permanently in deficit from the mid-1980s. Privatisation – 'selling the family silver' – failed to create popular capitalism but made the economy, skewed by predatory monopolies, more vulnerable to global fluctuations. Wider home ownership undertaken by a gullible public not just anticipating but *welcoming* inflation, created a vast private debt. The systematic assault on the less fortunate left almost a third of the urban population below or close to the poverty line.

This wasn't something that bothered Locate in Scotland, advertising in Germany in 1992: 'Salaries and wages – gratifyingly low. In Scotland the salary and wage-level is under the British average. In the assembly area in particular Scottish hourly wages are, by European standards, among the lowest.'

'Whaur's yir John MacLean noo?' Trade union membership fell as unemployment rose; stroppiness was being corralled in the public sector – among teachers or health service workers. But factory closures were fiercely contested; the need to regenerate the areas affected brought the state back on the scene, and Labour, the unions and the SNP on to the streets. Investing in Scottish manufacturing was a marginal calculation for multinational companies: winning North Sea oil cost them £9 billion in 1980 and £70 billion by 1994. But this was reined in after 1985, and their rationalisation programme CRINE (Cost Reduction in the New Era) decimated jobs: the labour-less workplace of the future could be discerned. Oil production was by 1998 – with 144 fields on stream – at record levels but it made little news impact, despite (or perhaps because of) the fact that the £2 billion revenue the UK got from it was only a third of what Norway, with its unfashionably publicly owned Statoil, derived from similar output.

This made the modish free marketeers of St Andrews University, in the Conservative party, the Institute of Economic Affairs and the Adam Smith Institute, less plausible. (Although St Andrews was the most English of the Scots universities, it also produced dissidents – from Alex Salmond to Fay Weldon.) As the achievement toppled over, the natives felt self-justified – 'Ah tellt ye!' – if also outraged that such idiocies were bankrolled by 'our oil'. But the messianic ideology had purposes and an audience. Large houses and luxury cars – not only in south-east England – showed that one class had done very well indeed.

Scotland remained a trophy landscape. The hills were alive with the sound of arms dealers, oil sheikhs and Wall Street traders having fun. About 13 per cent of Scotland's territory was still under large landowners and, in 1995 alone, 200,000 acres – 1 per cent of all Scottish land – changed hands. Sporting estates, peculiarly uneconomic, still characterised the highlands, but now met a resistance which was symbolic and cross-party; with co-operative takeovers in West Sutherland and Eigg crofting attained a profile it had only reached in the 1880s, not least because of the energy of Dr James Hunter, a historian who more than anyone else proved the clout of the profession when he founded the Scottish Crofters' Union in 1985. Yet only a trifling proportion of crofters' income came from agriculture, and the position of those farmers who actually made their livelihood from the land was steadily declining, along with the Common Agriculture Policy subsidies on which over 80 per cent of their income depended. £11,000 a year from an average hill-farm was unattractive to a new generation. Only half of the family farms were likely to continue. No less imperilled were the fishermen – 25 per cent of the British fleet – facing relentless foreign competition and dwindling stocks.

On the other hand, if the Scots were in any way to survive this torrent of change, they had to use the resources which were to hand. Ireland had picked up spectacularly, moving from 56 per cent of UK GDP in 1976 to near-parity twenty years later. But the Scots hadn't, like the Irish, a favourable demography (lots of young trained workers coming on to the market), nor had they a European political presence. What they had was paradoxical: a complex network of financial connections with leading industrial areas, born of the country's industrial past, and the post-war tradition of expertise in attracting inward investment.

Charlotte Square was where cotton magnates, jute barons, shipbuilders and shipowners had parked their gains, rather than invest them in modernising their industries. Edinburgh, the old pioneer of capital export, became a paradigm of a new global order, coming fourth in Europe after London, Frankfurt and Paris, with a financial sector employing one in thirteen workers by 1994, and £100 billion under Life Office management. Ten of the fifteen largest Scots companies were in the financial sector, and employment had gone from 5–6 per cent of the Scots total (7 per cent in UK) to 15 per cent by the late 1980s (17 per cent in UK). Its companies were international in scope; the assets of the biggest, Standard Life, grew from £500 million in 1959 to £40 billion in 1995. Their scale of operations was far beyond that of any Scottish government, which would handle about £14.5 billion annually. Despite ritual obeisance to Adam Smith, financial services were unconcerned either with the trickling-down of wealth to the lower orders, or any notion of society being held together by sympathy. In fact, the Life Offices (with two-thirds of their 21,200 jobs in Scotland) stood to gain by the withering-away of the welfare state.

In 1995 Edinburgh was the city most business executives wanted to move to, and was counting on 2.3 per cent growth in production, against London's forecast 1.2 per cent. Yet financial services were troubled. The Life Offices were badly hit by pension mis-selling, which brought about a 30 per cent fall in business in 1994–5. In 1996 it was no better; Scottish Amicable moved south, and 4 per cent of business was lost. 'Perth is more than where we have our world headquarters,' said a General Accident advert in 1995, 'it's also where our heart is.' A year later it moved its investment arm to London.

Matters were not much better with manufacturing, now down to only 300,000 jobs, fewer than those in local government. Though they had their protean moments, between 1974 and 1993 the number of Scots-owned and Scots-based companies sank from 150 to 80, and in 1985–6, when two-thirds of Scottish manufacturing capital was sold south, the Guinness takeover of Distillers involved villainy on a transatlantic scale. Seduced by the notion of Edinburgh as the headquarters of a major multinational, Charlotte Square – headed by Sir Thomas Risk and Sir Charles Fraser – had played along with 'deadly Ernest' Saunders. It was only when Saunders reneged that the whistle was blown.

What were the politics of Scottish business? It called itself unionist and echoed the Tory party, but was this sincere? The remaining big Scottish firms – the Royal Bank, Scottish and Newcastle, Standard Life – were streetwise and innovative. It was the banks who facilitated the capital supplies that built up Kwik-Fit into Britain's largest car-repair concern and made the privatised companies First Bus and Stagecoach, and Scottish Power, successful predators. The Royal Bank in particular was saved by George Younger from takeover in 1981, and blossomed under the bankers' banker, Charlie Winter. The rule of the Taipans, the great Far Eastern merchant families of Jardine, Matheson, Keswick and Herries, passed to Younger himself in 1991, and the bank became under George Mathewson, late of the SDA, a dramatic innovator in post-privatisation operations and insurance through its Direct Line subsidiary. Nationalist sympathies were not unknown among its senior staff.

Yet takeovers decimated headquarters staff and fewer and fewer small businesses started up. Scotland was remote from Rhenish capitalism with its *Mittelstand* companies committed to local production, innovation and training, and rather too close to the gnashing teeth of Luttwak's turbo-capitalism. ICI – that prototype of the British firm – was being demerged; the great road hauliers, headed by Christian Salvesen, were changing into internal markets in which nominally independent lorry-owners bartered with the dominant centre. Textiles, swithering between quantity and quality production, struggled along in the Borders and the Western Isles, gloomily conscious of the export consequences if Honor Fraser's or Stella Tennant's hemlines got any shorter. Thus did the last representatives of two great dynasties, in land and chemicals, prescribe! Production in the NICs was a very small part – maybe 3 per cent – of global investment but there were few places where its profits and losses seemed so indelible.

Everyone with some cash got it through a 'hole in the wall', and nearly everyone in the ABC1 classes worked with a personal computer. Manufacturing a large European chunk of such things, Scotland's electronics industry was 11 per cent of the labour force in 1992 and 42 per cent of exports. It had managed a fourfold increase in production in the 1980s, though employment – 42,523 in 1983 – didn't grow much. But only 12 per cent of the incoming firms' purchases were from the Scottish sector, while attempts at high value-added local concerns generally flopped.

Scots had helped set up some of the huge multinationals who were now inward investors. Hyundai, which Sir William Lithgow had helped set up to build giant tankers in South Korea, was by the 1990s locating part of its electronics division in Scotland, along with other Korean firms, eager for access to the EU market. But in 1998 the little tigers suddenly looked very endangered – what would happen to Chungwa at Newmains or Hyundai in Dunfermline? The American software concern Cadence was induced to settle – an executive was surfing the net and hit on the Locate in Scotland website – but this was only the first instance of large-scale, high-value-added production settling down. Cadence announced that it would require 4,000 car parking places – LIS didn't bat an eyelid – but this raised a problem of cultural as well as economic compatibility.

'THIS IS THE JUNK MAIL, CROSSING THE BORDER . . . '

Silicon Glen was expatriate California: its factories identical to American prototypes, but leafier. Generating vast amounts of road traffic, their executives flying to and fro, they plugged into one sequence of Scottish development. Could not, the Edinburgh planners argued, Scotland's disparate economic specialisms be

210

aligned through the accessibility and cultural presence of the country: 'Scotland the Brand' as David McCrone called it?

But this raised issues of access. Scotland – *pace* September 1997 – was more of a nation than Wales – but was it as effective as a European region? Newport was scarcely an hour from Heathrow, or the link to the Channel Tunnel, and *between* Ireland and Europe; Scotland was remote. Moreover, the evolution of European logistics – which could provide up to 25 per cent of GNP – was towards huge, Europe-wide concerns which might think of only a single hub for their entire British business. Scotland could have had a hub but didn't: only three competing medium-sized airports, from which it often cost less to fly to New York than to Frankfurt.'Trains to the south, now privatised, were slow on Richard Branson's West Coast route, and over-crowded on GNER's East Coast. Eurostar bilked on its promised through passenger trains, and proposed sleepers from Scotland to the Continent were ditched without protest or even discus-sion. Ro-ro ferries were endlessly mooted but never arrived. How much was this eccentric mobility based on costs which had been kept artificially low by subsidised road and airport construction, and the failure to extract environmental taxes? If rationalisation were to come about, how would Scotland be placed?

In forty years, 1955–95, there had been a sixfold increase in road traffic. The environmentalist David Spaven wrote that car culture dominated society – 'leaving those without cars perceived as second-class citizens, often with significantly poorer and relatively more expensive public transport than they enjoyed thirty years ago'. The Scottish Office was less 'green' than England's transport ministers. It gained an increased road programme in 1995; theirs fell by 34 per cent. No grant for road–rail freight transfer had been given since 1987, and an ambi-tious plan to expand rail and bus transport in Central region was shelved without explanation by the Labour authority. Increasing opposition, particularly by the young, in a Real World coalition of environmental groups, faced parties whose motives and policies were confused. Yet the paradox was that as public transport continued to deteriorate – bus passengers down 23 per cent between 1986 and 1996 – it became an exciting and prof-itable area of City speculation, in the flourishing of Scottish concerns like Stagecoach and First Bus.

GNER was owned by Sea Containers, based in the Bahamas. It and Branson were stars of the hedonism industry: the gin-palace-on-wheels of the Orient Express was up against Jumbojets, radio, condoms and balloons. Transport and tourism in fact raised acute problems about social and moral values. Tourism would be the world's major transnational trade by 2000, but was almost wholly unknown to economic analysis and touted by a largely corrupt press; few travel articles, even in the broadsheets, were more than paid-for plugs. This set Scottish enterprise at a discount. Yet studying tourism yielded information about which other publications were discreet. Exactly who could afford an overnight at Peter de Savary's Skibo Castle, at £425 for two? Half that sum could keep a Glasgow family of four for a week; a calculation that might have occurred to the place's one-time owner, Andrew Carnegie, but was unlikely to trouble de Savary's clients. The Edinburgh Festival, supplemented by a Hogmanay mini-fest which attracted over 300,000 and a spring Science Festival, contrasted with Glasgow's 'short-breath' problems, particularly when its city boundaries no longer yielded adequate finance. But how far it had drifted from its democratic 1940s origins came out in a *Financial Times* ad for:

> ... The Proscenium Club. One of the few instances where the Edinburgh Festival is totally, utterly and irrefutably elitist ... It's only open to 40 corporate members at a fee of £5000 ... there's the Edinburgh Festival Director's selection of best tickets for a start ... plus excellent opportunities for corporate entertainment and employee benefits.

This wasn't without costs. Edinburgh acquired the seamy 'rest and recreation' side of the conference economy: Mrs Noyce's Danube Street brothel, said to do exceptional business when the Fathers and Brethren were in town for the Kirk's General Assembly, now seemed the prototype for burgeoning sauna and massage parlours in which prostitution was tolerated. A student told the *Scotsman* she wasn't proud of 'turning a few tricks' in one, but she could make more in a week than in a vacation's waitressing.

Given a chronically unpredictable economy, where did the operations of the market, the universal pander, end? The 'unanticipated consequences' of the eighteenth-century *literati* took on new, endlessly contradictory guises. Between 1988 and 1990 a

212

flutter on becoming European City of Culture, plus smart politicking with a Garden Festival and a clever advertising campaign let Glasgow flourish as a tourist centre. A crass attempt by Scottish Office ministers to crack down on drug addicts' needle exchanges, which made Edinburgh the HIV capital of Europe, broadened the task of coping with a drug problem into the supervision of *maisons tolerées*. In 1996 the sudden interest of big media money in rugby union ended the amateur game and galvanised local clubs and local patriots in the cities and the Borders, only to leave some of them sadly adrift. In 1998 commercial pressures forced the second-division football team Clydebank to resite itself in *Dublin*, while the 'Geordie nutter' imported by Rangers occupied more pages at the front of the tabloids than at the back. A Congregational minister let rip at a devolution conference about Scotland being 'married to a prostitute', meaning England, but the implications of the leisure and servitor-capitalist economy meant that parts of the nation were rather too literally on the *qui vive*.

SOCIETY: SETTLED, INSECURE, EXCLUDED

This element of serendipity complicated attempts to fathom society. In the 1940s the social anthropologist James Littlejohn had surveyed the parish of Eskdalemuir, near Lockerbie, to produce a fascinating picture of Scottish country life. A follow-up in the 1990s would have had to account for the fact that half the population were Buddhist monks. Exoticism apart, was Scottish society greatly different from the south? A survey by Bill Miller in 1996 found attitudes deviating by only about 10 per cent – though this scale of magnitude also applied to differences with West Europe in general.

Still, the economy retained a more substantial state sector, which involved opposition politicians in consensual activities and public–private sector partnerships, while in provincial England the municipal socialist ethos, if not in abeyance, was subordinate to commercial pressure. In the city centres or in the new towns this showed itself as trim, neat and purposive, but a bus trip from Motherwell via Blantyre and Rutherglen to Glasgow passed through a different landscape, of derelict heavy industry, problem schemes, struggling small entrepreneurs, vast supermarkets: confused, lurid, difficult to read.

In the 1980s the talk had been of a 'two-thirds' society, in which the well-being of the majority was to some extent purchased at the cost of the least well-off. But a Scottish Council Institute report in January 1998 found a more ominous tripartite division into settled Scotland, insecure Scotland and excluded Scotland. These boundaries didn't necessarily fit existing classes; location, age and health also played a part.

The settled Scots were a mixture of the wealthy and the soundly guaranteed – businessmen and civil servants, teachers and local government employees, and those who had got themselves golden handshakes from their employers – the folk who had bought their houses for four-figure sums in the 1960s, and whose pensions kept Charlotte Square running. They had their big stone-built flats, country cottages and golf clubs, their yachts and Italian holidays. The 240,000 members of the National Trust for Scotland might, if multiplied by a notional family size of four, give their dimensions. They weren't as affluent as the small *haute bourgeoisie* of the 1900s, nor were they in general as politically active, but they kept a civic society going: theatres, literary associations, bookshops and art galleries. This circuit functioned effectively, but it wasn't expanding. Or rather, in order to service it through the operations of hard-nosed fund managers, the life-chances of others were being diminished.

The insecure Scots could simply be the same but younger. Entrants to journalism and broadcasting, academia and research were now on contract rather than tenure. Between a third and a half of new jobs were part-time, and many manual and white-collar workers now did business on their own account where earlier they would have been on the establishment of substantial firms – lorry drivers, for instance, or employees of Compaq Computers who built up a supplementary labour force to come in 'on call' when a big order turned up. Insecurity wasn't new. Up to 1960 most Scottish males had worked outside, or at sea, or underground, in the fields, on railways or building sites. Exhaustion was general, and injury and illness frequent. The completion of a ship or contract could bring the dole. But inside and outside the pastel-coloured blocks of the new economy, these problems didn't diminish. In William McIlvanney's novel *Strange Loyalties* (1991) his detective Jack Laidlaw, investigating the death of his teacher brother, run over by a car, finds his fate a metaphor of the impact of 'the machine' on flesh-and-blood. Laidlaw's zig-zag journey across southern Scotland becomes an inquest on *bourgeois* Scotland's implication in a social order indifferent to personal outcomes, from the accident which kills the ex-boxer Dan Scoular, hero of *The Big Man* (1985), to the old man run over by Glasgow students in the 1960s, the primal crime which poisons a hopeful generation.

Death was closer than it ought to have been. Although wages had risen roughly to the British average, patterns of expenditure were different. Thirty-eight per cent of Scots families lived in flats, compared with 17 per cent in the UK; they shopped locally rather than in malls. These were plusses for notions of community. But they bought fizzy drinks, canned soup and chocolate biscuits half as much again as the British average; drinking and smoking were a third higher. This was something which issued in truly horrendous statistics of death and disease. In the mid-1980s the Scottish male death-rate from all causes was at 1,318 per 100,000, the highest in Western Europe. A health service enquiry found that 'Men in the manual classes had death-rates 45 per cent higher than men in the non-manual classes, and women had death-rates 43 per cent higher.'

And under all of this was a trap waiting to spring, and project the insecure down into the excluded. Some were almost fore-doomed. As conventional marriage collapsed – 1,800 divorces in 1955, 12,000 in 1995 – but the urge to couple continued, the teenage kids who were marginalised by the new relationship started with little going for them, and even less after 1988, when they were deprived of social benefits. Ill-health could also stem from 10 to 15 percent of unfit homes, as well as from diet, drink and poverty. These could rapidly imprison, as could confine-ment in problem schemes – every town had them – which exhibited multiple social deprivation. On top of this came drugs. Virtually unknown in Scotland in the 1970s, their salience rapidly grew in the next decade, particularly in areas which had suffered a complete industrial wipeout, such as Paisley after the Linwood closure, or the village of Drongan in Ayrshire, built to house the miners from the Barony Colliery, which had by 1995 one of the worst per capita problems in Britain.

'There is no such thing as society, only individuals and families' was perhaps Mrs Thatcher's most notorious statement, and a cap-tious break with a Tory attitude to the old seamless web which, from Edmund Burke onwards, had never been less than subtle. How sincere anyway was she about shifting responsibilities to individuals or families, when her allies in media, advertising and acquisitive consumerism could not have survived an assault on the welfare state? Her entourage wasn't a monument to marital stability or – drink and drugs being around quite a lot – to puritanism. Image substituted for action and, in Scotland, Thatcher's image didn't fit.

A survey of stereotypes in 1997 by the sociologist Isobel Lindsay disclosed a pervasive and frankly irrational anti-English irritation. This was class-based, however, and seldom had Anglicised 'winners' been more in evidence than in the Thatcher years. The August migration to the highlands and universities of the wealthy and their noisy offspring, salient after half-a-century of obscurity, bred mutterings about 'Yahs', 'white settlers' and 'FEBs'. Reactions got harsher after the false dawn of 1992, yet there was a certain ripe irony in Michael Forsyth attempting to reanimate Tartan Toryism by denouncing constitutional change as an Islington plot.

UPPIES AND DOONIES

Where did all this leave the 'estates', the traditional guarantors of civic nationalism in Scotland? Although they got their own apologia in Lindsay Paterson's *The Autonomy of Modern Scotland* (1995), their health was variable. Law and local government found themselves implicated in political changes. The first shared in the increasing criticism by the judicature of the legislature and executive that marked the Thatcher and Major years. This was somewhat ironic since the Woolsack passed from Lord Hailsham, almost a caricature Oxford and Inns of Court figure but a devolver, to Lord MacKay, a Scot of puritan integrity, reforming zeal and fierce unionism. Lawyers who had been hostile to devolution, such as Judge David Edward, became favourable to it indirectly, through experience in the European courts, and by 1996 the Court of Session wasn't above cuffing the government's ears when a prime-ministerial broadcast was suddenly scheduled just before Scottish local elections. Local government politics are difficult to disentangle from parliamentary ditto, so most of them will irrupt in the next chapter, but let it be noted that attempts to abrogate these in favour of (theoretically) the private sector meant state action and this, out of sheer inertia, and a reluctance to offend everyone all the time, meant the Scottish state.

In education Scottish comprehensives had a prestige denied their English counterparts; independents were comparatively few. In 1994 53 per cent of Scottish pupils got over five GCSE equivalents, compared with 39 per cent in England, and 43 per cent went into higher education, against 30 per cent. With the introduction in 1981 of parental choice, however, the worrying tendency of the district school to reinforce social divisions was aggravated. In 1990 62 per cent of candidates at Dunblane High got more than three Highers, and in sixteen Glasgow secondaries no-one got anything. There was a continual tug-o'-war over policy. Heads and parents, as much as politicians, rejected attempts to break up educational authorities by opting out. Government forced the publication of league tables of schools, against protests that these ignored social make-up in the catchment areas. In 1989 Mrs Thatcher intervened to try to save Paisley Grammar, on the prompting of its old boy Andrew Neil of the *Sunday Times*, the beginning of a brief but fateful involvement in Scottish affairs, but the national tradition appeared to survive intact. 'Appeared' because it had effectively become more meritocratic, with informed parents propelling their children towards schools with an academic record.

In the *Scotsman* in 1998 the same Andrew Neil, now the editor-in-chief appointed by the Barclay brothers (and, as far as anyone knew, not actually a parent) would harp on about the state sector assaulting centres of excellence. Since most commentators regarded him as dumbing down the paper according to the prescription of his former master Rupert Murdoch, the honours were more or less even. But any school had a hard fight against an Americanised commercial culture peddling inane materialism and conformity, while provoking among pupils an increasing foreboding about future security.

Between 1989 and 1994 university numbers rose 70 per cent and higher education passed into the remit of the Scottish Office. University expansion was one means whereby unemployment statistics were curbed; it doubled the number of Scottish universities, and in 1997 the dream of a University of the Highlands and Islands looked like becoming a reality. But events at some of the new foundations made even advocates pause for thought, not least because funding grew at only half the rate of student expansion. At the end of 1996 the vice-chancellors of four universities – Edinburgh, Cambridge, Warwick and University College London – were muttering, rather tactlessly, about the need for a 'big league'; some were more equal than others. The broad, philosophically based curriculum, all but obscured under an avalanche of vocational courses, seemed likely to expire before devolution became reality.

The profile of the Churches remained high, though not always for the best of reasons. In 1996 only 13 per cent of the Scots were regular attenders, though this was good in comparison with England (10 per cent) or Wales (8 per cent). But, in this period, was the Protestant tradition central? Arguably Catholicism was more salient, claiming 800,000 adherents in 1980, 250,000 of whom greeted the Pope when he visited Scotland in May 1982. But 120,000 had already lapsed. The drift was as fast as that from Protestantism, as Catholics were secularising and their children entering higher education. True, there had been earlier successes – Wheatleys, Brogans and Cronins, Matt Busby, Sean Connery – and this had applied also to the Italians, Scandinavians or Jews, who provided the Coias and Contis, the Magnussons, Daiches and Rifkinds. After 1970, however, Catholics contributed generously (perhaps even disproportionately) to the Scottish elite.

Only in the mid-1990s, with the cease-fire in Northern Ireland, were the Scots' western cousins – 'a fell dour den, but oor ain' – as John Buchan had put it, beginning to be talked about. The Catholics' Scots loyalties may have been aided by reflection on the conflict, something which both severed traditional links and increased the determination to hold to an idea of civil society. In part a variant on the dynamism which was transforming the Irish republic, these changes implied a critical citizenship, detached from older institutions, closures and prejudices, *and* a mundane politics of manipulation and patronage. An earlier generation might have chosen vocations, now historians such as Tom Gallagher and Tom Devine, novelists like William McIlvanney, writers such as Bob Tait, Pat Kane and Andrew O'Hagan and entertainers like Billy Connolly dominated a culture which was simultaneously Scots and international.

218

IN THE POSTMODERN MEGASTORE?

'When was Wales?' asked Gwyn Williams in 1983. 'Where was Scotland?' would be apposite for the mid-1990s. Was it in Europe? The political class thought so. Or part of Anglo-America, as so much of Scottish consumer and popular culture tended to assume? It was easier and cheaper to reach New York by plane than all but a few European destinations. The 1990s was the USA's decade of triumph, but the politics of post-nationalism, submitting to dollar imperialism, didn't reassure the Scots elite, particularly in their old domain of Canada. Was Scotland postmodern or neo-modern? Such questions prompted Nairn's *Janus Revisited* and enjoined a backward glance.

In what ways did these changes become ideology? The notions of Nairn or McCrone or your man seemed to assume a cumulative marginalising of the union cause. This raised the pervasive and moulding effect of literary culture and historical research. If one examined Glasgow's literary radicalism, of which the work of Alasdair Gray, James Kelman, Liz Lochhead, Agnes Owens, William McIlvanney or Jeff Torrington was only a part, it emerged as something quite different from literary politics elsewhere. This lay in the commitment of its writers to their own city and their own people, countervailing the market to give a voice to 'folk on low incomes', with its decent and rational ideal – seemingly moribund in the south – of a 'Scottish Cooperative Wholesale Republic'.

Nonetheless, this wasn't straightforward. Glasgow ran through rather a lot of literary and cultural ventures and venues. Mayfest, around for twelve years, expired in 1997. The worker's city writers spurned the merchant city as being tourism cooked up by entrepreneurs: the loot of the Burrell Collection, a controversial Gallery of Modern Art, the 'Mockintosh' lettering which only served to remind how shabbily Glasgow had treated its greatest architect. This was almost a miniature of European confrontation – Ossies versus Wessies – though lightened by a sharp irony to be found in the sculptures of Ian Hamilton Finlay and George Wilkie. The arts were part of 'insecure Scotland': they also presented a fascinating, continually changing world quite different from the social or confessional monoliths of the past. As the critic Joyce Macmillan remarked in 1994 in her summing-up of arts policy for the newly devolved Arts Council, they were faced with overcoming the division between high and community arts and with empowering traditionally disadvantaged groups, not least women.

'If there was hope, it lay with the proles'? That would be too easy. Orwell hadn't reckoned with pervasive insecurity and third-generation unemployment. Even enthusiastic leftists had to admit that the cool seemed as salient in Scotland as elsewhere, especially after *Trainspotting*: kids bunking off school, swaggering as clotheshorses for Adidas, subliterate, aggressive, bored. But civil society was minatory, defensive. When Tom Nairn cited the unavoidable nature of nationality, this was a *jetée* to the eighteenth century when Adam Ferguson's sociology contrasted with that of Saint-Simon and Comte. While the latter saw society evolving circumspectly from the religious through the metaphysical to the positive or scientific stage, Ferguson stressed continuing conflict between the in-group and 'the other', and the menace of luxury and corruption which commerce brought in its wake. Effectively this endorsed the 'strong' – quasi-political – institutions which the Scottish estates embodied. The irony, as Nairn observed, was that – largely thanks to Gellner – the 'softer' version was being touted round an East Europe desperate for a voluntarist substitute for the all-pervasive Communist state.

The Scottish tradition was important, because at a crucial point – the 1830s – Carlyle synthesised Ferguson and Saint-Simon *in the interest of England*. This anticipated the followers of Comte – from Emile Durkheim to Vilfredo Pareto – who accomplished between 1880 and 1920 what Stuart Hughes calls 'the reorientation of European social thought'. Caught between Marx and Bismarckian militarism, they detected beneath mass society huge substructures of habit, superstition, sex-drives and ethnic patriotism, and tried to bind these into their explanations. This had a strong Scottish element: the social anthropology of Robertson Smith and J. G. Frazer, the vast myth-kitty of *The Golden Bough*, culminating in the regional studies of Patrick Geddes, and the pioneering of psychoanalysis which produced Maurice Nicoll, Ronald Fairbairn, A. J. Brock and ultimately R. D. Laing. This investigation of time, mind, society and sex was interwoven with the achievement of Mann and Proust, Joyce, Yeats, Eliot, Pound and MacDiarmid: 'we moderns' as the young Edwin Muir would christen them in *The New Age*.

Yet Muir found Glasgow – the 'technopolis' *par excellence* – sheer hell, after his edenic Orkneys. This belied tensions between town and country, people and institutions. Neither civics nor modernism were democratic. Glasgow's 'municipal socialism' was run by middle-class rentiers, by 1912 scared stiff of organised Labour, deploying civic capital to steer society from class conflict. Schools, town government, universities, research institutes and museums, not to speak of huge intellectual enterprises like the *Oxford English Dictionary* or the *Cambridge Modern History* were either civic or British – one reason for the eclipse of Scottish consciousness at this time.

These also led, in finance, either to social democracy or to tariffs and imperialism. The latter not only increased the risks of war, but re-enthroned the anti-modern, in military elites and military technology – a vicious circle which completed itself in 1914–18. What emerged was the totalitarian modernism of Soviet communism and authoritarian ethnic nationalism, fascism, again exploiting technology. The conflict of both with one another and democracy lasted until 1989–91. The victory of the moderns – the Fukuyamas and Dahrendorfs – was short-lived, but ensured that Scotland's renascent nationalism coincided with market and information revolutions which shattered structures and hierarchies, leaving a hyper-individuation exhausted by its technology, and overwhelmed by its data: deconstructed texts, rejected canons, literature or culture fixed in local constellations. After the psychodramas of Thatcherism, Britain imploded, leaving isolated bits of modernism as *micropoli* – small, essentially political clans camping out in the ruins. 'Policy communities' replaced statesmen, 'culture industries' took over from F. R. Leavis's 'great tradition', and ran on *chutzpah* plus the rewards provided by global capitalism. A hugely inegalitarian information-market rewarded the successful while exorcising the problematic.

Scotland was struggling into statehood in a world dominated by three history-less communities: Germany and Japan wanted to forget their pasts; America's Anglo-Saxonist frontier had been swamped by multicultural masses and magpie plutocrats. Within – and beyond – such societies the *micropoli* appeared as life-style communities, global *and* defensive or, in the case of the internet, open *and* paranoid. These varied by income, social background and age and, perhaps because Scottish identity was so complex and inviting, there was hardly a part of the affluent world which didn't have its *Schottlandkenner*. Guelph in Canada and Columbia, South Carolina, were long established, but the University of Eastern Tennessee, Kobe University in Japan and Mainz-Germersheim on the banks of the Rhine were catching up.

Was there the embryo of a new and positive international society here, with a potential central *locus* in Scotland? Civic nationalism – preached by Tom Nairn and vibrant in Alasdair Gray's Scottish Cooperative Wholesale Republic – wasn't cool. When the Campaign for a Scottish Assembly's *Claim of Right* appeared in 1988, it was framed by quotes from Adam Ferguson and Scott: community as real but narrow and aggressive, modulating into community as commodity. The Enlightenment had given Scotland an advance dose of modernisation, and to go back to this experience, made Scottish history a good instructor. The problem was that the institutions of research associated with the nation, such as sociology, had declined, while media-hype had gone ballistic.

One streetwise *savant*, the American Ben Bradshaw, suggested that postmodern society was dividing into two ideological streams, combating *anomie* in different but dynamic ways: McWorld and Jihad. Scotland, typically, produced simultaneous paradigms of both.

Irvine Welsh was the author of *Trainspotting* (1993), the tenth most significant book ever, or so Waterstones said. Welsh was like Scott in writing a powerful and credible *patois* – though on a crude monotone – but his ideology (Dave McSpart, as Kenneth Roy put it) tinkled away in received pronunciation sociologese. There may originally have been a political purpose in these tales of the semi-qualified insecure of McWorld and their instant gratification, but the mark of the MBA was there. Welsh shrewdly commodified the result into 'books for people who don't read books, exploiting the satanic kailyard of the chemical generation as professionally as *No Mean City* had milked working-class Glasgow in the 1930s, or as 'Ian MacLaren' had played the Mid-West in the 1890s.

Welsh's shivering junkies shared the billboards with Mel Gibson's *Braveheart* (1995). Tinseltown had (yet again) discovered Caledonia Stern and Wild. This version of Jihad was more ominous, as although it massaged crude ethnic nationalism, Scots and (after jumping through some weird dynastic hoops) English, it exemplified Gibson's extreme right-wing politics. This was a proto-Darwinian, individualist as hero figure, all too keen on settling complicated problems with a broadsword, not out of the dressing-up box of Thatcherism, but out of the bestiary of the American nightmare.

THE REVENGE OF CALIBAN

One terminus of the Scottish *Sonderweg* could be the events of May and September 1997. Another, far less inspiriting, could be the town of Dunblane, and the crime of 13 March 1996: a horror which went round the world. The action of Thomas Hamilton was so extreme as to stifle discussion, but it wasn't a simple case of a psychotic misfit, business failure and sexual deviant running amok in the entry class at a primary school, killing sixteen inno- cent 5-year-olds and their teacher before putting one of his four fast-action handguns in his mouth and blowing his brains out. Dunblane held the headlines for a week, until the scandal of BSE – also painful for Scotland – broke. Then within a month a 'copycat' struck, even more lethally, in Tasmania.

The catastrophe generated no grief industry, but an agitation which gained a wide-ranging ban on hand-guns. In political terms, this disadvantaged the Conservatives, whose Home Affairs Committee MPs' pro-gun report was condemned, and the monarchy, through an insensitive intervention by the Duke of Edinburgh.

But the perpetrator wasn't, as so often, someone who 'kept himself to himself'. Hamilton was quite high-profile. He had organised youth clubs in various parts of central Scotland, including camps and athletic contests. He was suspected of paedophilia, but no-one could pin anything on him. One attempt ended in 1984 when he took his accuser to the local government ombudsman and won. Michael Forsyth, his MP, had congratu- lated him on this, but what alternative had he? Hamilton also had supporters on the local Labour council. Dunblane had stood out against his youth schemes. Was this why he revenged himself there?

Hamilton was 43, the product of a crazily dysfunctional family (illegitimate, he was brought up by grandparents who told him he was an orphan, while pretending his mother was his sister) and had lived with his father until they had split in 1992. He had tried to become a scoutmaster in 1974, but had been dismissed for incompetence in managing a weekend hike. Then he had run his clubs (for which there was no form of regulation) with the help of a 'staff' of teenage youths, and several hundred boys had, over the years, attended them. He liked photographing them, stripped to the waist, wearing baggy shorts like the Hitler Youth. But there were also echoes of General Gordon, Robert Baden-Powell, or Patrick Pearse. How many youth movements in the past had counted on some such mixture of motives to supplement the dedication required to keep them moving? Ian Jack, writing in the *Independent*, remembered a rather similar character from his Fife boyhood, always organising things, spouting bright ideas, but with a manner which soon made people avoid his company.

Following the James Bulger case in Liverpool, when two small boys had tortured a toddler to death, Hamilton appealed to local authorities for support for his clubs, as discipline and healthy exercise which would keep kids off the streets. But suspicions remained after his court case, and he became involved in a homosexual incident. Did this push him over the edge? Or had his disturbance global as well as local roots? In 1995, members of an extreme right-wing American militia, like Hamilton obsessed with weaponry, had blown up the Federal Building in Oklahoma City killing 167, including twenty toddlers.

Hamilton chose to revenge himself on a town of 9,000 which represented Scotland at perhaps its most successful and integrated. Dunblane was called 'a close-knit community', but in fact its breadwinners commuted to workplaces within the central belt, when they didn't work at Stirling University. Children who went to Dunblane High School were the best academic performers in Scotland; the town was represented in parliament by the Secretary of State, and his shadow, George Robertson, lived there, as did Canon Kenyon Wright, leader of the Scottish Constitutional Convention. Did Hamilton decide on his own execution, and determine on a crime to match it, to be as damaging a legacy as he could leave?

Several worrying questions were latent. Five-year-olds were innocents, but truant teenagers another matter. In Glasgow nearly 20 per cent of schoolkids were bunking off; most people, confronted with 14-year-olds, hanging around, smoking, vandalising, swearing, 'could have seen them far enough'. In various central Scottish towns Hamilton's clubs were a solution, not a problem. 'Wear them out. Get some discipline into them' was what he was offering, in a bundle of mixed motives. And from other mixed motives – particularly a decline in community activities – the offer was accepted. Membership in the Scouts and BBs and their sister organisations had dropped by 20 per cent in the eight years to 1996, and the usual reason given was lack of volunteers who could motivate the kids away from forms of entertainment – TV, videos, Walkmen, Nintendo – which were simultaneously over-individualised *and* conformity-inducing, sedentary *and* violent. As George Rosie noted in *Scotland on Sunday*, the old, autonomous culture of kids had been evicted by an imported, chiefly American juvenile consumerism: 'cool' and 'attitude' discouraged communication. Most adults were hard put to compete and this left the gifted, the committed and the eccentric.

'Close-knit' in the case of Dunblane seemed to be an antipode to 'unravelling' in less fortunate places. A third of marriages ended in divorce, so more children were reared in households where there was no father, or (perhaps worse) a new partner unconnected and uncommitted to them. One in three children were anyway growing up into poverty. As career prospects diminished, rationality and skill acquisition fell far down the list. The market rewarded some types of exploitation, and the law penalised others. Welsh's novels and plays, the *dernier cri* of 1995–6, offered extreme experience as hyper-hedonism. In *Marabou Stork Nightmares* (1995) several graphic pages of gang-rape were followed by poster-like inserts plugging 'zero tolerance' of it. But was the novel being read for this elevated message?

This was a society which offered personal development as an antidote to economic dislocation. Sometimes literally. A poignant TV documentary showed how unemployed steelworkers in Coatbridge became body-builders, exercising in the huge empty halls where they'd once worked. This drew the community around them, but what then? As the collective tide of churches and unions and political parties went out it left, lurking here and there in the unvisited parts of central Scotland, forlorn grouplets and individuals pursuing their own *idées fixes* – UFOs, Orangeism, hypnotism, the occult. *Motherwell People*, a Lanarkshire freesheet, had a weekly column of advice on family and work problems, not by a minister or social worker but a tarot card reader. Perhaps there was more of this sort of thing than in England, given a Scots shyness and reluctance to get drawn into things which affected the traditional voluntary sector: something in its way parallel to the troubles of poor white America demonstrated at Oklahoma City. Andrew O'Hagan's *The Missing*, which came out in 1995, suggested that society, as well as some of its inhabitants, had gone AWOL: that it had drifted far away from what was comprehensible even in terms of his own youth in the 1970s.

Along with globalisation came a recoil from the state. This was pre-modernist; its militancy showed the downside to Fergusonian sociology, with Oklahoma a chilling *réprise* of the militia agitation of the 1760s and 'the right to bear arms'. Was it mere speculation to hypothesise similar forces behind a break-down like Dunblane? The snapping of the individual, when the bolt of society was too tight or too loose – this time coupled with a torrent of troubled information and opinion about a troubled world?

Scotland's reckoning with itself was, at best, ambiguous. Poetry was confident of place and landscape, though the masters – Norman MacCaig, Sorley MacLean, George Mackay Brown – were departing. The novel was not. Among the characters invented to typify modern Scotland or, in the salience of the crime story, the notion of solipsism was pervasive. 'It will be horror' as James Kelman observed, lapidarily, of everyday life. Whether in the cases of Inspectors Laidlaw or Rebus, or the tormented characters and encoded plots of Ian Rankin, Frederic Lindsay, Iain Banks, Ian MacEwen or even Allan Massie, a divided, fathomless and largely male society was on view, naked before the winds of a terrible century. A feminist critique wasn't absent, but it came in at a different angle, through an autobio-graphical re-examination of personal histories: Meg Henderson's *Finding Peggy* (1994) or Kay Carmichael's *For Crying Out Loud* (1995). To these were fused subtle despatches from the front by younger writers – A. L. Kennedy, Janice Galloway, Liz Lochhead – and a recovered history of their own, in which the neglected and forgotten could revive: writers like Catherine Carswell, Willa Muir and Naomi Mitchison, who looked as if she would beat the century at both ends. For most women horror was never far away, given worries about children, domestic violence, ill-health, ageing relatives. Yet they had kept some sort of society going, so often *against* church, school, medical professionals, and men whose culture had become totally dysfunctional. If women got equal representation in the Scottish parliament, this would be overdue recompense: it would also be a revolution.

The problem was that Scots sociology, for all its salience, was impressionistic rather than systematic. Other bourgeois states would have been more considerate in furnishing material for theoretical historians. A hundred and eighty years earlier, John Galt had drawn on the *Statistical Accounts*, but the *Third Statistical Account* was published over too broad a period to provide comparative data. In this period academic sociology had been evicted by market research, which simply didn't want to know about the 33 per cent too poor to qualify. The nation-building concerns of Nairn or McCrone were not likely to include them either. A *Scottish Affairs* article concluded that if you really wanted to hide from history, you should be female, poor and worried about the environment.

REVERSING INTO HISTORY

In this upheaval was regionalism, or civic nationalism, yet another lifestyle, or could it reform the state? Getting history right was critical, in recovering a trajectory which was civic rather than ethnic or commercial-exploitative. The Scottish renaissance of the 1980s looked eccentric because metropolitan politicians and intellectuals were deserting the nation. Their new cultural vocabulary was ahistorical and non-discriminatory, but its priorities were those of accountancy which seemed, in the universities and the arts, to be weakening experiment and inter-disciplinarity.

The Scottish political tradition had stood out against a culture divided from history. It was England which had gone tartan, devising a heritage market round a canon, rigid and ritualised, aimed at cultural tourism, themed around Shakespeare, the Brontës or Bloomsbury. Such 'internationally viable projects' – with their hierarchies turned into political institutions – hadn't just evicted social criticism of the Richard Hoggart or Raymond Williams sort. Turbo-capitalism reduced political economy from a *Staatsphilosophie* to narrow management studies or propaganda for the market which covered only a fraction of the discipline. Adam Smith was a rhetorician, but his rhetoric was inclusive. Market men might have been winning, but they sounded more and more like Social Crediters or bimetallists. The project of stakeholder capitalism – a broadly European, Keynesian economic order once identified with New Labour – was buried in quicklime by Gordon Brown, in favour of Anglo-Saxon *laissez-faire*, and no-one noticed.

Brown was not the only history man of the left to surrender. John Lloyd had been far-left at Edinburgh University. With flowing hair and John Arden glasses, he went even further left as a member of the International Marxist Group: only one of those whose Damascus-like conversion to the market saw a left vocabulary – 'projects', 'commitments', 'cultures' – harnessed to commercial and technological practices far smoother than the chaos they were used to. ('You were the one who was supposed to bring the pamphlets!') They admired the 'sheer professionalism' of the Blairite project; and concerned themselves little with its ideological narrowness, its dependence on rigid party discipline and mysterious external finance.

Scots, still aware of national structures which locked history and politics together, could see how rapidly such projects fall apart. New Labour was loud on messages and mission statements, but quiet about policy and about its negotiation with the New World barons, the Murdochs and Gateses. Its communitarianism – Macmurray, Etzioni, etc. – seemed cosmetic, with control freaks backstage. Was this exportable to the evolving European state? No. Marketism provoked mass-action to protect Keynesian gains. Job losses and cuts in welfare and public services identified competitive reform with the owners of capital. German trade unionists knew that DM 150 billion a year flowed into tax havens. Environmentalists saw American growth bought by dodging the requirements of the Rio summit. But in a metropolitan left lacking any social philosophers cognate with Hans Küng or Jürgen Habermas, dissent was virtually impossible.

If compartments were opened, and the global constrained, then the Anglo-American model looked dubious. With road and air transport covering only a third of their environmental costs, reforms aimed at safeguarding the climate would start to bite. The fall of the little tigers, and the electrocution of Russia by the shock therapy of the market might only be the first stages in a shift back to regulation.

Would this be democratic regulation? The Murdoch–Neil agenda put Scottish internationalism in a different context. Ayn

Rand was all but unknown in Scotland, but her super-capitalist hero John Galt bore a Scottish name. This Russian emigré rightist was big in the States, with hyper-individualist epics such as *The Fountainhead* and *Atlas Shrugged*. The enthusiasm for these among the American elite – from Hilary Clinton to Alan Greenspan of the Federal Reserve and the scientific racist Charles Murray – suggested that in a future more likely to resemble a global mall, fenced off for the security of the wealthy, than a postmodern supermarket, co-ordination would come through a pitiless capitalist authoritarianism, derived from Herbert Spencer and Rudyard Kipling. One could look at Wall Street, Microsoft or News International – and at Skibo Castle – and see a lot of this Social Darwinism in place: James Hogg's Gil-martin on a global scale.

8

FACING THE CUILLIN
Politics 1986–2000

Thar lochan fala clann nan daoine,
thar breòiteachd blàir is stri an aonaich,
thar bochdainn, caithimh, fiabhrais, àmghair,
thar anacothrom, eucoir, ainneart, ànraidh,
thar truaighe, eu-dàchas, gamhlas, cuilbheart,
thar ciont is truaillidheachd; gu furachair,
gu treunmhor chithear an Cuilithionn
's e'g èirigh air taobh eile duilghr.

Somhairle Macgill-eain, 'An Cuilithionn', 1939

RIFKINDISM

A political narrative, of clever manoeuvre, inept appointments, clumsy mistakes – 'events, dear boy, events' but *Scottish* ones – cumulatively skewed London policy on Scotland. In retrospect the drama could be divided into three acts, with two turning-points, in 1986 and in 1992. To state this is to open again the Thatcher inquest. Her demonisation by so many in Scotland (the present writer included) conceals too much. The Scots didn't care all that much for Kinnock or Blair either. Was she an English nationalist, as she told Michael Ancram? But English nationalists around her wanted the Scots to clear out, carrying with them the toxins of Celtic collectivism. Was she a British imperialist? If so, she was an incompetent one, letting the Scottish Unionists collapse when some superficial devolution compromise (of the third chamber sort entertained by Edward Heath) might have given them room for manoeuvre. Or was she, on this as on other issues a typical Westminster product, aiming at party advantage, unconcerned as to ultimate ends?

230

Until oil prices collapsed in 1986, she maintained and was maintained by an orthodox welfare state. Her monetarist *démarche* – the details of which were Geoffrey Howe's – was a shambles. She had to change course in 1981, treading water desperately until the Falklands happened in the following year. As the *Guardian* remarked after the election of 1983, it was Beveridge that won it for her, keeping most of the discontented off the streets at any one time. Privatisations were opportunistic: mainly selling off the oil industry while earnings were high. The full forces of the state were flung against the miners, true, but the relevant minister, Peter Walker, counted as a wet and was after 1986 to be a vastly popular Welsh Secretary, cheered as a bipartisan force in the valleys whose pits he closed.

After 1986, with austerity in view, Thatcher became more ideological, and Scotland bore the marks. At Westminster a near-terminal crisis blew up when she let the Americans rather than the Europeans take over the British helicopter industry. Westland was clumsy and panic-driven, and Thatcher was only saved from Michael Heseltine and oblivion by the fact that Neil Kinnock was clumsier. Heseltine resigned, and the Scottish Secretary George Younger succeeded him at Defence. Malcolm Rifkind went to St Andrew's House.

There were two types of Secretary, and these types cut across the unionist/home rule divide: the manager or the ideologue. The latter were pretty rare. The first was prepared to go with the flow of the Scots (or at least the Scots who mattered); the second would challenge them, on policy and nationalism. The first usually had to be a grandee in the party, a whip like James Stuart or a magnate like John Maclay. The second, a Johnston or an Elliot, had to be very clever and persuasive; and was for that reason unlikely to be completely sound on the Union.

In 1979 Thatcher lost her pet Clydeside calvinist Teddy Taylor. But how sound was he? Many recollected a crypto-nationalist phase, and old Scottish Office hands found the 'redneck populist' of this book's first edition to be friendly and consensual far beyond the call of duty. To Southend and Bob Marley he went; he returned in 1990 at Michael Forsyth's invitation, only to shake his head. Younger, his replacement, was a classic manager – economic grandee plus power-broker – but his expert finessing of the damage of the petro-pound and sado-monetarism depended on oil revenues.

With these on the slide, and businessmen outraged by rising rates, Younger hatched the Poll Tax. The unionism of its begetter, the Adam Smith Institute, might have been checked out. Madsen Pirie, its founder, was a root-and-branch independence man; Forsyth, the chief of its younger *fauves*, had in 1983 suggested floating the £ Scots against sterling. But Rifkind picked up the Poll Tax and ran with it. A *ci-devant* devolver, he was clever, ambitious, unsocial (in 1993 his drinks bill at Defence was £30, Douglas Hurd's at the Foreign Office £30,000). He had defied Thatcher from 1976 to 1979, to no avail. It had been shown on 1 March 1979 that the Scots weren't worth going out on a limb for, so he reappeared as an acolyte. In Miss Jean Brodie mood the premier called him 'the greatest Secretary of State Scotland has ever had'. He was, like Giotto, her favourite. But this didn't stop him being briskly hammered in the 1987 election. The result was what Alan Lawson, the gifted editor of *Radical Scotland* (a bite-your-bum opinion sheet), called the Doomsday Scenario: the Tories in power in the south and facing oblivion in the north.

Rifkind invoked the authoritarianism of eighteenth-century 'improvement' and presented himself as a latter-day Dundas. He made the Poll Tax – and bus and electricity privatisation – weapons against what he called 'dependency culture', boasting about this to the Adam Smith boys and an oddball hard-right outfit called the Campaign for a Free Britain, run by a mysterious property speculator David Hart. As far as the marketising of government – in the health service, housing and education – was concerned, Scotland would evolve from sloth to guinea-pig.

A learning curve, one might say, little different from Tony Blair's. But as Secretary of State, Rifkind was saddled with his leader. After 1986, Mrs Thatcher's mind seemed fixed on the north, much as Edward I's had been in 1300. The Scots felt their bile was justified. In fact, she had tippled on neat ideology enough to endow the place with the entrepreneurialism of her mid-period: the old misreading of the Enlightenment, with economic 'mechanism' shorn of Ferguson's 'society' or Adam Smith's 'sympathy'. Her court had Scots hard-righties tripping over each other, and ultimately she fell over them. The problem was that this ideological phase allowed constitutional agitation to catch up with and convert latent discontent into something far more formidable.

FROM CAMPAIGN TO CONVENTION

A year after the disaster, in March 1980, the Campaign for a Scottish Assembly, consistent agitator of the issue for what turned out to be a generation, was founded by Dr Jack Brand of Strathclyde University. The CSA's premise was that things had changed in the 1970s, and permanently. In this sense it resembled the second stage of Hroch's intellectual nationalism, organising ideas into policies affecting culture and socialisation. But intellectual spirits were muted. Jim Ross, the civil servant once in charge of devolution, remembered a fringe meeting at the Scottish Labour Conference in 1981 when he and Jim Boyack, an architect and dogged home ruler since the days of the Covenant, were the only people present. Only in the run-up to the 1983 election did it begin to take off, with centre-left politicians at the Assembly Rooms in Edinburgh, and academia and the literati in the corridors: Tom Nairn, Hamish Henderson, Edwin Morgan, Tessa Ransford and Joy Hendry. Graham Watson, later a Liberal Democrat MEP and then personal assistant to David Steel, helped organise a London branch; this may have had some effect on the latter's positive attitude to a Constitutional Convention, which drew others into the Campaign, particularly from voluntary organisations and the Churches.

If it was an uphill struggle – precarious 'rallies', dismissive politicians, a minute budget – it could only be judged thus on strictly political terms. In the cultural sphere much more was going on and there was, weirdly enough, encouragement from Wales. The campaign for a Welsh language TV channel showed how a cause could fight its way not just off the carpet but back into the boxing-booth. When in 1981 Gwynfor Evans threatened a fast unto death if the channel were not granted, someone said that two Scottish intellectuals had threatened to drink themselves to death in the Assembly cause. The joke was barbed, as the annual expenditure even of activists on politics wouldn't have covered a couple of evenings' refreshment on Rose Street. But S4C had a considerable effect on an initiative so far little recorded. Billy Wolfe – out of mainstream SNP politics because of an apparently anti-Catholic statement at the time of the Falklands War – worked his way back by organising a cultural campaign which gave a particular political quality to the renaissance of the early 1980s, in periodicals like *Cencrastus* and

Chapman, the Heritage Association of Scotland and the movement for a Scottish Poetry Library.

Literary chartered accountants are unusual. Wolfe was assiduous and few could express any sort of interest in Scottish culture without getting signed up for a donation, if not a more active role. The campaign of the 1970s, as Neal Ascherson remarked, had been politics *pur*, without much cultural input; consequently it was easy to derail. Efforts like this helped create a network, many of whose activists were to figure in several roles as time went on. This involved people like Tom Gallagher, Angus Calder, the Rev. Will Storrar, Tessa Ransford and Ian Barr, then head of the GPO in Scotland, and the practically full-time work of two retired public servants, Jim Ross and Paul Scott. (Political change always tends to imply youth; in Scotland it would never have happened without the input of energetic oldies.)

It was in this sustaining atmosphere that, after 1984, the CSA started campaigning for a Scottish Constitutional Convention. Although it would come to be equated with cross-party agreement, this notion had also a profile on the far nationalist left, the John MacLean Society and the Scottish Republican Socialist Party, who thought in terms of a Constituent Assembly. Initially, this struck few sparks with the Labour or Liberal parties. It didn't come up in the programme 'Grasping the Thistle' that I made for the BBC in the autumn of 1986, which involved interviews with all the Scottish leaders; yet it was in the air when, during the run of *Scotland 2000*, Alan Lawson arranged a 'Declaration Dinner' in late February 1987. Kay Carmichael and I addressed it, but the key performer was Kenyon Wright, then Secretary of the Scottish Churches' Council. By then the informal organisation of the Convention, reflected in the great and good who drafted *Scotland's Claim of Right*, could be seen in embryo.

Lawson was peddling the idea that, should the election go against the Tories in Scotland, but not in England, politics would have to move away from Westminster. The Scots might have, as a Labour MP put it, 'to live a little dangerously'. There had been signs of unrest from the trade unions during the miners' strike and the long-drawn-out campaign for Ravenscraig and, with the appointment of a known home ruler, Campbell Christie, as General Secretary of the STUC in 1985, this tapped into an important if threatened political group, which (not least because of its Communist traditions) had good links with the arts. In the 1987

234

election traditional party loyalties abated somewhat, in the interest of creating Tory-free zones. Rifkind helped. He allowed the right its head – with young, often English, acolytes from a group called TSAR (Turn Scotland Around) being parachuted into impossible Scots seats. One *enragé* was even clamouring for the abolition of the Kirk as well as the Scottish Office. Tory success in England, with a gain on the party's 1983 poll, turned sour, as the Scots *bourgeoisie* found that a tactical vote could hurt. The Tory vote dropped only from 28 to 24.4 per cent, but the number of MPs fell from 21 to 10.

Another endangered species was represented by Kenyon Wright. The Kirk *appeared* anti-Thatcherite, but polls showed lay members to the right of Scots society and sympathetic to her individualism; fundamentalists looked to Reagan's America. If Scotland was to be turned round, why not start here? A subtler performer could have made something of it, but Mrs Thatcher's performance before the General Assembly in 1988 was a disaster, less for her speech than for an earlier interview in a women's magazine, in which she uttered the line 'there is no such thing as society, only individuals and families'. The Assembly coincided with a report of the Church and Nation Committee on urban deprivation, and the Moderator, the Rev. Prof. J. H. Whyte of St Andrews, a figure very much in the tradition of John Baillie and the social reformers of World War II, ceremonially handed her a copy of it. With the Poll Tax seemingly in breach of the Act of Union, and likely to make the poor poorer, the Kirk's wrath was roused as it had seldom been since the days of the Disruption.

The Constitutional Convention would meet ten months later and in the same place, chaired by Kenyon Wright. It was a response to a declaration *Scotland's Claim of Right* – a grand covenanting title – drafted by a distinguished but ostensibly apolitical committee under the planner Sir Robert Grieve (a Catholic) and submitted on 6 July 1988. The catalyst came when Bruce Millan, the last Labour Secretary of State, decided to go to Brussels. Kinnock had appointed Donald Dewar as his successor in 1983 and Dewar (an ecumenical devolutionist in 1979) endorsed the *Claim's* Convention idea. This was not in direct response to the Govan by-election that returned Jim Sillars, but in a more general sense this concentrated Labour's mind on a repetition of the 1970s situation, with such a formidable opponent in the ring.

235

The Poll Tax led to unprecedented mass-lawbreaking, but didn't stop Thatcher intervening further. Her instrument was Michael Forsyth, Education Minister in Rifkind's team. A working-class socialist converted to free enterprise at St Andrews University, he had gone south almost immediately on graduation and started his political career on Dame Shirley Porter's Westminster City Council. His public relations firm had waxed in the balmy atmosphere of health care privatisations. Mrs Thatcher put him into the Scottish office to 'mind' Rifkind, and he rapidly ruffled the feathers of the Scottish education establishment. She made him Scottish party chairman in 1989, and he got access to a special fund outside the control of the Scottish executive. Almost methodically, Forsyth set out to rile every official in this eventide home, importing young ideologues whose manner (though not their policies) belonged on the outer shores of militant socialism. 'Young Conservatives do it with the woman on top' or 'Devolution sucks' would scarcely have tripped off the tongue of Arthur Balfour. But aggressiveness, money and even manpower from Reagan's America, weren't given a chance. Hubris and incompetence set in, and the coil of Thatcher's power unravelled rapidly. The old guard and Rifkind – incandescent with fury – fought back, and Forsyth was dislodged from the Chairmanship, though not from the Scottish Office. Rifkind waited a few weeks, and on 22 November 1990, took his revenge.

A STAY OF EXECUTION

Mrs Thatcher's Scottish excursions piled up opposition votes like windfall apples, fermenting into the discontent which carried the Constitutional Convention into the Edinburgh Assembly Hall in March 1989; provoking groups such as Charter 88 which demanded more widespread constitutional change in Britain. Would things be different with John Major? In 1991 Major became the most popular premier since opinion polling began despite – because of? – the platitudes he mouthed, the archaic English decencies – cricket, warm beer, old ladies cycling to church – his public relations men equipped him with.

A general election impended, and Scottish politics went into a manic-depressive phase reminiscent of 1978. Major's standing was buoyed up by the Gulf War, in which many Scots were involved, both as service personnel and as expatriates working in the oil industry. In two by-elections in Paisley the Conservative vote held up. But in November 1991 another, held in the Tory seat of Kincardine and Deeside, was won by a Liberal Democrat, and Doomsday again hove into sight. In the Constitutional Convention the Labour, Liberal Democrat and Green Parties, the churches, local authorities and trade unions deliberated and got a commitment out of the Labour Party to a form of proportional representation in Assembly elections: an event almost amounting to *perestroika*. A 'leading role of the party' which gave Labour a dominance in certain parts of the country, without parallel anywhere in Europe, was to be ditched. At the same time, the SNP's detachment from the Convention was apparently validated by the popularity of its new leader Alex Salmond, and polls which put independence in Europe almost abreast of devolution.

On 8 January 1992 British Steel announced the closure of Ravenscraig, with the loss of 1,800 jobs and 40 per cent of Scottish rail freight traffic. On 23 January Rupert Murdoch's *Sun*, which had printed a Scottish edition since 1987, backed independence. The Tories wobbled. Douglas Hurd was believed to be chairing a committee to settle the Scotland issue, should there be a hung parliament, or a Tory majority coexisting with a wipe-out in Scotland. Yet the Major and Gulf War factors got the Tories up from 16 per cent to around 25 per cent in the polls. The home rulers weren't benefiting from the end of the Lawson boom, and industrial stagnation and unemployment spreading north. The Convention couldn't save Ravenscraig. It had to struggle to make an impact; a fate which tended to overtake all constitutional forums from 1848 on. Although polls showed that between 70 per cent and 80 per cent favoured home rule, only 17 per cent of the electorate had heard of it.

Why, anyway, had the home rule question established itself? Among Scotland's political class, or, as Andrew Neil of the *Sunday Times* would insist, 'chattering class', the obsession was obvious. He would argue that it went no further. It was usually about sixth or seventh down the ordinary voter's scale of priorities. In 1987 this meant after unemployment, increasing health and education spending, reducing taxes and tackling AIDS. But these staples were pretty variable. Improving health and education spending and reducing taxes tended to cancel one another out, unemployment was less important by the mid-1990s, AIDS a momentary panic – though the issue remained serious. Home rule sustained itself as a primary demand, not least because it could be mixed with other policies.

Nevertheless, there was an element of complacency around in 1991. In May 1991 *Radical Scotland* unexpectedly closed. Was it needed, now that the *Scotsman* and *Herald* were 'sound'? All the polls were indicating a coming Conservative wipe-out, and they were broadcast by an overall sympathetic press, radio and TV. The SNP's coup with the *Sun* meant that Jim Sillars wrote a column and page 3 girls did their patriotic bit with black and yellow rosettes. Why, one might ask? To split the Labour vote? Perhaps. To expand the *Sun's* market share? Insofar as the *Sun's* politics mattered, most certainly. Its circulation rose from 200,000 in 1987 to 400,000 in 1994.

In the SNP headquarters, the day after the 1992 election, a mute tableau summed it all up. On a table stood an untouched bottle of champagne and an empty bottle of whisky. The first-past-the-post system had played another of its jokes. The Liberal Democrats, although only 11 per cent in the overall poll, held nearly all their seats. The SNP's vote rose by seven percentage points to 22 per cent but they picked up no marginals and were still far behind Labour in the central belt. Sillars went out at Govan, dourly fulminating against 'ninety-minute patriots'.

Why had the Tories recovered? The absence of the Thatcher factor? The impact of the anti-Poll Tax campaign (almost a third had refused to pay) which debilitated local government and consequently left-wing forces, and perhaps cut the electorate by 2 per cent? (John Curtice of Strathclyde said no. Iain McLean of Nuffield said yes – Lady Thatcher agreed with him.) The Conservatives used the manoeuvrability of a minority, piled vast resources into postal voting and telephone canvassing, and rose from 24 to 25.9 per cent. They appealed specifically to English incomers, after the 1988–9 house-price boom, with some success. A survey found that 28.6 per cent of English-born voted Tory, compared with only 19 per cent Scots-born. Ian Lang, under-rated as a political animal, remained in charge.

TAKING STOCK

Depression settled, haar-like, on the enthusiasts. 'Just conceiv-ably,' gloomed Andrew Marr, 1992 was 'the end of Scottish politics as a tale in its own right'. There were certainly some unfriendly secular trends. The SNP's membership (c.12,000) was unimpressive. The membership of *all* Scottish political organisations had been falling for a decade. Labour admitted to 16,000 in 1992, a fall of 8,000 from the previous year, though it subsequently recovered; the Tories claimed 40,000, but these were mostly over 65. The young Conservatives, once a huge institution for rural courtship, had almost ceased to exist. This political deterioration wasn't specifically British. Throughout Europe, from Sweden to the new democracies of the East, the mutual sector shrank as the seductions of the market escalated, as in the career-change of Douglas Hurd.

Were people becoming less social, withdrawing to a hedonistic or traumatised individualism? Or were greenish bodies like the National Trust for Scotland, which had gone from 40,000 to 240,000 members between 1971 and 1993, more of a pointer? Not least at the implications of the tidal wave of early retirement which had swept across the professions in the 1980s? The Scots sneered at the materialism of the Tory heartlands of the southeast, and the residual strength of churches and trade unions may explain why the country was spared urban violence both in 1981 and in 1991 – given even more desolate housing schemes than in England. There was a whiff of the 'unco guid' in this, but also a sense of priorities other than those of the market.

What had happened to Scottish economic unionism? It was certainly *there*. Research for *Scottish Business Insider* showed widespread hostility to devolution among the Chambers of Commerce and Charlotte Square, not to speak of the Scottish branches of southern firms. It was a brave businessman who would admit that Europe's best-behaved national movement, following the route of every other European region, would not be an economic disaster. Yet while in November 1932 hundreds of grand, mainly Glasgow-based capitalists – shipbuilders, steelmakers, coal-owners – along with noblemen, clergy and university principals, had signed the notorious 'Ragman's Roll' protesting at any move toward a Scottish parliament, sixty years later the grandson of one of the original signatories, Viscount Weir, could only get a dozen or so – including two elderly Tory clergymen, the novelist Alan Massie and the singer Moira Anderson – to declare against devolution. As Weir's firm had been rescued in 1982 by the Scottish Development Agency, this distrust seemed churlish, and a whispered subtext spoke of none-too-subtle pressure from headquarters. In November 1990 the *Financial Times* had asked Bill Hughes, Vice-Chairman of the Scottish Conservatives and head of the Grampian retailing chain, how he would react to the looming depression. The answer came pat: transfer investments to Europe. This was honest in its way – an earlier generation would have obfuscated – but it explained as nothing else could the limitations of 'unionism' and the unpopularity of Scottish business.

The creation of a Scottish ideology – the second stage of Hroch's model – meant an institutional alignment which, if not explicitly nationalist, marginalised such anti-national behaviour. The estates were now defensive rather than, as late as the 1970s, divisive: religion had reverted to its common-sense role, along with social philosophy, as a mediating influence in the democratic movement, personified by the endless power-broking of Kenyon Wright. And a new axis had sapped the power of Edinburgh – London. Europe, from being a bogey in 1975, when the Scottish left united to battle against it and lost, became as magic a word as community, with devolution-minded officials and politicians, from Judge David Edward in Luxembourg to Councillor Charles Gray on the Committee of the Regions, distancing themselves from Conservative formulations of Little England nationalism as well as from a stingy Whitehall. This showed in elections for the Strasbourg parliament. In 1979 the Conservatives had five out of eight MEPs and 34 per cent of the vote. By 1994 the contest was between Labour with six and 43 per cent and the SNP with two and 33 per cent. Relations with Europe also preoccupied the Scottish Council in its international forums, the universities – Edinburgh honouring Thatcher's bogeymen Kohl and Delors – and ultimately even the Scottish Office. Scotland Europa, with a high-powered Brussels office, was launched in 1992.

The irony was that the paymaster, the Tory government, was steadily disadvantaged by its rigidity over the constitutional issue. The list of plausible appointees had to include opponents – three out of four of Ian Lang's nominations to the Committee of the Regions in 1994 were home rulers – but there was no underlying strategy, no Conservative equivalent to the SNP's Scottish Centre for Economic and Social Research, or the Labourite John Wheatley Centre. Somewhere on the right was a David Hume Institute and – at least momentarily – a John

Buchan Club, but their delivery mechanisms were faulty, and no-one in London bothered about them. Major was both less étatist and more emotionally English than Thatcher. But while Madsen Pirie, a constitutional nihilist if ever there was one, said he had far readier access to the premier than to Thatcher, Anthony Seldon's biography shows that, for all his panicky rhetoric, Scottish politics preoccupied Major scarcely at all.

But his background in the PR side of the Standard Chartered Bank had left its mark. Although the City lauded her, Mrs Thatcher had hated its fast buck ethos: quite incompatible with inter-war Grantham. Major recognised that the balance had shifted, but not the rapidity with which 'luxury and corruption' was undermining his government. Breaking up the central state, through privatisation, or agency operation, inevitably had a centrifugal effect, and equally inevitably Scottish institutions – banks, bus and power companies, as well as government – were waiting to pick up and reassemble the pieces.

Although the simple *Weltanschauung* of the neo-classicists side-lined regional policies for regenerating the Scottish economy, 'planning failure' on a British scale made Scotland look comparatively impressive. By the end of the 1980s Scots cities were rated by businessmen far superior to the ungoverned, congested, over priced shambles of London. 'Britishness', as much as the welfare state or the firm itself, was being sapped by the market: both on a populist level, and through the heritage industries. Scots found that their history was both salient and marketable, and were apt to compare themselves favourably (not always with good cause) with the South. Part of the formulae of democratic nationalism seemed to have been met, as a former critic, the playwright John McGrath admitted in 1986:

> [The Scots] are using language with a sense not only of discovery but of origination and invention, compared with the rather arid, academic way that the English writers and theatre-makers are trying to force language to obey issues and obey concepts. This is very, very important and again relates to the same thing: a sense of contact with humanity in Scotland which I find lacking amongst the intelligentsia and writers in London.

On Friday 11 September 1992, Major visited Scotland as part of a process of taking stock of the Scottish question. Momentarily, there seemed something earnest in this solicitousness, although press briefings indicated that Scots opinion would be met by with further privatisations and the accelerated dismantling of the regions. Within hours, however, Major had even less credibility than the (notionally) unionist worthies paraded before him in Bute House. Sterling, whose exchange rate he had defended before the Scottish CBI in Glasgow, collapsed against the Deutschmark.

Political realities meant that once out of the ERM, Britain was no longer at the heart of Europe. Although the enforced devaluation helped economic recovery, it joined Italy on the margin: as an over-centralised, under-efficient polity. The irony was that the discourse of Thatcherite nationalism continued. The subsidiarity insisted on at Maastricht was to be interpreted as a continuing excuse for the British nation-state to persist in the very policies which had brought it to the verge of collapse.

Or was it? Government policy was to maintain a sanitised version of the *status quo* in Scotland, to introduce legislative devolution in Northern Ireland by agreement with the confessional parties and the Dublin government, to make the Hong Kong constitution more representative. This inconsistency was at least transparent, compared with a total vagueness about what the constitutional and electoral consequences of closer European union would be. In consequence, the government's Scottish policy came under fire from every reputable *conservative* newspaper in London, from the *Daily Telegraph* to *The Economist*. For two main reasons. Any Scottish gain in administrative autonomy would mean that relations between Whitehall and Scottish power-groups would pose continual, wasting problems for a Secretary of State representing only an 'English' majority at Westminster; while the logic of the increasing regionalism of European politics suggested that representative supervisory bodies were now essential.

The Major government's strategy was either a high-risk battle for the Scottish soul or a case of sleep-walking into disaster. In the 1970s, local government reform meant devolving power to the regions to frustrate a move to a Scottish authority. The resulting upheaval increased support for the SNP. Undeterred or uninstructed, in 1993 the Conservatives set about removing the regions to create weak, single-tier local authorities, in some cases gerrymandered to keep their few remaining councils in power. This time the Thatcherite notion of the 'withering away of the state' no longer applied. The attempt to privatise Scottish water and sewage was met by a crushing 97 per cent to 3 per cent defeat in a referendum arranged by the doomed Strathclyde region. If such functions as education and health were taken from councils, they would settle at an over-bureaucratised national level, overseen by a Scottish Grand Committee which could only become a focus for national discontent. Yet on top of this, Lang determined on the full administrative devolution of higher education and cultural policy: the traditional weaponry of national institution-building.

Government claimed it saw a renaissance of unionism, but it was independence – vaguely defined – which grew. In the 1970s, even with the oil bonus to hand, it had stuck at around 20 per cent in the polls; but after 1979 it started to climb, to around 30 per cent by 1987. By 1992 it was level-pegging with the devolution option, at between 35–40 per cent, and some polls in 1992 and 1993 showed it ahead. Underneath Major's unionist rhetoric, was there now the realisation that any compromise along devolution lines now lacked the consensus that would make it work? Taking stock turned out a risky Habsburg expedient of authoritarianism plus cultural nationalism.

WALKING WITH DESTINY

On 12 May 1994, John Smith, the Labour leader, died suddenly in London. Convivial and accessible, he had since replacing Neil Kinnock been regarded almost uncritically in Scotland. The mass nature of the response was significant – in some respects a Scottish version of the uninhibited grief that greeted the death of Diana, Princess of Wales, three years later. But he seemed to sum up an openness and social awareness which was seen as particularly Scots, still visible in the 1997 referendum campaign which implicitly bore his subtitle 'unfinished business':

> Last night I dreamed a weary dream
> Ayont the Isle of Skye
> I saw a dead man win a fight
> And I knew that man was I.

According to Hroch, the nationalist take-off comes when cultural and political movements fuse. In Scotland after 1994 this

243

happened, but unstraightforwardly. Smith, it turned out, left something to be desired as a constituency MP, and Helen Liddell only just scraped in against the SNP in Monklands East, one of Labour's rottenest burghs. In the spring of 1995 Sir Nicholas Fairbairn, whose baroque style decorated a huge talent ruined by alcohol, died and the SNP took his Perthshire seat on 25 May. The Tory came third. A month later Major, deemed unsound on Europe by a dwindling but increasingly frantic Tory rank-and-file, was challenged by one right-wing proconsul, John Redwood, Secretary of State for Wales, where he had, in Dafydd Wigley's unforgettable line, 'gone down like a rat sandwich'. He was, surprisingly, defended by another: Forsyth, now a Home Office minister.

Forsyth got Scotland as a reward, but appeared in Edinburgh as a new man, a benign manager *cum* cultural nationalist. He courted Campbell Christie and the STUC, recruited the SNPers Sillars and Dick Douglas into his quangos, and strutted his stuff in a kilt (the only Secretary of State ever to wear one). When in 1996 Mel Gibson reanimated William Wallace, Forsyth was up there, getting Gibson to advise him on film policy. Braveheart's big deal was the return of the Stone of Destiny, thieved by Edward I in 1296 and kidnapped in 1950, to Edinburgh on St Andrew's Day 1996. The Queen was not amused.

Could he have got anywhere? Forsyth the Gael increased support for Highland projects, including the multi-campus and internet University of the Highlands and Islands. He ticked off his younger self, who had bawled about subsidy junkies, to announce successful raids on the pork barrel as jubilantly as Willie Ross. 'The best Secretary of State' was a verdict which managed to unite Jim Sillars and Allan Massie. When the cloven hoof showed itself, the results could be risible. On Europe Day, 1996, Ken Munro, the EU's Representative in Scotland, asked whether public buildings could fly the European flag. No, replied the Secretary, the Union Jack would fly, to put Brussels in its place. Throughout Scotland, provosts searched for star-circled banners or failing that, saltires – while the general public reflected that Union Jacks had indeed got distinctly rare, and didn't mind at all.

After 1995 it was evident that the Tories faced a grim future, if the local election results were extrapolated. But the polls gave them no mercy and neither, ultimately, did their activists. As the

1997 election loomed, their Scottish effort, bad even by the standards of a shambolic campaign, was dominated by a sequence of scandals and in-fighting. This felled not only Allan Stewart, their 'safest' MP (alcohol and adultery) but the chairman of the party, Sir Michael Hirst (accusations of a homosexual past). The Conservatives had in 1979 taken advantage of the chasm-like divisions between the home-rule parties, and flogged first-past-the-post for all it was worth. The English electoral system certainly moulded Scottish party loyalties into a rigidity as severe as that of the traditional estates – a source of turbulence, initially satisfactory to them. But after 1987 the electorate discovered that it had a four-party system, more flexible than the individual parties, and started to use it to belabour the Tories. In 1997 it destroyed them.

On 1 May 1997 they did five points better than the 12.5 per cent that they got in the 1995 local elections but lost all of their MPs, including the two who would remain on 1995 projections. This was less tactical voting than surgical decapitation. Forsyth cut his losses. He might have made the case against devolution – in particular over tax-raising powers, given the fragility of the Scottish financial sector – into a means of regrouping his party. The new leader, William Hague, could have kicked some knight of the shires upstairs and given him Commons credibility. But Sir Michael scuttled off to Robert Fleming and the City, and silence fell from and on him.

This might account for the galvanising of Tony Blair. Before the election his Scottish *démarches* were ill-received, and he stood the chance of becoming even more unpopular than Neil Kinnock. This rose to a peak with the proposal that devolution legislation be preceded by a referendum, denied then produced and even multiplied, to placate a southern constituency, which all but derailed George Robertson, his Scottish spokesman. The suspicion was that Blair wanted a majority so big that he could forget the Scots, as his hero Sir Henry Campbell-Bannerman had forgotten the Irish in 1906. After the upsets of the election campaign, Blair was on the spot. The result had demonstrated how soft the anti-Tory vote now was. So the promise of a prompt referendum was fulfilled, and slated for 11 September, a token of rapid action that few had seriously expected.

The 'Yes–Yes' campaign was not helped by a rash of political scandals in the Glasgow area, and the suicide of the Labour MP for

Paisley South, Gordon MacMaster. Sir Bruce Pattullo, the Governor of the Bank of Scotland, took over the tartan-tax issue from Forsyth, which initially gave some headway to the 'Think Twice' unionist group, but then exposed how few Scottish business leaders there actually were. Not for nothing had two-thirds of Scottish manufacturing capital been sold south in 1984–5! Lord Weir was silent; Sir Alastair Grant of Scottish and Newcastle was effectively neutral; Brian Souter of Stagecoach, which had gone from buses to a multinational eyeing the revival in public transport, came out as a Yes–Yes man.

The challenge only goaded the home rulers into co-operation, and allowed the Labour spin-doctors to do their stuff. 'Think Twice' obliged with incompetence. One little-noticed Tory success in the 1980s had been the recruitment of Catholic yuppies – Gerry Malone, Mary Scanlan, Liam Fox – from a hitherto Labour-voting and, indeed, Labour-unionist group. The No campaign was fronted by Donald Findlay QC, high-profile but *a Rangers director*: which turned off a third of the voters *like that*. By contrast, Dewar and his deputy Henry MacLeish cleverly made up ground lost before the election by Blair and Robertson. The co-operation of Alex Salmond in the 'Yes–Yes' cause would otherwise have been impossible. The inner-party opposition kept quiet, save for Tam Dalyell. He had a certain scarcity value, but as a debater he was no match for Dewar, as he had been no match for John Mackintosh twenty years earlier. Moreover, the *status quo* was itself prejudiced by the scandals in the West; for every one who said that these would characterise Scottish politics, three insisted that things would be worse without change.

These threats were just moving in on Labour when the news broke of the death in a Paris accident of the Princess of Wales and her lover Dodi Fayed (incidentally the heir to a highland estate). The 'Think Twice' campaign tried to use the Diana factor to stress Britishness, but this backfired. The contrast between a decorous truce in the north and uninhibited orgies of grief and directionless – anti-monarchic, pro-monarchic? – emotion in London suddenly seemed to crystallise civic differences, growing for so long. The historian Angus Calder wrote to *Scotland on Sunday* that the 'Evitafication' of the Princess made him want to vomit. This produced no protest, and those turning out at local commemorations and laying flowers were at most 14,000 compared with perhaps two million in London.

The 'Scotland FORward' alliance got off to a very slow start, which worried its backers in the Campaign for a Scottish Parliament. A poll on 6 September showed 45–37 per cent for taxation powers which, if extrapolated, would menace even the first Yes. But 'Think Twice', already hampered by the non-participation of Rifkind and Forsyth, started to fall apart. It was finished by the 'fraternal assistance' of Lady Thatcher, said to be £30,000 to the better after a foray to Scotland to address travel agents. She ritually denounced home rule, and this was reckoned as worth a few more percentage points for it.

The press was broadly supportive. The BBC was a much more professional outfit than the infant Radio Scotland – the equivalent of Ally's Tartan Army – had been in 1979. The *Herald* under Harry Reid was consistently and energetically 'Yes'; the *Scotsman*, which had been far more enthusiastic in 1979, withstood the attempts of Andrew Neil to drag it into a unionist course, but was considerably weaker in its support, while its 'objective' reporting (for the best of reasons) undermined Labour by energetically following up the sleaze stories. But the fact that its platforms were open showed how weak the 'Noes' were in taking them up. The *Record* published twenty patriotic pages on 11 September, mentioning the SNP once, and the *Sun* (unlike in Wales) was not to be outdone. Only the Dundee press remained predictably loyal to the Unionists in their last ditch.

Polling day, when it came, was worryingly quiet. There were lots of Yes–Yes posters, but not much going on in the streets. A gang of literati – Neal Ascherson, William McIlvanney, Joyce Macmillan, Will Storrar – who had been touring Scotland in a minibus, stopped in the cleft of a highland pass, regarded the moon, and hoped however distrustfully, for a good deliverance. It came. The poll was slightly lower than in 1979 (which had been fought on a new register) but the Yesses reached 74 per cent (turnouts were low in the industrial cities, but promisingly high and positive in the 'new' Scotland of the suburban central belt). Orkney and the Borders defeated the taxation clauses, but only narrowly. The swing in Scotland, compared to 1979, was 40 per cent. Which was as well, because the Welsh would have to manage 150 per cent on 18 September. This they only just did.

THE PARTIES AND THE SETTLEMENT

Almost immediately, one symbol bit the dust. Dewar decided that the Royal High School would not be the parliament. Although – perhaps because? – its mighty Doric portico had projected the struggles of the Campaign and Convention during the 1980s, it was reckoned too small. The new site would be Holyrood, opposite the Palace, where Scottish and Newcastle's brewery had been. This gave a distinctive tone to a short-tempered interlude. The effect of the referendum success shielded Labour from the SNP at the Paisley South by-election and got Salmond stick from his fundamentalists. Then a ministerial resignation (Malcolm Chisholm) over benefit cuts, the to-ing and fro-ing over the parliament site, and the refusal of a knighthood to the SNP-supporting Sean Connery – did he really want to be up there with Elton John and Cliff Richard? – put them upsides again. The SNP was now what it and Labour had not always expected: the only opposition in town.

Some sort of consensus would be enforced by the new electoral system, with 73 single-member seats (the present constituencies with one extra for the Orkneys) plus 56 elected on a list system based on the eight notional Euro-constituencies (notional because these would vanish in favour of an all-Scotland list when PR was introduced for the Euro-elections in 1999). Would this bring about a Labour–Liberal Democrat coalition? One or two polls, narrowing the 12-point gap at Paisley, suggested that the SNP might run Labour close. It might even, Salmond hinted, come to an agreement with the Liberal Democrats over issues like Europe and proportional representation.

But first there was the Government of Scotland Bill itself. The principle had changed from 1979. The Bill specified the powers Edinburgh would be denied, not those to be granted. Foreign affairs and defence were obvious; these would have been withheld from Ireland by Gladstone or Asquith. But others were bound to be more troublesome. The Health Service was devolved, but not Social Security. Roads and passenger transport, but not railways. Education and arts, but not media – where old Reithian centralisation persisted, and the responsible minister was Brian Wilson, a convinced if silent unionist. Who was actually discussing the clauses? The Tories demanded a committee of the whole House, and got it. But it operated with a guillotine; when time ran out, clauses were passed. No more than 30 MPs turned up: the SNP, the relevant ministers, some Liberal Democrats, Tam Dalyell, and a few Tories, mainly English, under Michael Ancram. Otherwise there were about six Scottish Labour MPs, more nationalist than the Nationalists, whom Salmond allowed to get on with his job. The rest of the House couldn't be bothered.

Yet, what precedents were there for such legislation? Not in the methodical world of German federalism. Spanish quasi-federalism was part of a grand Statute of Autonomy, although its elements operated at different speeds; to a lesser extent this applied to France and Italy. And who bothered? After briefly registering the fact of constitutional change in late 1997, the rest of Britain now cared less than ever about the fate of Scotland.

The first elections were down for early May 1999. What would happen if the SNP was the biggest party? In the 1970s there had been much talk about the 'mandate for independence', about whether the SNP would have to capture a majority of Scotland's Westminster seats, or (in addition) a majority of the Scottish vote. Devolution changed this. The SNP in power in Edinburgh could move for a referendum on outright independence. But elsewhere several nationalist majorities in federal provinces had fallen at this hurdle. Before then the economic case would have to be established and sold. If Scotland really had public expenditure running 23 per cent in excess of income, and oil prices were sinking – in 1997–8 from $21 to $12 a barrel – then the SNP would have its work cut out. On the other hand, little was actually known about taxation and expenditure. Since most of Scots industry was in the hands of London or multinational concerns, corporation and other taxes were paid at headquarters (or not paid at all); while government expenditure on items like public transport or defence contracts seemed strongly biased to the south-east. With subventions for the Docklands and Jubilee lines, the fast links to London Airport and the Channel Tunnel running into at least £12 billion – each Jubilee line tube station cost between £70 and £100 million – and the Greenwich Dome threatening to be a millenial shouting-match, the case for further investigation seemed strong.

How would the parties operate at Holyrood? After a decade of reform under Kinnock, Smith and Blair, the Scottish Labour monolith was now split four ways. A third of its MPs – sixteen

– were ministers, and ten or so young, ideology-light New Labourites observed them like vultures. An atavistic 'Old Labour Scottishness' remained, discredited and rather disconsolate, mainly in the west, but it was proving difficult to demolish that Glaswegian monument to survival, Lord Provost Pat Lally. Only half-a-dozen committed home rulers looked to Holyrood (Dewar, McLeish, Home Robertson, Canavan, MacAllion, Chisholm). Would some of them ally with the far-left, under Tommy Sheridan, which might do well under PR? The Liberal Democrat MPs, representing textile workers in the Borders and oil workers in the north-east and the islands, and tactical voters everywhere, played down the free-market rhetoric their colleagues used in England, but didn't manage to shake off the accusation of being ten separate parties. PR could facilitate a Conservative come-back, but the party remained paralysed. There was no need for it, said such old lefties as Jimmie Reid in the *Herald*: New Labour was doing the job just fine.

What would the parliament actually do? With only limited tax-varying powers, amounting to about 5 per cent of its income, redistribution was out. But not reorganisation. The 1960s and 1970s showed how important a considered and debated strategy was – one that would *not* produce three airports without rail access, or roads which destroyed Scots cities without giving a safe link south, or high-rise flats and atomic power stations. The parliament could use 'virement' of resources between sectors, as well as extending democracy and empowering the disadvantaged. One priority was local government, for which a majority probably existed in all parties. PR would be essential to prevent the abuses of one-party government; there was also a case for executive provosts elected on long enough terms to tackle comprehensive planning programmes. Wearily, MSPs would have again to tackle the boundaries so hastily thrown together in 1993, perhaps replacing a thicket of *ad hoc* joint boards with a modified two-tier system.

Industrial policy would be divided between Whitehall and Holyrood, with control of Scottish Enterprise largely in the north. This was important as so much of employment creation – notably in multiplying call centres, which could be a route to high value-added investment – depended on education and training. Arts policy was in a similar situation. It had been a surrogate for politics in the 1980s, giving an unprecedented power to the intelligentsia. David Stenhouse, the BBC commentator, argued that: 'many thousands of people have the opportunity to consume art products which are produced according to parameters set by the actions of a tiny, highly informed elite'. In a self-governing Scotland, however, this could squash liveliness through the imposition of a corporate style – a national theatre or film school – instead of a pluralistic, post-national approach. Stenhouse's paradigm was Ireland, not the official Ireland of the Abbey Theatre, but Dublin's Temple Bar, with its cafés, small theatres and galleries. But by mid-1998 the Scottish arts were in trouble: local government 'reform' had restricted the cash base, museums and libraries were shutting down for longer periods. In 1997 Glasgow's Mayfest closed down completely. As arts earnings were, with tourism, some £3 billion, one of Scotland's main industries was overdue a comprehensive policy.

The two major areas of government expenditure were the education and health service. The first had always operated to higher standards, but in the universities this had also involved educating many English students. Would this practice be reduced, and what would the consequences be? In the health service an extensive shift in resources from curative to preventive medicine could in the long term reduce expenditure, by cutting down smoking, sweeties, fry-ups and drink. But, since much of Scotland's high morbidity stemmed from poverty, the redistribution question couldn't be dodged. Sooner rather than later the demand to take over social security would gain majority backing, and with it would come a major confrontation.

The outcome of this would depend on who could co-opt people, right across the spectrum of Scottish politics, whether employees of the Scottish state sector – teachers, doctors, administrators, clergy – or of voluntary societies and the unions, to link autonomy with social and environmental issues. Who could best incorporate women, the young, and ethnic minorities? Did the battleground lie with the social or the national? With a Labour party obsessed with internal discipline? Or with the Nationalists?

The second point was forecast by the contents of the previous chapter: a chamber whose priorities were social would have to be well informed about its policy options. Social and economic planning would have to be reinvented, and priorities established which the market was unlikely to come up with. And this in turn would depend on re-inventing the Scottish tradition of social investigation and social philosophy.

Foreign policy was reserved to Westminster, but Europe intervened dramatically in the devolution debate. Anglo-British centralism meant the need to consult London over every major policy issue, effectively doubling the distance from Brussels, while Europe, war-defeating and internationalist, was seductive. Closer up it was a huddle of acronyms, bureaucrats, lobbyists and tortuous academicism. But as the powers of the constituent states were progressively federalised, this gave a chance to the regions and culture-nations, Catalonia, Brittany, Scotland. Westminster's hostility was positive encouragement.

Then, in 1989–91, matters changed. Compact, federal West Germany gained an instant Ireland, an immigration problem and huge economic burdens. Pressure from the new democracies would make for a baggier Europe, with a drastic gradient of wealth. The brief flourishing of nationalism and economic freedom merely postponed the reckoning with other intractable problems. In the 1970s the home rule movement was against social-democrat centralisation but in favour of its Keynesian consensus. SNP economics were growth-based, with oil as a new source of investment. Nothing much had changed by 1998; the SNP hadn't gone for the market; yet it was also, in comparison with Plaid Cymru, less than green.

The prestige of politics had ebbed – in 1987 MPs weren't much ahead of estate agents in popularity – but an acute awareness of the peculiar 'condition of Scotland', the interdependence of society, politics, economy and ecology, had emerged. If autonomy produced a higher quality of government, this revival of Gellner and Nairn's 'strong' civil society might be transmitted internationally: a reservoir of 'civic virtue' for co-operative regional politics in Europe. Targeted reform – improving the housing stock, for example – could inaugurate a virtuous circle in lowering curative health costs. Raising transport energy prices, for ecological reasons, could make a European oil resource, and other forms of energy such as wind and wave power, a particularly rich Scottish endowment.

If the strength of its autonomous corporations made it more than a myth, how were Scottish democracy's ideas and criticism to be integrated effectively into the governmental process? The SNP suggested a Senate composed of MEPs and local-authority representatives supplementing the single-chamber legislature. This could detach issues from direct party pressures: initiate, scrutinise and advise on legislation, but not impede it. The Irish Senate has had a valuable role as an alternative civil service for the elected members, reporting on the working of legislation, examining controversial planning and development proposals, scrutinising government departments, authorities, and state and private industry. It has also given a voice to minorities and cultural groups which elected members cannot always represent. Would something similar be an alternative to advice being 'bought' from consultants – who often had material interests in the subjects on which they were advising – incorporating expertise within the legislative process?

Bagehot's 'dignified parts of the constitution' presented their own problems. Scotland had grown republican in the 1980s and 1990s, partly because neither Labour nor the SNP would accept political honours. A knighthood for political and public services was like a leper's bell. Scottish attachment to the Royal family was – according to one poll in 1997 – a minority taste. Its highly-publicised problems distracted attention from social and environmental issues. The SNP had its own quietly republican plan to create a head of state out of the Chancellor of Scotland, presiding officer of the parliament. Were this the case, could an Australian situation be far off, with a Scottish version of Mary Robinson or Richard von Weiszäcker representing exportable national traditions?

There remained the 'British question'. The aftermath of 1989–91 showed the limitations of nationalism but stressed the need for a responsive politics on a mezzanine level – not necessarily the nation-state – between Brussels and regional capitals. In this, the British Isles could be a pointer to something more positive. Symmetrical federalism seemed out, since the combined population of Scotland, Northern Ireland and Wales was less than a fifth of that of the UK, and there was little prospect of regional legislatures in England, but the option of a Council of the Islands, rather surprisingly tabled at the Anglo-Irish negotiations over Northern Ireland in 1998, might provide a framework for confederal institutions which could deal with common cultural, transport and environmental issues. Drawing on the reawakened Scots interest in Ulster, a Scots-Irish Agreement, involving two nations which really had an intimate interest in Northern Ireland, might offer flexibility, and a *quid pro quo* for further autonomy.

MONSTROUS REGIMENT?

In November 1997 Naomi Mitchison, novelist, poet, socialist, patron, celebrated her centenary. Over fifty years earlier she had written to Roland Muirhead:

> It seems to me that you are bound to assume that a self-governing Scotland is going to be immediately morally better, and I don't see it *unless there has also been a revolution*. I can't see how the people who are likely to govern Scotland under any democratic system are going to be any different from the undoubted Scots who are in positions of local power.

They *were* going to be different, because half the MSPs would be women. Some sort of revolution was predictable. In Germany the SPD and Greens set had levels of at least 40 per cent in cabinets and councils, and catcalls of *Quotenfrau*! gave way to real respect for the women who took office in *Länder* and cities, and the way in which they reoriented policy away from the preoccupations of '45-year-old male motorists'.

This also had implications for social class. In 1947 George Orwell, on one of his trips to Jura, noticed the difference between an 'English or anglicised upper class' and 'a Scottish working class which speaks with a markedly different accent, or even, part of the time, in a different language ... a more dangerous kind of class division than any now existing in England'.

Although Christopher Smout accused the welfare state of sapping Scots workers' democracy, it probably calmed down precipitous changes in the economy, and women would have disagreed about democracy anyway. What real conviviality was there about a society divided by sex, with work, sport and drink on one side, and house and shop on the other? It was women who kept up the linkages between families and generations, neighbourhoods, trade unions and religion which contributed to Emanuel Todd's family-political structures with their will towards innovation and success. The parlous nature of excluded Scotland – affected by longer-term changes in marriage and housing, with routes opened out of the working class and links broken with its losers – wasn't the women's fault.

Civic nationalism of the sort Dewar, or for that matter the Salmondite SNP, represented was institutionally still within the top-down Westminster tradition. In common with Victorian democrats such as Leslie Stephen and James Bryce – or the paternalists of *fin-de-siècle* municipal socialism – it believed it could offer the masses extensive concessions in order to preserve the state and their hegemony over it. The year 1999 would join 1867 and 1918 as victory through tactful concession, avoiding the sort of conflict that might have nullified its gains. In *Capitalism, Socialism and Democracy* the Austrian economist Joseph Schumpeter, who had experienced the dominance and fall of European liberalism, endorsed such diplomatic concession. But would it work now, given its opponents, left and right?

In 1981, the Glasgow political scientist Bill Miller wrote *The End of British Politics*. This burial of the concept of British political homogeneity advanced by Jean Blondel and David Butler seems definitive, but leaves a ghost. While Welsh devolution fits into a manageable European regional framework – Newport is less than two hours from Heathrow – Scotland is more remote, more powerful, and touchier. If English opinion presses for reduced Scottish expenditure and fewer MPs at Westminster, Scots would either reach for the oil 'weapon' or make menacing gestures at Trident in Loch Long, or both.

It was assumed that home rule would diminish Scotland's role in the Union, but the opposite was likely to be the case. There was a brief drama in December 1997 when the Foreign Secretary, Robin Cook, made a bid for the Scottish premiership. 'People call Robin Machiavellian, but at least you knew where you were with Machiavelli': Cook's patriotism had been as tortuous as his private life. A left Unionist who in the 1960s regarded the Scottish Office as an impediment to British socialism, he fell for devolution in 1974, spurned her in 1979, was back on the doorstep with a bouquet in 1983. The 1997 bid was doused, but what would Cook as First Minister have meant?

There was a German precedent. If the Union were to stay, then Scottish Labour could become the UK equivalent of the Bavarian Christian Social Union: a semi-independent party with a leading role in any UK government. The presidential role of the premier, which Thatcher practised and Blair envied her for, would no longer work, as a Scots rival would have his or her own power base. Dewar saw off the Cook challenge, but he would be 65 in the middle of his first term. As First Minister he would have to square an effervescent multi-party system with the smoke-filled rooms of West Central Scotland, and keep on doing so under the cool eye of the Secretary of State, whoever that might be, and Alex Salmond MP.

We were back to John MacLean's metaphor. If the stream of history was running ever faster, could devolution do much to slow this? John Major had broken popularity records in 1991; in early 1992 commentators were glooming over a 'Japanese scenario' with an impregnable ruling party. Only months later his decline seemed unstoppable. Labour was enjoying an extraordinarily long honeymoon, with – devolution apart – little to show for it. If the politics of dismay among its activists were to prove contagious – and 1998 polls for Holyrood showed the SNP pulling ahead – then the 1999 Scottish election could be close, with PR speeding the change. Dewar might yet end up in the same situation as John Galt's arch manager Archibald Jobbry, looking balefully at the new men of 1832: 'I had indeed a sore heart when I saw the Whigs and Whiglings coming louping, like the puddocks of Egypt, over among the right hand benches of the House of Commons, greedy as corbies and chattering like pyets.' Majorities, as Galt also remarked, could vanish 'like snaw aff a dyke'. They might not even be there.

Whether the future actually was with the nationalists depended on two things: Scotland's economic viability and the orientation of British politics. The first did not *prima facie* favour the SNP, with 'lavish' government expenditure, faltering inward investment, falling oil prices and cuts in the EU's regional programme. But the SNP's economic researchers were clever at ferreting out details of taxation and income. Second, a continuing gulf between Scottish Labour and New Labour was shown in the 1998 Scottish Labour Conference. Blair wanted to settle such mutinies by transforming the event into an American-style Convention, filleted of ideology – 'Lots of balloons and things', as a visiting spin-doctor put it – but this assumed an extreme degree of tolerance amongst the Scottish comrades of the appeal to Middle England as the yardstick of policy. If there was a Labour split, exploiting it would require a lot of forebearance among the Nationalists, but might bring them quite rapidly to their goal.

AT THE MIDNIGHT HOUR

At the midnight hour of the millennium, with the world singing 'Auld Lang Syne', Scotland would awake to freedom. A technicality: parliament would have been in session for six months. In July 1998, however, polls for the Holyrood parliament showed the SNP ahead. Would an SNP-led government confront Westminster, with conflict already brewing over university fees, local government sleaze, nuclear waste and inward investment? Facing the salience of an independence bid, the parties unprecedently vetted candidates. While 'settled' and 'insecure' Scotland did well, 'excluded' Scotland remained just that.

Then the Tartan Army, weirdly accoutred, sailed for France. 'Out of strands of ginger nylon the Scots have fashioned their own, richly deserved, laurels' hymned the London *Times*. The World Cup was in 1998, it seemed, 'more important than life and death', and the Scots inaugurated a carnival spirit which as it spread overwhelmed the loutishness many had feared. The triumph of a multicultural French team saw off the neo-fascist Front Nationale, in the same week that Orange intransigence the most toxic element of Black Scotland – fumed to a standstill on the Garvaghy Road. Was this post-nationalism?

In Brazil, who beat Scotland in the first match and went on to the final, the population of São Paulo would increase, 1990–2010, by five million: the same as Scotland's. Every one of whom could either be ignored or regarded as having 'the self-same soul as the superfinest lord-lieutenant'. Carlyle left his mark here – as radical humanist and toxic racist. But the voice of a man who died in 1996 reminded of the 'merely human'. Sorley MacLean's people lived on the edge of hunger and fought bravely, were sold with estates and cleared from the land; yet they wrote and sang one of the world's greatest literatures. MacLean's Cuillin, in its beauty and danger, was also his country and his world:

Beyond the lochs of the blood of the children of men,
beyond the frailty of the plain and the labour of the mountain,
beyond poverty, consumption, fever, agony,
beyond hardship, wrong, tyranny, distress, beyond misery,
  despair, hatred, treachery,
beyond guilt and defilement; watchful, heroic, the Cuillin is
  seen
rising on the other side of sorrow.

BIBLIOGRAPHICAL ESSAY

This essay has necessarily to be dualistic. It must give some idea of the sources and secondary literature that propelled the first edition of *Scotland and Nationalism*, but it has also to suggest to the contemporary reader where he or she can further explore the themes which the book raises. This is no easy task, as in the seventeen years since the book was published, the historical *lacunae* against which it protested were, most of them, briskly filled in. I have tried to take cognisance of this in rewriting, and in some areas, notably the Victorian period, my interpretation has been significantly altered. Elsewhere I find that a lot of hunches and informed guesses have been borne out, enabling details to be added but the flow of the original text to be retained.

The first section of this essay deals with the major secondary sources, and how they have changed. There then follow sections which cover the themes of the individual chapters.

GENERAL SOURCES

The two 'finds' which originally got me started were of two different types. The first was Wallace Notestein's engaging *The Scot in History* (London: Cape, 1946), an essay of great perceptiveness by a notable American seventeenth-century historian who was usefully of Scots and Jewish descent. This gave central emphasis to the ideological, and specifically religious, framework of the Scottish intellect, and although J. G. A. Pocock suggests a more secular modification of this in *The Machiavellian Moment* (Princeton: Princeton University Press, 1975), this approach still convinces me that there was, and is, a Scottish political tradition.

The second find was the huge Scottish Secretariat archive, the Papers generated by Roland Eugene Muirhead, in the National Library. Scottish nationalism's sugar-daddy suffered from a fatal lack of charisma but his generosity meant that practically everyone connected with nationalism and left-wing politics between World War I and the 1960s had to explain themselves to him. Other archives consulted were the Cabinet Papers in the Public Record Office at Kew, the papers of Tom Johnston, Hugh MacDiarmid, Walter Elliot and John Buchan (in the Blackwood Papers) at the National Library of Scotland; the Scottish Liberal Association in Edinburgh University Library; the Labour Party in Walworth Road, London; the Independent Labour Party in the London School of Economics; and the Bryce Papers in the Bodleian Library, Oxford.

MAIN SECONDARY WORKS

Like everyone writing on Scotland in the 1970s I was greatly influenced by T. C. Smout's ground-breaking *A History of the Scottish People, 1560–1830* (Glasgow: Collins, 1969) in its attempt both, as G. M. Young put it, to ask the questions that people in the past were asking, and to quantify the data of Scottish social change; his *A Century of the Scottish People, 1830–1950* (Glasgow: Collins, 1986), while impressive and stimulating, is remoter from his main research field and somewhat less magisterial – particularly about institutional influences – though still fascinating. With Jenny Wormald he edited *The New History of Scotland* (8 vols, 1980–81, reprinted Edinburgh: Edinburgh University Press, 1990–93), which has been deservedly successful, as has Michael Lynch's *A History of Scotland* (London: Century, 1991), although they do not altogether replace Gordon Donaldson's and William Ferguson's volumes in the *The Edinburgh History of Scotland* (Edinburgh: Oliver and Boyd, 1965 and 1968). The *Sunday Mail History of Scotland* (Glasgow: Mirror Group Newspapers, 1990), despite its dubious origins in the last days of the Maxwell Empire, has many expertly written essays and much unfamiliar and interesting visual material. Briefer collections are: David McCrone (ed.), *The Making of Scotland: Nation, Culture and Social Change* (Edinburgh: Scottish Academic

Press, 1989), and Rosalind Mitchison (ed.), *Why Scottish History Matters* (Edinburgh: Saltire Society, 1991).

Social affairs now have T. M. Devine, R. Mitchison, W. H. Fraser, James Treble and Tony Dickson (eds), *People and Society in Scotland, 1760–1990* (3 vols, Edinburgh: John Donald, 1988–92) and David McCrone's *Scotland: The Sociology of a Stateless Nation* (Edinburgh: Scottish Academic Press, 1992). Although there is still a need for an economic history which takes adequate cognisance of the Victorian period, S. G. E. Lythe and John Butt, *An Economic History of Scotland* (Glasgow: Blackie, 1975), and Roy Campbell, *The Rise and Fall of Scottish Industry* (Edinburgh, John Donald, 1980) provide adequate general accounts. Anthony Slaven and Sidney Checkland (eds), *Dictionary of Scottish Business Biography* (Aberdeen: Aberdeen University Press, 1986ff.) is typical of the much more elaborate range of reference sources that are now available.

There are now two good treatments of politics: Michael Fry, *Patronage and Principle: A Political History of Modern Scotland* (Aberdeen: Aberdeen University Press, 1987), and Ian Hutchison, *A Political History of Scotland, 1832–1922* (Edinburgh: John Donald, 1985), plus a wealth of monographs, and articles in learned journals. The articles in Ian Donnachie, Christopher Harvie and Ian S. Wood (eds), *Forward: A Hundred Years of Labour Politics in Scotland* (Edinburgh: Polygon, 1988) and William A. Knox, *Scottish Labour Leaders, 1914–1939* (Edinburgh: Mainstream, 1989) were frequently consulted, as was Ian MacDougall's massive *Labour Records in Scotland* (Edinburgh: Scottish Labour History Society, 1976). MacDougall, and Billy Kay, have also played remarkable roles as encouragers and editors of the history that has been recorded by ordinary people, in volumes such as *Voices from the Hunger Marches* (Edinburgh: Mainstream, 1990) and the *Odyssey* sequence (Glasgow: BBC, 1986–8).

Cultural coverage, too, has enormously improved, thanks particularly to Cairns Craig, littérateur, teacher and computer wizard. His work as editor-in-chief of *The History of Scottish Literature* (*HSL*) (4 vols, Aberdeen: Aberdeen University Press, 1988–90) produced a collective achievement both monumental and indispensable. Duncan MacMillan, *Scottish Art, 1460–1990* (Edinburgh: Mainstream, 1990) and John Purser, *Music in Scotland* (Edinburgh: Mainstream, 1990) complete a hat-trick.

There are now Penguin architectural guides to the main Scottish towns and counties and, for the geographical background, there is Chalmers M. Clapperton (ed), *Scotland: A New Study* (Newton Abbot: David & Charles, 1983). Hamish Henderson's collected essays *Alias MacAlias* (Edinburgh: Polygon, 1992) must be added at this stage, as not only bearing out Fletcher's famous line about the potency of the national ballads, but for introducing the democratic intellect in its most convivial form.

Periodical literature has been, throughout, of great importance. The *Scotsman* and the *Glasgow Herald*, now the *Herald*, have always weighed in at the level of the London qualities, and seem to have avoided the latter's overrunning by public relations handouts. Much serious historical writing and criticism is contained in them. Other periodicals have not quite shown their resilience, but on the whole the torch gets carried on. Many have been referred to in the main text. In the inter-war period there are the *Scots Independent* and the Scottish National Development Council's *Scotland*, whose contemporary equivalent is *Scottish Business Insider*. On a more academic level *The Scottish Historical Review* and *Scottish Economic and Social History*, and *The Scottish Literary Journal* (with its review and language supplements) are all important. *Cencrastus* and *Chapman* have much to offer, as have newcomers like *Gairfish*. *Radical Scotland* is much missed, but *Scottish Affairs* carries on the tradition.

1 THE BALLADS OF A NATION: POLITICAL NATIONALISM, 1707–1945

For theoretical approaches to nationalism I drew on Elie Kedourie, *Nationalism* (London: Hutchinson 1960), and on K. W. Deutsch, *Nationalism* (New York: Knopf, 1969). Stalking horses were provided by A. V. Dicey and R. S. Rait's *Thoughts on the Union between England and Scotland* (London: Macmillan, 1920), David Fernbach's Penguin edition of Marx's writings yielded *The Revolutions of 1848* (Harmondsworth: Penguin, 1973) and Michael Hechter, *Internal Colonialism: the Celtic Fringe in British National Development* (London: Routledge, 1975). Benedict Anderson, *Imagined Communities* (London: Verso, 1983) presents many useful critical concepts, as does Tom Nairn's fierce, feisty, and frequently hilarious *The Enchanted Glass: Britain and its Monarchy* (London: Radius, 1988).

261

For the religious input, in particular the Covenanting tradition, there are essays in Tom Gallagher and Graham Walker (eds), *Sermons and Battle Hymns* (Edinburgh: Polygon, 1991), and for Fletcher there are David Daiches (ed.), *Andrew Fletcher of Saltoun: Selected Political Writings and Speeches* (Edinburgh: Scottish Academic Press, 1979) and Paul Scott, *Andrew Fletcher of Saltoun* (Edinburgh: Mainstream, 1993). Harry Hanham turned up a vast amount of material on political nationalism in his short spell in Edinburgh. In *Scottish Nationalism* (London: Faber, 1969) it is not always digested, but the book remains stimulating. See also his 'Mid-Century Scottish Nationalism: Romantic and Radical', in R. Robson (ed.), *Ideas and Institutions of Victorian Britain* (London: Bell, 1967) and 'The Creation of the Scottish Office, 1881–7' in the *Juridical Review*, vol. 10 NS (1965) pp. 205–36. St Andrew's House gets the (inside but awfully judicious) treatment from John S. Gibson, *The Thistle and the Rose* (Edinburgh: HMSO, 1985) and George Pottinger, *The Secretaries of State for Scotland* (Edinburgh: Scottish Academic Press, 1980).

Tom Nairn's first bout with the beast was the hostile 'The Three Dreams of Scottish Nationalism', in Karl Miller (ed.), *Memoirs of a Modern Scotland* (London: Faber, 1970); his more sympathetic 'Old and New Scottish Nationalism' in *The Break-Up of Britain* (London: New Left Books, 1977) was suggestive about the Scots anticipation of nation-building. Nicholas Phillipson, 'Nationalism and Ideology' in J. N. Wolfe (ed.), *Government and Nationalism in Scotland* (Edinburgh: Edinburgh University Press, 1969) pp. 168–86 is suggestive about the persistence of 'semi-independence', while Murray G. H. Pittock, *The Rediscovery of Scotland* (London: Routledge, 1991) argues stimulatingly if not altogether convincingly for nationalism as a Jacobite tradition. George Elder Davie's argument in his seminal *The Democratic Intellect: Scotland and her Universities in the Nineteenth Century* (Edinburgh: Edinburgh University Press, 1961) was supplemented by *The Crisis of the Democratic Intellect: The Problem of Generalism and Specialism in Twentieth Century Scotland* (Edinburgh: Polygon, 1986); his *The Scottish Enlightenment and Other Essays* (Edinburgh: Polygon, 1991) suggests important links between the Enlightenment and the civic humanist tradition of the renaissance, dealt with in Arthur Williamson, *Scottish National Consciousness in the Age of James IV* (Edinburgh: John Donald, 1979). John Robertson, *The Scottish Enlightenment and the Militia*

Issue (Edinburgh: John Donald, 1985) discusses one aspect of the above, while Craig Beveridge and Ronald Turnbull, *The Eclipse of Scottish Culture* (Edinburgh: Polygon, 1989) give a pugnacious overview of the Scottish politico-philosophic tradition from Fletcher to Nairn.

There hasn't been a comprehensive study of Franco-Scottish radical movements since H. W. Meikle, *Scotland and the French Revolution* (Glasgow: Maclehose, 1912), but see Kenneth Logue, *Popular Disturbances in Scotland, 1780–1815* (Edinburgh: John Donald, 1979). On the Whig intervention which climaxed in 1832, both Fry and Hutchison (*vide supra*) have much material, as does William Ferguson in 'The Reform Act (Scotland) of 1832: Intention and Effect' in *The Scottish Historical Review*, vol. 45 (1966). Karl Miller got the Whigs on to the psychiatrist's couch, intriguingly if not always relevantly, in *Cockburn's Millenium* (London: Duckworth, 1975).

Thomas Kleinknecht, *Imperiale und internationale Ordnung: eine Untersuchung zum Gelehrtenliberalismus am Beispiel von James Bryce, 1838–1922* (Göttingen: Vandenhoeck und Rupprecht, 1985) is a perceptive study of what was different about nineteenth-century Scottish liberalism; I have done my bit in this direction in 'Scotland: Enlightenment to Renaissance', in Keith Stringer and Alexander Grant (eds), *The Formation of Social Identities in the European Past* (Copenhagen: Copenhagen University Press, 1993) and 'Gladstonianism, the Provinces, and Popular Political Culture' in Richard Bellamy (ed.), *Victorian Liberalism* (London: Methuen, 1990).

For the relations between the labour movement, nationalism and land reform James Hunter's work is near-definitive, in his 'The Politics of Highland Land Reform, 1873–1895' in *Scottish Historical Review*, 53 (1974) pp. 46–63, and his rightly acclaimed *The Making of the Crofting Community* (Edinburgh: John Donald, 1977). For the miners and early socialists and their nationalism see Alan Campbell, *The Lanarkshire Miners, 1775–1874* (Edinburgh: John Donald, 1979) and Kenneth O. Morgan, *Keir Hardie: Radical and Socialist* (London: Weidenfeld and Nicolson, 1975) and David Marquand, *James Ramsay MacDonald* (London: Cape, 1977).

Nationalist political party history began with John MacCormick's romantic *The Flag in the Wind* (London: Gollancz, 1955). This has been qualified by Jack Brand, *The National Movement in*

Scotland (London: Routledge 1978). I am much indebted also to the forthcoming doctoral thesis on 'Scottish Nationalism, 1886–1934' by Ruth Drost of the University of Munich. Literary nationalism is displayed in MacDiarmid's *Albyn, or Scotland and the Future* (London: Kegan Paul, 1927), and interpreted in Alan Bold, *Hugh MacDiarmid* (London: John Murray, 1988) and in Duncan Glen, *Hugh MacDiarmid and the Scottish Renaissance* (Edinburgh: Chambers, 1964) but much in Glen has now been overtaken by Susanne Hagemann's *Die Schottische Renascence* (Frankfurt: Peter Lang, 1992). For World War II politics see Graham Walker, *Thomas Johnston* (Manchester: Manchester University Press, 1988), and my own 'Labour and Scottish Government, 1939–1945: the Age of Tom Johnston', in *The Bulletin of Scottish Politics*, 2, Spring 1981, and 'Scottish Labour and World War II' in the *Historical Journal*, 1983.

2 AN ACHIEVING SOCIETY: UNIONIST SCOTLAND, 1707–1945

Roy Campbell, 'Scottish Economic and Social History: Past Developments and Future Prospects' in *Scottish Economic and Social History*, vol. 10 (1990) pp. 5–20, provides a good survey of the writing. T. M. Devine, 'The Union of 1707 and Scottish Development', in *Scottish Economic and Social History*, vol. 5 (1985) pp. 23–40, questions the notion of 1707 as a catalyst. John Butt and K. Ponting (eds), *Scottish Textile History* (Aberdeen: Aberdeen University Press, 1987), and C. J. A. Robertson, *The Origins of the Scottish Railway System, 1722–1844* (Edinburgh: John Donald, 1983) deal with the two main motors of industrialisation down to 1850; Paul Robertson, 'Scottish Universities and Scottish Industry', in *Scottish Economic and Social History*, vol. 4 (1984) pp. 39–54, deals with an important area of industrial-cultural interface.

The absence of a history which synthesises work done on Victorian industry still makes it necessary to go back to David Bremner, *The Industries of Scotland* (1869, Newton Abbot: David & Charles, 1969) for an overview. It can be compared with C. A. Oakley, *Scottish Industry Today* (Edinburgh: Moray Press, 1937); John Butt, *The Industrial Archaeology of Scotland* (Newton Abbot: David & Charles, 1967); and with Tony Dickson (ed.), *Capital and Class in Scotland* (Edinburgh: John Donald, 1982).

On social conditions see Smout, *Century* (*vide supra*), and Devine *et al.*, *People and Society* (*vide supra*), supplemented by R. A. Houston and I. D. Whyte (eds), *Scottish Society, 1500–1800* (Cambridge: Cambridge University Press, 1988) and L. M. Cullen and T. C. Smout (eds), *Comparative Aspects of Scottish and Irish Economic and Social History, 1600–1900* (Edinburgh: John Donald, 1974). G. F. A. Best, 'The Scottish Victorian City', in *Victorian Studies*, vol. 11 (1967–8) remains very stimulating in the questions it asks, when taken with Ian Levitt, *Poverty and Welfare in Scotland, 1890–1948* (Edinburgh: Edinburgh University Press, 1988), and Ian Levitt and T. C. Smout, *The State of the Scottish Working Class in 1843* (Edinburgh: Scottish Academic Press, 1979), not forgetting J. Cunnison and J. B. S. Gilfillan (eds), *The Third Statistical Account of Scotland: Glasgow* (Glasgow: Collins, 1958). W. Hamish Fraser, *Conflict and Class: Scottish Workers, 1700–1838* (Edinburgh: John Donald, 1988) adds a subtlety of interpretation not on the whole present in that old war-horse, influential in its time and still powerful, Thomas Johnston, *History of the Working Classes in Scotland* (Glasgow: Forward Publishing Company, 1921).

J. M. Robertson, *The Perversion of Scotland* (London: Free-thought Publishing Company, 1886) goes for the Victorian Kirk with a meat cleaver. A. L. Drummond and J. Bulloch, *The Church in Victorian Scotland, 1843–1874* (Edinburgh: St Andrew Press, 1975) is over-diffuse as a defence, and in its social aspects superseded by Callum Brown, *The Social History of Religion in Modern Scotland* (London: Routledge, 1987). Stewart Jay Brown, *Thomas Chalmers and the Godly Commonwealth in Scotland* (Oxford: Oxford University Press, 1982) is masterly in explaining the obsessiveness of Free Kirk politics, and William Storrar's *Scottish Identity: A Christian Vision* (Edinburgh: Handsel Press, 1990) brings the story up to date, as well as demonstrating the demanding quality of Scots theology. Hugh Cunningham, *The Volunteer Force* (London: Croom Helm, 1975) shows how religion and community mesh with 'radical militarism'.

Gordon Donaldson, *The Scots Overseas* (London: Robert Hale, 1966), a general survey, has been joined by R. A. Cage (ed.), *The Scots Abroad: Labour, Capital, Enterprise, 1750–1914* (London: Croom Helm, 1985). Towering over the lot is Angus Calder, *Revolutionary Empire* (London: Cape, 1980). W. Turrentine Jackson, *The Enterprising Scot: Investors in the American West after*

265

1873 (Edinburgh: Edinburgh University Press, 1968) is good on capital exports, and Janet Adam Smith, *John Buchan* (London: Rupert Hart-Davis, 1965) is much more than a biography of the proconsul as thriller-writer. Jenni Calder (ed.), *The Enterprising Scot* (Edinburgh: Royal Museums of Scotland and HMSO) 1986 unites the industrial and emigration drives.

For social reform movements and critiques of the inter-war years see Ian S. Wood, *John Wheatley* (Manchester: Manchester University Press, 1990), G. M. Thomson, *Caledonia or the Future of the Scots* (London: Kegan Paul, 1926) and J. A. Bowie, *The Future of Scotland* (Edinburgh: Chambers, 1939).

3 THE INTELLECTUALS, 1707–1945

David Craig, *Scottish Literature and the Scottish People* (London, Chatto and Windus, 1961) was my starting-off point: a dramatic achievement in the Marx–Leavis canon, although his critical view of Scottish culture suffered from an excessive scientific materialism. To this Davie acted as a corrective, and Robert Crawford, in *Devolving English Literature* (Oxford: Clarendon, 1992) inverts the former discussion, setting 'British' in the context of Scottish literature. Derick Thomson (ed.), *The Companion to Gaelic Scotland* (Oxford: Blackwell, 1983) is invaluable for the third of the country whose culture is quite distinctive, as is, for Lallans, Billy Kay's *Scots: The Mither Tongue* (Edinburgh: Mainstream, 1986), and Hamish Henderson's ever-stimulating *Alias MacAlias* (Edinburgh: Polygon, 1992).

Of books on the Enlightenment there have been many since the 1960s. Alexander Broadie's *The Tradition of Scottish Philosophy*, (Edinburgh: Polygon, 1990) sets it in a philosophical continuum with the internationalism of the schoolmen. Davie and Phillipson have already been mentioned, and T. M. Devine (ed.), *Improvement and Enlightenment* (Edinburgh: John Donald, 1989), R. H. Campbell and Andrew S. Skinner (eds), *The Origins and Nature of the Scottish Enlightenment* (Edinburgh: John Donald, 1982), emphasise the social context. Jennifer Carter and Joan H. Pittock (eds), *Aberdeen and the Enlightenment* (Aberdeen: Aberdeen University Press, 1987), N. T. Phillipson and R. Mitchison (eds), *Scotland in the Age of Improvement* (Edinburgh: Edinburgh University Press, 1970), and Douglas Young (ed.), *Edinburgh in the Age of Improvement* (Edinburgh: Edinburgh University Press, 1967) stress the local impact.

Alan Bold's *Sir Walter Scott: The Long-Forgotten Melody* (London: Vision, 1983) was one of the first reappraisals of Scott, his successors and contemporaries, mightily supplemented by the coverage of the Victorian period in Douglas Gifford's volume of *HSL*. Robert Anderson, *Education and Opportunity in Victorian Scotland: Schools and Universities* (Oxford: Clarendon, 1983) and W. M. Humes and H. M. Paterson, *Scottish Culture and Scottish Education* (Edinburgh: John Donald, 1983) are crucial on educational infrastructure, and William Donaldson's *Popular Literature in Victorian Scotland: Language, Fiction and the Press*, (Aberdeen: Aberdeen University Press, 1986) registers what amounts to a paradigm shift. Hugh Miller, *My Schools and Schoolmasters* (Edinburgh: Edmonstone and Douglas, 1854) is a remarkable contemporary account of literary, psychological and social tensions, expanded by George Rosie's selection *Hugh Miller: Outrage and Order* (Edinburgh: Mainstream, 1980).

For the hidden depths of the Kailyard see Ian Campbell, *Kailyard* (Edinburgh: Ramsay Head, 1981) and Christopher Harvie, 'Behind the Bonnie Brier Bush: the Scottish Kailyard Revisited', in P. N. Furbank (ed.), *Proteus*, Summer 1978. Helen Meller's *Patrick Geddes* (London: Routledge, 1991) is first-rate on the early history of geography and sociology in Scotland. For the literary nationalism of the 1920s and 1930s MacDiarmid's *Collected Poetry* (London: Martin Brien & O'Keefe, 1983) is basic, as is his *Contemporary Scottish Studies* (1928, reprinted by the Educational Institute of Scotland, 1973). See also Hugh MacDiarmid, *Albyn, or Scotland and the Future* (London: Kegan Paul, 1927), *The Company I've Kept* (London: Hutchinson, 1966) and Alan Bold, *MacDiarmid: A Critical Biography* (London: John Murray, 1988). Gibbon's *A Scots Quair* is now available in several editions; for biography and criticism see Iain S. Munro, *Leslie Mitchell: Lewis Grassic Gibbon* (Edinburgh: Oliver & Boyd, 1966) and Douglas Gifford, *Gibbon and Gunn* (Edinburgh: Oliver & Boyd, 1988), Glen (1964), Hagemann (1992), etc., (*vide supra*).

4 LEADERS TO NO SURE LAND: UNIONIST SCOTLAND, 1945–1979

For the post-war period William Donaldson's model holds good to a great extent, in the sense that so much work has to be done in newspapers and magazines. Edwin Muir's *Scottish Journey*, from which the passage took its cue, was reissued by Mainstream in 1984 with an introduction by T. C. Smout; there are two good volumes on Motherwell and Wishaw, written by Robert Duncan and published by the District Council in 1988 and 1991; these typify a much higher standard of local history, often indebted to the work of colleagues in the Open University. For the economy Alec Cairncross (ed.), *The Scottish Economy* (Cambridge: Cambridge University Press), is basic, supplemented by Richard Saville (ed.), *The Economic Development of Modern Scotland, 1950–1980* (Edinburgh: John Donald, 1985) and the Scottish Council's *Scotland*, useful throughout this period. Particular attention must be paid to the Council's *The Scottish Economy, 1960–61* (The Toothill Report), and its *Oceanspan* project, 1968.

On the left Gordon Brown's famous *Red Paper on Scotland* (Edinburgh: Edinburgh Student Publications Board, 1975) edited by an altogether fiercer person than the present Shadow Chancellor, included a high count of well-informed economic analyses, including pieces by John Firn, Vincent Cable and John Foster. Gavin Kennedy (ed.), *Scotland: the Radical Approach* (Edinburgh: Palingenesis Press, 1976) has also much of interest from an SNP perspective. John Foster and Charles Woolfson, *The Politics of the UCS Work-In* (London: Lawrence and Wishart, 1986) goes into depth about the problems of the heavy industries on the Clyde, although a general view of multinational capital and Scotland has yet to be written.

5 NOTHING ABIDES: CIVIL SOCIETY, 1945–1979

Victor Kiernan's various analytical writings: 'A Scottish Road to Socialism', in *The New Left Review* (1975) and 'Notes on Marxism in 1968', in *The Socialist Register* (1968) were basic to my approach, as was Neal Ascherson's 'Return Journey', in *Question* (1, Edinburgh, 1975), supplemented by 'Devolution Diary', in *Cencrastus*, 22, 1986; important too were many of the contributions to Gordon Brown's *Red Paper*, especially those by Tom Nairn and John McGrath. On local government see Michael Keating and Arthur Midwinter, *The Government of Scotland* (Edinburgh: Mainstream, 1983), Frank Bealey and John Sewel, *The Politics of Independence* (Aberdeen: Aberdeen University Press 1981), is very useful for the pre-regionalisation period, as is John Mackintosh's *The Devolution of Power* (Harmondsworth: Penguin, 1969). See also the *Third Statistical Account* volumes for Glasgow and Edinburgh, G. Gordon (ed.), *Perspectives of the Scottish City* (Aberdeen: Aberdeen University Press, 1986) and G. McLachlan (ed.), *Improving the Common Weal: Scottish Health Services, 1900–84* (Edinburgh: Edinburgh University Press, 1987).

On church affairs Callum Brown (1987) and William Storrar (1990) update John Highet, *The Scottish Churches*, (London: Skeffington, 1975) and Anthony Ross in Duncan Glen (ed.), *Whither Scotland?* (London: Gollancz, 1971). On education see T. R. Bone in Glen, and, very important, the painstaking work of the Edinburgh educational sociologists, notably Andrew MacPherson, 'An Angle on the *Geist*', in Humes and Paterson (*vide supra*). See also W. M. Humes, *The Leadership Class in Scottish Education* (Edinburgh: Edinburgh University Press, 1986) and Andrew MacPherson and Charles Raab, *Governing Education* (Edinburgh, 1988).

6 A DANCE TO THE MUSIC OF NATIONALISM, 1945–1979

For the post-war career of the SNP see Brand (1978), Hanham (1969), Fry (1987) and MacCormick (1955) (*vide supra*), supplemented by Billy Wolfe, *Scotland Lives!* (Edinburgh: Reprographia, 1973). More detailed studies are John Bochel and David Denver, 'The Decline of the SNP: an Alternative View', in *Political Studies*, vol. 20 (Sept. 1972) and Raymond Levy, *Scottish Nationalism at the Crossroads* (Edinburgh: Scottish Academic Press, 1989). The *Yearbook of Scottish Politics*, 1976–1992 (Edinburgh: Edinburgh University Politics Department) gives a wealth of contemporary material, including Chris Allen's useful bibliographies. On the role of Scotland in British politics see William L. Miller, *The End of British Politics: Scots and English Political Behaviour in the Seventies* (Oxford: Oxford University

Press, 1981). The Labour Party situation is dealt with by Michael Keating and David Bleiman, *Labour and Scottish Nationalism* (London: Macmillan, 1979) and Tam Dalyell was typically forthright in *Devolution – The End of Britain?* (London: Cape, 1977). For the Tories see James Mitchell, *Conservatives and the Union* (Edinburgh: Edinburgh University Press, 1990).

The political manoeuvres of the late 1970s feature in David Steel, *Against Goliath* (London: Weidenfeld & Nicolson, 1989) and the diaries of Tony Benn (London: Cape, 1989–92). For North Sea oil see my own *Fool's Gold: The Story of North Sea Oil* (London: Hamish Hamilton, 1994), Cordula and Lothar Ulsamer, *Schottland das Nordseeöl und die britische Wirtschaft* (Schondorf: Kriebel, 1991), and Donald MacKay and Tony MacKay, *The Political Economy of North Sea Oil* (Oxford: Martin Robinson, 1975) and Christopher Harvie and Stephen Maxwell, 'North Sea Oil and the Scottish National Party, 1970–79', in T.C. Smout (ed.), *Scotland and the Sea* (Edinburgh: John Donald, 1992). John Bochel, David Denver and Allan Macartney edited a wide range of evidence into *The Referendum Experience* (Aberdeen: Aberdeen University Press, 1981).

7 ON THE EVE

Scottish politics, society and economy after 1979 is covered and well illustrated in Ken Cargill (ed.), *Scotland 2000* (Glasgow: BBC Publications, 1987). Also see Magnus Linklater and Robin Denniston (eds), *Anatomy of Scotland Today* (Edinburgh: Chambers, 1992). *The Yearbook of Scottish Government* functioned from 1977 to 1992, and was effectively replaced by the quarterly *Scottish Affairs; Radical Scotland* (1982–92), alas, was not. What with other casualties such as *Scottish Child* (1989–96) and *Harpies and Quines* (1992–4) there's a lack of longer than broadsheet-length articles about Scottish economic and social life, and culture in the 1980s, which may be a reflex of the material available on websites. The Scottish Office's one is particularly important, and the *Online Scotsman*, the work of the late great Bobby Campbell, is a model of what an internet newspaper ought to be. Lindsay Paterson's *The Autonomy of Modern Scotland* (Edinburgh: Edinburgh University Press, 1995) is a study which, as it ranges wider than its political theme, ought to be mentioned at this point.

In terms of economics we are dependent on the specialist or the economic journalist, on the *Scottish Economic Bulletin*, papers of Scottish Enterprise or the Fraser of Allander Institute, or the *Herald, Scotsman, Scotland on Sunday* and *Scottish Business Insider*. See these for treatments of financial services in particular. Peter Payne, in Tom Devine and Richard Finlay, *Scotland in the Twentieth Century* (Edinburgh: Edinburgh University Press, 1996) is patchy, but impressive in 'The End of Steelmaking in Scotland' in *Scottish Economic and Social History*, vol. 15, 1995. See also Andrew Hargrave, *Silicon Glen: Reality or Illusion?* (Edinburgh: Mainstream, 1985). On oil, *Fool's Gold* and *Wasted Windfall*, Channel 4's TV series, have been joined by John Foster, Charles Woolfson and Dieter Beck, *Paying for the Piper* (London: Constable, 1996). For the Dr Jekyll side of financial services there is Richard Saville, *Bank of Scotland: A History, 1695–1995* (London: Constable, 1996) and for the Mr Hyde side Nick Kochan and Hugh Pym, *The Guinness Affair* (London: Croom Helm, 1987).

David McCrone, *Understanding Scotland: the Sociology of a Stateless Nation* (London: Routledge, 1992) and McCrone *et al.*, *Scotland the Brand* (Edinburgh: Polygon, 1995) have to be seen in the context of Tom Nairn, *Janus Revisited* (London: Verso, 1998), Emanuel Todd, *The Causes of Progress* (Oxford: Blackwell, 1987), Paul Halmos, *Solitude and Privacy* (London: Routledge, 1952), and Ronald Frankenberg, *Communities in Britain*, 1969 (Harmondsworth: Pelican, 1973). In terms of social conditions Tommy Sheridan, *A Time to Rage*, (Edinburgh: Polygon, 1994) is much more than socialist polemic, just as Andrew O'Hagan, *The Missing* (London: Paladin, 1995) is much more than a study of 'Mispers'. Particularly important are Meg Henderson's *Finding Peggy* (London: Sphere, 1994) on a Catholic girlhood in Glasgow, and Kay Carmichael, *For Crying Out Loud* (Glendaruel: Argyll, 1994) on the Scots' – and others' – problems with their emotions.

I. S. Wood, (ed.), *Scotland and Ulster* (Edinburgh: Mercat, 1993), and Graham Walker, *Intimate Strangers* (Edinburgh: Polygon, 1985) add a lot to the largely unresearched area of Scots-Ulster relations, as does William Marshall, *The Billy Boys* (Edinburgh: John Thomas, 1996). Glasgow – city and commercial culture – was covered by Ian Spring in *Phantom Village* (Edinburgh: Polygon, 1989), and Michael Keating, *The City that Refused to Die: Glasgow* (Aberdeen: Aberdeen University Press, 1988). We have so far been spared *Irvine Welsh's Edinburgh . . .*

Cairns Craig, *The History of Scottish Literature, The Twentieth Century* (Aberdeen: Aberdeen University Press, 1989) has been partly updated by Gavin Wallace, *The Novel in Scotland since 1979* (Edinburgh: Polygon, 1993). The imaginative literature of this period has been dealt with in the main text, and my references are necessarily limited, but I would stress the contributions of Alasdair Gray – *Lanark* (Edinburgh: Canongate, 1982), *1982 Janine* (London: Cape, 1985) and *Poor Things* (London: Bloomsbury, 1992) as 'theoretical histories' – synoptic, though also very subversive – comparable with Scott and Galt. The sensitivity of William McIlvanney's realism, in his detective story *Strange Loyalties* (London: Sphere, 1991) ought to be read alongside his social criticism in *Surviving the Shipwreck* (Edinburgh: Mainstream, 1992). Douglas Gifford and Dorothy McMillan, eds, *A History of Scottish Women's Writing*, (Edinburgh University Press, 1997) at last gives those hidden-from-history their due.

8 FACING THE CUILLIN: POLITICS 1986–2000

Andrew Marr, *The Battle for Scotland* (Harmondsworth: Penguin, 1992, 1998) unfortunate in the year of its birth, is bright, accurate and irreverent. Arnold Kemp, *The Hollow Drum* (Edinburgh: Mainstream, 1993) has a lot of interesting interview material but is somewhat daunting to the inexpert, and Alan Clements, Kirsty Wark and Kenny Farquharson, *Restless Nation* (Edinburgh: Mainstream, 1995) has a reliable narrative but rather disappointing photographs. Kenyon Wright, *The People Say Yes* (Glendaruel: Argyll, 1997) is an inside view of the Scottish Constitutional Convention by its convener. Raymond Levy's *Scottish Nationalism at the Crossroads* (Edinburgh: Polygon, 1992) hasn't the comprehensiveness of James Mitchell, *Strategies for Self-Government* (Edinburgh: Edinburgh University Press, 1996).

As to the 'auld enemy', Margaret Thatcher, *The Downing Street Years* (London: HarperCollins, 1996), is source material of a sort though bearing the fingerprints of many ghosts. Eric Evans, *Thatcher and Thatcherism* (London: Routledge, 1997) sorts out the main themes. Anthony Seldon's *John Major: a Political Biography* (London: Weidenfeld, 1997) is careful but almost wholly uninformative on Scotland. David Graham and Peter Clarke, *The New Enlightenment* (London: Macmillan, 1985) and the Adam Smith Institute's *Omega File on Scotland*, (1983) are slugs of marketism *pur* at which even the lady would have blanched, while Noel Annan's *Our Age*, (London: Fontana, 1993) is an apologia for a social-democratic elite in retreat.

Paul Anderson and Nyta Mann, *Safely First*, (London: Granta, 1997) is so far the best guide to New Labour and its policies. Ian McLean deals with Scotland in Anthony King (ed.), *New Labour Triumphs* (London: Chatham House, 1998) though David Butler and Dennis Kavanagh, *The British General Election of 1997* (London: Macmillan, 1997) are rather thin on Scotland. A study of election and referendum should appear from Edinburgh before this edition is published. Definitely in print in summer 1998 is the Open University/Dundee University *Modern Scottish History* (East Linton: Tuckwell) course, in five volumes of teaching material, sources and essays.

'And what were they going to do with the grail when they found it, Mr Rossetti?' Max Beerbohm's Benjamin Jowett made a point relevant to Scottish politics in 1998, with a surprising dearth of discussion of policy options in the popular press and media. C. H. Lee, *Scotland and the United Kingdom* (Manchester: Manchester University Press, 1995) examined the financial background, restating the Scottish indebtedness theme. It doesn't convince me – see my review in the *Scottish History Review*, 1996 – but I would say that, wouldn't I?

INDEX